Planning an Appropriate Curriculum for the Under Fives

Planning an Appropriate Curriculum for the Under Fives

A Guide for Students, Teachers and Assistants

Second Edition

Rosemary Rodger

David Fulton Publishers
London

David Fulton Publishers Ltd
The Chiswick Centre, 414 Chiswick High Road, London W4 5TF

www.fultonpublishers.co.uk

First published in Great Britain by David Fulton Publishers 1999
Second edition 2003

British Library Cataloguing in Publication Data
A catalogue record for this book is available from the British Library.

ISBN 1 85346 912 2

Typeset by Servis Filmsetting Ltd, Manchester
Printed and bound in Great Britain

Contents

Preface

The Foundation Stage curriculum was launched in September 2000. In the three years since then there has been a great improvement in the provision for children from three to five in the Foundation Stage, whether they are in nursery schools, nursery classes, pre-schools or private nurseries. It is probably too early to say there has been the same rate of improvement in reception classes. Reception classes generally have had further to travel to improve their provision, especially the use that is made of the outdoor environment as part of children's learning. As a result, the early years is being given a much higher profile politically and in schools than it was when the first edition of this book was published in 1999. I hope that you find that the amendments in this edition reflect the major changes. The dilemma always when writing a book that covers the whole Foundation Stage is that you do not feel able to reflect everything that is happening in the field. In this edition, I have added more information about the leadership roles of the various managers in the Foundation Stage, included more references to Sure Start and Early Excellence centres and tried to reflect the situation as it is in settings across the country. My prime audience is the young people setting out on their careers in the early years. You are entering a profession at an exciting and innovative time. Much has changed and very rapidly in recent years. Opportunities to develop a career in the early years are better than ever. The Foundation Stage matters in primary schools. Headteachers acknowledge that if staffing and other resources are channelled into the Foundation Stage there will be longer-term benefits as children progress through school. Unfortunately, we are also living at a time when there is child poverty and neglect; the first sign that there are difficulties with a child's personal circumstances may well be when he/she starts preschool. This brings added pressures to the role of leader in the early years. At last, there is total commitment by a government that is trying to eradicate some of the effects of social, economic and physical deprivation in our youngest children. It will take time to see the benefits of the social inclusion policy in those areas that have Sure Start, where deprivation is being tackled at the very heart of its inception; before children are born and through guidance to vulnerable young people in school.

The tone of the book may reflect changes to my professional role in recent years. I make no apologies for that. The inspection of schools in the past ten years has been a powerful agent for change, not least in the early years. The increased self-evaluative strand to inspection, and working in partnership with registered inspectors and teams is a robust and rigorous, if at times, stressful process for head-teachers and all others involved. This process contributes very effectively to school improvement. It is with great pleasure that I acknowledge the professional relation-ships I have developed with several outstanding practitioners in the early years through inspection and consultancy work. An invitation to speak to early years staff in Hertfordshire about target setting and accountability in the early years recently was a salutary reminder that the early years has come a long way in recent years!

Rosemary Rodger
Durham, May 2003

Acknowledgements

I extend my thanks to all the schools, nurseries and children's centres with which I have had involvement over the past few years, in particular, the staff and children of Manchester City Council's children's centres. My thanks also go to Anne at David Fulton Publishers for the gentle way in which she has cajoled me to complete the revisions to this manuscript. For the impetus to revise and share excellent practices, I am indebted to Heather Steed, headteacher of Boston nursery school, Lincolnshire, and her staff for making what could have been a stressful experience professionally rewarding, to Maureen Vickers, headteacher of Grosvenor nursery school, Bolton, for her inspirational leadership and inclusive curriculum. Closer to home, the headteachers of Houghton community nursery school and Pennywell Early Excellence Centre who have cheerfully and professionally embraced Performance Management and made target setting appear so integral to effective early years practice. Finally, my thanks to my husband Iain, for his support and encouragement.

I acknowledge the permission of Manchester City Council to reproduce material from Brown *et al.* (1997) *Education and Physical Education in the Early Years*, Manchester City Council Education Department.

Abbreviations

ASPECT	Assessment Profile on Entry for Children and Toddlers
CD	Creative Development
CLL	communication, language and literacy
DES	Department for Education and Science
DfEE	Department for Education and Employment
DfES	Department for Education and Skills
EAL	English as an additional language
elg	early learning goals
IEP	individual education plan
kuw	knowledge and understanding of the world
MD	mathematical development
NFER	National Foundation for Educational Research
NLS	National Literacy Strategy
NNS	National Numeracy Strategy
Ofsted	Office for Standards in Education
PD	Physical Development
PIPS	Performance Indicators in Primary Schools
PSED	Personal, Social and Emotional Development
QCA	Qualifications and Curriculum Authority
SEN	special educational needs
SENCO	special educational needs co-ordinator
SIP	school improvement plan
TTA	Teacher Training Agency
THRASS	teaching handwriting, reading and spelling skills

To Jake, whose energy and zest for life act as a reminder to us all that learning in the early years is the start of a great adventure

Introduction

Introduction

The opportunity to revise this book comes at time of considerable change in the early years. An increase in the range and structure of provision for young children to include greater rigour and accountability for childminders, full day care, sessional care, crèches and out of school care is to be welcomed. The move towards greater integration of services providing education and childcare is increasing. Early Excellence centres, neighbourhood nurseries and extended schools are all part of the developments to provide parents with a choice of services for their children. From September 2001 Ofsted (Office for Standards in Education) took over the regulation of all childcare for the under eights. This entailed the creation of one national system for the regulation, inspection, investigation and enforcement of under eights childcare. There is one database listing all providers and one set of national standards as a baseline for quality. Information about the national standards can be found later in this chapter. The overall aim of Ofsted is to ensure that children are safe, well cared for and take part in activities that contribute to their development and learning. This initiative is in the early stages for development and has not as yet provided details of the curricular implications of the work of practitioners in settings other than through the national standard concerned with care, learning and play, more of which is mentioned later. The DfES (Department for Education and Skills) are due to report on the play and learning requirements for children under three in 2003.

In the first edition, I shared the concerns of several early years specialists that the early learning goals (QCA 1999b) to be reached by the time children completed their time in the reception class would lead to an over concentration on the outcomes of learning at the expense of the processes by which children learn (Sylva 1997, Blenkin and Kelly 1997, Anning 1998, Scott 1998 and David 1999). The reality, as I hope to show, is that the guidance provided by the Qualifications and Curriculum Authority (QCA 2000) has provided practitioners with a workable curricular framework which clearly acknowledges the differing stages of development of children from three to five years of age. The group of under fives whose needs have been met less well in the past, i.e. children in reception classes (Pugh 1996, Mills and Mills 1997, Ghouri 1998a), now have a much better chance of experiencing a wider range of appropriate learning experiences, due, in part, to the priority being given to the Foundation Stage in inspections of primary schools and the training carried out through the Early Years and Childcare Development Partnerships (EYCDP) throughout England. Children in preschools, in the care of a childminder or in private or voluntary settings are expected to have the same level of quality in their provision as any other child in a preschool environment. Inspections of preschools, independent and voluntary settings did not take place in the period from August 2001 to March 2002 to enable Ofsted to develop and pilot a new model of combined section 122/Children Act inspections to meet a commitment to reduce the burden of inspection on providers. The inspection of funded nursery education on a four-year cycle using the combined model resumed in September 2002.

As a result of this there was a dearth of evaluations from Ofsted on the impact of the statutory curriculum for the early years both in the maintained and in the private and voluntary sectors. The most recent survey carried out by the early years directorate, *Nursery Education: Quality of Provision for 3 and 4 Years Olds 2000–01* (Ofsted 2000), is based on an analysis of 5,562 inspections of funded nursery education carried out between September 2000 and July 2001. For the first time there is a report on three-year-olds. The outcomes show a positive picture of improvement and maintenance of high standards. As many of the inspections were re-inspections of settings requiring a subsequent inspection only one to two years since their previous inspection, it is likely that the findings of the survey may underestimate performance. This data alone is a positive indicator that the implementation of the Foundation Stage is successful.

This book aims to describe good practices in a range of early years settings and offer guidance on an appropriate curriculum to those practitioners wishing to specialise in the early years either as qualified teachers, or teaching assistants or as students about to enter the profession. The views expressed are my own, but I have attempted to reflect on what happens in early years settings through reference to research evidence and from case study material gathered from my work with early years practitioners across the country. My views tend to support the move towards greater emphasis on *what* young children do, as the worthwhileness of an activity or experience in terms of interesting, motivating and providing children with the opportunity to learn is frequently down to the activity and the inspirational guidance of an informed adult as well as intrinsic factors such as the emotional and social well-being of the child.

This chapter analyses the *status quo* in the early years in order to provide a rationale for the overall view reflected in the book, which is organised in such a way that practitioners can dip into chapters as they are appropriate to their needs. As a text for those working in the Foundation Stage in a range of settings, it reflects the way it is in early childhood settings with regard to the curriculum. Hopefully, it will raise questions and inform ongoing debate about the relationship between early learning and the way in which settings interpret the national requirements to meet the needs of the children in their care. An analysis of the current research into the characteristics of effective teaching and learning for children under five is a central strand to each chapter. Central to this review is the fundamental importance of the adult role, either as a parent in the home or an educator in a nursery setting. The terms educator, practitioner and teacher are used synonymously throughout the book and all refer to the adults who are employed to work with young children whether they are qualified teachers or not. Similarly, the early years establishments in which young children are educated are referred to by a variety of titles: setting, preschool, nursery class, school or reception class.

Previously, I have looked at the way in which other countries claimed to be ahead of England in their definition of what an appropriate curriculum should include. In this edition, I intend to explore the recommended curriculum for children in England and illustrate through examples of good practice how practitioners are including all 286 early learning goals in their plans. As Wales has removed the distinction between the Foundation Stage and Key Stage 1, Chapter 2 makes reference to the Welsh philosophy for the early years and considers whether it would be appropriate to extend the Foundation Stage curriculum, beyond the reception class. Each chapter covers an area of learning: personal, social and emotional development; communication, language and literacy; mathematical development; knowledge and understanding of the world; physical development; and creative development. There are examples of effective planning and case study material to illustrate good practice. In addition, there are chapters covering leadership and management in the Foundation Stage, inspection and preparing an action plan, writing an early years policy, guidelines on curriculum planning, assessment, and record keeping. The use of performance data, i.e assessment information to show how well children are making progress, and the implications of government initiatives, especially performance management, and the increases in funding available for managers of settings, especially nursery schools, will be discussed in the the light of the changing leadership and management roles of headteachers and managers.

It is important that critical analysis informs the mind of the reader to question, interpret and evaluate the effectiveness of the curriculum they provide for their children in whatever kind of setting they work. It is now a requirement that provision for children in the Foundation Stage takes account of the six areas of learning defined by QCA (2000). Since 2002, this stage has been officially included as the first phase of education and is part of the National Curriculum for those children taught in the maintained sector. QCA have stated that the requirements of the National Curriculum programmes of study for Key Stage 1 can be achieved by children in six terms excluding the reception year. Consequently, the assumption can be made that four-year-old children in reception classes will be provided with effective learning opportunities, some planned and others self-initiated using the six areas of learning as the basis for planning the curriculum. This is reducing the pressure on reception class teachers to plan and teach the National Curriculum programmes of study. Examples of practice show it is not uncommon for children in the latter months of the reception class to be following the requirements of the National Curriculum programmes of study as they have already met the early learning goals in each area of learning. The recently introduced statutory assessment requirement for children at the end of the reception year acknowledges there will be children whose needs are most effectively met through the challenge provided by National Curriculum-based activities.

The national context

A previous edition of this book outlined the changes in provision for the early years in the past ten years in great detail. I do not propose to rehearse that debate in this edition, as there have been many changes in the past four years that carry on from the changes outlined in the previous edition. Government has invested heavily in both education and childcare in order to give children a more equal start in life. Good early years education and childcare, they claim, can play an important part in improving educational standards and help to reduce child poverty and social exclusion. There is now a universal entitlement to nursery education for four-year-olds, most three-year-olds and a much higher number of childcare places. Seven hundred thousand places have been created since 1997. Many of the plans are outlined in the Green Paper 'Building on Success' (DfEE 2001a). The next section will outline some of the changes that will help to provide the context for this new edition.

Leadership and management in the early years has changed dramatically, especially for headteachers of nursery schools. Gone are days of part-time provision for small groups each day, the nursery closed more often than it was open and parents bemoaning the lack of childcare for their children when they wished to return to work. Instead we are seeing, increasingly, wrap-around care, provision for noughts to threes and multi-agency, on-site support for families and children. Bidding for additional funding, such as Seed Challenge, New Deal for Schools or Neighbourhood Nurseries, may be taking the nursery headteacher increasingly away from the core of his/her work, that is, assuring the quality of provision for the children day by day. The changes are exciting, but they are also very demanding and require leadership and management skills of a different order. The career path for the committed and professional early years practitioner has never been so well mapped out. This can be seen on the DfES website www.childcarecareers.gov.uk. This has tremendous potential for all the young graduates entering the early years profession. These are some of the reasons for a separate chapter on leadership and management in the early years. The changes referred to in this chapter include:

- Sure Start;
- registration and inspection of day care and childminding;
- the statutory requirements of the Foundation Stage Curriculum;
- educational inclusion;
- the Foundation Stage Profile.

Sure Start

In a recent speech, 'Quality and inequality in schooling', the school standards minister, David Milliband, summed up the potential of Sure Start.

> Education cannot eradicate the effects of home life. They live with children throughout their lives. But everything communities and Government can do to help tackle worthlessness, social decay and social dysfunction is right in itself, and important for what it makes possible in education . . . The delivery of Sure Start promises that every child be 'ready to learn' at age five is a vital and radical investment.
>
> ('Learning or Leaning? Lessons to be Learned from Pisa', London, January 2003)

As a result of the government's ambitious proposals to work towards preventing social exclusion, the Sure Start strategy to improve services for young children under four and their families in areas of need was set up in 1999. The basic aim of Sure Start is to work with parents-to-be, parents and their children to promote the physical, intellectual and social development of babies and young children, particularly those who are most disadvantaged, so they can grow and flourish at home and when they go to school, and thereby break the cycle of deprivation for the current generation of young children. Since 1999, the growth of Sure Start centres has been significant. It is expected there will be 522 Sure Start local programmes by 2004. A relatively recent development is to set up Children's Centres in disadvantaged areas offering education, childcare, health and family support to be integrated with existing Sure Start programmes. The concept of the extended school is a new idea. Legislation is currently being put in place to enable there to be more childcare, health and family support on school premises. There is a training programme that seeks to ensure that the employment created via these developments can be filled with appropriately qualified staff. What will the impact of this be on provision in the Foundation Stage? Will three-year-olds now have a better start to their education? Will there be less disadvantage in terms of language delay or social and emotional behaviour? Will parents be more aware of the educative role they have with their own children? This book may answer some of those questions, but having checked the evaluations of Sure Start so far it may be that there is still some way to go.

Early indications from the national evaluations are that the early Sure Start programmes suggest that implementation has been beset with accountability and management difficulties. A key aim of the programme is to improve children's ability to learn. Eradicating impoverished language skills is an important strand in promoting learning. City University (Harris 2002) was commissioned to devise a language measure for two-year-olds with the aim of setting a national baseline of language skills for two-year-olds. This work is still ongoing. Key findings so far show that the average word count for two-year-olds is 46 out of 100. Eighty five per cent of two-year-olds put words together and 78 per cent of parents have no concerns about their child's language development. Sure Start is an ambitious and potentially critical key in the drive to eradicate social inequalities in young children. Early programmes are innovative. Crucial first steps have been taken to bring about joined-up working between education, social services, health, local community groups and the voluntary sector at grassroots level. Some programmes are led by social services, others by health or education. Communities are centrally involved. There are initiatives to support pregnant mums and reduce the high incidence of teenage pregnancies.

Registration and inspection of day care and childminding

In September 2001, the Office for Standards in Education (Ofsted) became responsible for the registration and inspection of day care and childminding. Previously these services were regulated by 150 local authorities which set their own criteria and procedures (Ofsted 2003). Almost simultaneously, in May 2001, following extensive consultations, the Department for Education and Employment as it was then published the first *National Standards for Under Eights Day Care and Childminding* (Figure 1.1). Ofsted has four regulatory functions:

- The *registration* of providers, to ensure that those providing day care and childminding are suitable to do so and meet the national standards.

STANDARD 1 **Suitable person:** adults providing day care, looking after children or having unsupervised access to them are suitable to do so.

STANDARD 2 **Organisation:** the registered person meets required adult:child ratios, ensures that training and qualifications are met and organises space and resources to meet the children's needs effectively.

STANDARD 3 **Care, learning and play:** the registered person meets the children's individual needs and promotes their welfare. They plan and provide activities and play opportunities to develop children's emotional, social and intellectual capabilities.

STANDARD 4 **Physical environment:** the premises are safe, secure and suitable for their purpose. They provide adequate space in an appropriate location, are welcoming to children and offer access to the necessary facilities for a range of activities which promote their development.

STANDARD 5 **Equipment:** furniture, equipment and toys are provided which are appropriate for their purpose and help to create an accessible and stimulating environment. They are of suitable design and condition, well maintained and conform to safety standards.

STANDARD 6 **Safety:** the registered person takes positive steps to promote safety within the setting and on outings and ensures proper precautions are taken to prevent accidents.

STANDARD 7 **Health:** the registered person promotes the good health of children and takes positive steps to prevent the spread of infection and appropriate measures when they are ill.

STANDARD 8 **Food and drink:** children are provided with regular drinks and food in adequate quantities for their needs. Food and drink are properly prepared, nutritious and comply with dietary and religious requirements.

STANDARD 9 **Equal opportunities:** the registered person and staff actively promote equality of opportunity and anti-discriminatory practice for all children.

STANDARD 10 **Special needs (including special educational needs and disabilities):** the registered person is aware that some children may have special needs and is proactive in ensuring that appropriate action can be taken when such a child is identified or admitted to the provision. Steps are taken to promote the welfare and development of the child within the setting in partnership with the parents and other relevant parties.

STANDARD 11 **Behaviour:** adults caring for children in the provision are able to manage a wide range of children's behaviour in a way which promotes their welfare and development.

STANDARD 12 **Working in partnership with parents and carers:** the registered person and staff work in partnership with parents to meet the needs of the children, both individually and as a group. Information is shared.

STANDARD 13 **Child protection:** the registered person complies with local child protection procedures approved by the Area Child Protection Committee and ensures that all adults working and looking after children in the provision are able to put the procedures into practice.

STANDARD 14 **Documentation:** records, policies and procedures which are required for the efficient and self management of the provision, and to promote the welfare, care and learning of children, are maintained. Records about individual children are shared with the children's parents.

FIGURE 1.1   National Standards (DfEE 2001)

- The *inspection* of providers, to ensure they continue to be suitable.
- The *investigation of complaints* against providers.
- The *enforcement* action to ensure compliance with the national standards.

Ofsted apply the National Standards throughout England. This means that parents can be confident in the standard of childcare wherever they live. As the main focus for this book is the education of young children I do not propose to go into the full detail of the functions of the new regulatory body but to highlight those aspects that should have an impact on the education of young children. Essentially, Ofsted aims to ensure that all children are safe and well cared for, and that they take part in activities that will help them to learn and develop. Standard 3 – care, learning and play – states that a registered person must meet the children's individual needs and promote their welfare. They must plan and provide activities and play opportunities to develop children's emotional, social and intellectual capabilities. The systems for registering settings have been combined to ensure all settings and childminders are registered under the watchful eye of Ofsted. The extensive task of registering thousands of childminders has been completed. Actions to ensure providers meet the national standards have taken place and there are now fewer safety hazards and more appropriately qualified people providing day care. Organisation and staffing ratios are the areas in which standards have not been met.

Further initiatives are in place or planned which will have a major impact on the work of the regulatory body. Wrap-around care will provide services for children before and after school in primary and nursery schools. A range of services are currently being developed, to include nursery education and adult basic skills support via neighbourhood nurseries. This is an initiative to set up community nurseries in disadvantaged areas, some of which may be attached to playgroups. Home childcarers are a new category of childcarer appointed to look after children in their own home. There are plans to extend the number of Early Excellence centres to 100 by 2004. The intention is that they are encouraged to build on their training and dissemination functions to support other early years provision in the locality.

Pilot inspections (Ofsted 2003a) of 20 Early Excellence centres are taking place in 2002/03 to evaluate their quality and standards and identify strengths and weaknesses. They tend to be situated in areas of social disadvantage and have children with complex needs, have good outdoor facilities and good leadership and are achieving success in weaving together the various aspects of their provision and disseminating their practice. Surprisingly, the area which is less well-developed is early literacy and mathematical development, although a high priority is given to personal, social and emotional development. Physical development is a strength in one-third of centres. It will be important that centres that are heralded as the beacons of excellence do not lose sight of their core purpose. I was surprised at the Ofsted finding, based on my own experience of an Early Excellence centre in the North-East which has as its key aim a commitment to 'providing a high quality teaching and learning environment which is purposeful, efficient and effective'. A centre that has tackled head-on the issue of boys' under-achievement in literacy by using a wall mounted interactive whiteboard as a mark-making activity – raised from the floor so that disaffected boys would be motivated to use it because it required them to climb to reach the board. A centre that moved writing activities into well-resourced role-play areas such as building sites and garden centres. A centre that has a detailed training programme to assist social services staff make high quality assessments of progress towards the early learning goals in their key worker groups.

The statutory requirements of the Foundation Stage curriculum

The introduction of the Foundation Stage curriculum was generally welcomed. The DfES press release stated that 95 per cent of respondents to the consultation backed the proposed early learning goals. The proposed integration of play and learning was welcomed as a sensible way forward. The guidance provided to support the Foundation Stage (QCA 2000, 2001) in terms of principles and exemplification of the early learning goals initially, and subsequently in the planning guidance, have been heralded as a clear vision of what children should be able to achieve by the time they approach the age of six. The clear examples of planned activities through which young children can learn and develop are valued. Patricia Lacey, head of the Dorothy Gardener Early Excellence Centre said with reference to the guidance, 'Within the early years the emphasis has always been on delivering a differentiated curriculum that meets the needs of individual children and extends their learning in a stimulating and appropriate way.' Importantly, the government acknowledged the implications of the Foundation Stage curriculum for reception classes by allocating £13 million into the Standards Fund for classroom assistants in reception classes in 1999. However, to ensure that the provision promotes children's all-round development and learning, practitioners will need to have well-laid-out indoor and outdoor space (Ensing 2000).

The Foundation Stage begins when children reach the age of three. All settings that receive nursery education grant funding are required to offer high quality provision. Most children are expected to achieve the early learning goals by the end of the Foundation Stage. It is expected that those working with these children will draw on a range of teaching and care strategies and knowledge of child development. It is fundamental in working with young children that children are helped to develop their understanding by playing, talking, observing, planning, questioning, experimenting and reflecting with each other and adults. The curriculum is based on six areas of learning:

Personal, social and emotional development;

Communication, language and literacy;

Mathematical development;

Knowledge and understanding of the world;

Physical development;

Creative development.

Effective practice in early years settings will be based on twelve principles for early years education (See Figure 1.2).

Subsequent chapters will outline the requirements for each area of learning and provide illustrative examples of planning and case studies from a variety of settings.

Educational Inclusion

As already mentioned, the importance of meeting the needs of all children irrespective of their needs is crucial in the Foundation Stage. In order to define the key principles for inclusion I have referred to the definitions given for the statutory National Curriculum (DfEE 1999c). They are succinct and described as: setting suitable learning challenges; responding to pupils' diverse learning needs; and overcoming potential barriers to learning and assessment for individuals and groups of pupils. Diverse learning needs are defined as: pupils with special educational needs; pupils with disabilities; and pupils who learn English as an additional language. Reference to meeting the needs of all children was given scant attention in the previous edition; I will rectify this omission by threading issues related to inclusion into all chapters. Inclusivity as a concept is integral to all aspects of work in the early years. The basic principles encapsulated by QCA (2000) acknowledge the diversity of children's experiences. 'No child should be excluded or disadvantaged because of ethnicity, culture or religion, home language, family background, special educational needs, disability, gender or ability.' Inclusion is about equality, about celebrating the commonalities in individuals and being able to provide for the diversity of needs whatever they may be.

Early years practitioners have been and continue to be pioneers in the field of inclusivity through longstanding arrangements and funding to provide places for children with special educational needs to work and play alongside all children. Good early years practice is synonymous with inclusivity. But can this be achieved

These principles are drawn from, and are evident in, good and effective practice in early years settings.

1. **Effective education requires both a relevant curriculum and practitioners who understand and are able to implement the curriculum requirements.**
2. **Effective education requires practitioners who understand that children develop rapidly during the early years – physically, intellectually, emotionally and socially.** Children are entitled to provision that supports and extends knowledge, skills and understanding and confidence, and helps them to overcome any disadvantage.
3. **Practitioners should ensure that all children feel included, secure and valued.** They must build positive relationships with parents in order to work effectively with them and their children.
4. **Early years experience should build on what children already know and can do.** It should also encourage a positive attitude and disposition to learn and aim to prevent early failure.
5. **No child should be excluded or disadvantaged** because of ethnicity, culture or religion, home language, family background, special educational needs, disability, gender or ability.
6. **Parents and practitioners should work together** in an atmosphere of mutual respect within which children can have security and confidence.
7. **To be effective, an early years curriculum should be carefully structured.** In that structure there should be three strands:
   - provision for the different starting points from which children develop their learning;
   - relevant and appropriate content that matches the different levels of young children's needs;
   - planned and purposeful activity that provides opportunities for teaching and learning, both indoors and outdoors.
8. **There should be opportunities for children to engage in activities planned by adults and also those that they plan or initiate themselves.** Children do not make a distinction between 'play' and 'work' and neither should practitioners. Children need time to become engrossed, work in depth and complete activities.
9. **Practitioners must be able to observe and respond appropriately to children,** informed by a knowledge of how children develop and learn and a clear understanding of the possible next steps in their development and learning.
10. **Well-planned and purposeful activity and appropriate intervention by practitioners will engage children in the learning process** and help them to make progress in their learning.
11. **For children to have rich and stimulating experiences, the learning environment should be well planned and well organised.** It provides the structure for teaching within which children explore, experiment, plan and make decisions for themselves, thus enabling them to learn, develop and make good progress.
12. **Above all, effective learning and development for young children requires high-quality care and education by practitioners.**

FIGURE 1.2   Principles for early years education (QCA 2000:11)

in all situations? What constitutes 'good early years practice'? How many children with diverse learning, social, emotional and physical needs can a setting cope with? Nutbrown (1998) warns that early years settings must be fit to include, and educators equipped with, appropriate professional development and management support.

> Respectful educators will include all children; not just children who are easy to work with, obliging, endearing, clean, pretty, articulate, capable, but every child – respecting them for who they are, respecting their language, their culture, their history, their family, their ways and their very essence.

(Nutbrown 1996:54)

Clough and Nutbrown (2002) have reminded early years practitioners that the *Index for Inclusion* was launched in March 2000 and a copy was issued to every state school in England. A small-scale study was made of the impact of the *Index* on the work of five early years practitioners before and after using it. We are reminded that there are two major inclusion initiatives in the early years: Sure Start and Early Excellence centres. The outcomes for the practitioners using the *Index* were frequently personal and led to changes in attitudes: facing prejudices; questioning the title Special Educational Needs Co-ordinator (SENCO) and replacing it with Learning Support Co-ordinator.

Individual chapters for each area of learning share some of the ways in which inclusion issues are dealt with (see Chapters 6 and 11). Chapter 2 is based on the premise that all early years practices are inclusive.

The Foundation Stage Profile

QCA consulted with early years practitioners, LEAs, baseline assessment scheme providers, early years organisations, parents and other partner organisations. A consultation document was published in December 2000 which contained proposals for revising the statutory baseline assessment and the key issues that needed to be considered. This included a proposal to move the assessment to the end of the Foundation Stage (which for the majority of children is the end of the reception year in primary school) and assessing the progress made by each child towards the early learning goals. The consultation process showed strong support for a single national scheme. Consequently, the new profile was introduced in the academic year 2002/2003. Training on the implementation of the new scheme was slow to take place and many reception class teachers were unclear of the nature of the tasks ahead of them.

The handbook to assist practitioners assess each child's development in relation to the early learning goals was eventually published with the clear statement that the *Foundation Stage Profile* would provide a way of summing up the practitioners' accumulated knowledge of the whole child. This it was assumed was based on whatever existing assessment data was available. Guidance was based on existing good practice: that practitioners would carry out an assessment at three key points during the year to build up a profile of development to that point. However, this was optional: the statutory requirement is that the profile is completed at the end of the year during the summer term. This could mean that data from existing assessments could be transferred to the new profile. Criticisms of the 117 assessment points have been made, including comments that the system is too unwieldy and time-consuming for practitioners. Not a view shared by those in the field who have been successfully incorporating the stages towards each early learning goal (*stepping stones*) into their curriculum planning. Nursery staff have felt left out in this development and rightly so. What they do during the first part of the Foundation Stage has consequences for children's later development. LEAs, for example Lincolnshire and Sheffield, and early years partnerships are addressing this at a local level and devising modified assessment guidance based on the six areas of learning.

An inclusive curriculum for the early years

No child should be excluded or disadvantaged because of ethnicity, culture or religion, home language, family background, special educational needs, disability, gender or ability.

Introduction

The above principle taken from the *Curriculum Guidance for the Foundation Stage* (QCA 2000: 11) captures the essence of this chapter, radically revised in this edition to give a higher profile and recognition of the outstanding work in the field of inclusion by practitioners. In an attempt to define an 'inclusive curriculum' I have extended the definition beyond children with special educational needs. It is defined as 'creating equal opportunities for all pupils whatever their age, gender, ethnicity, attainment or background' (Ofsted 2001:1). In response to the Inquiry completed into the murder of Stephen Lawrence, the Macpherson Report (1999) highlighted the need to make race equality a reality for everyone through the responsibilities placed on each of us so that every individual, regardless of colour, creed, or race has the same opportunities and respect as his or her neighbour. How do early years practitioners value cultural diversity and 'build on what children already know and can do? In addition, references will be made to, and guidance will be provided on, the ways in which settings are meeting the requirements of the *Special Educational Needs Code of Practice* (DfES 2001). A range of curricular definitions will be shared to show how different ideas and methods have an impact on how practitioners interpret, plan and teach young children.

Promoting an awareness of cultural diversity

Close scrutiny of the principles for early years education (DfES 2000) shows how good practitioners meet the needs of all children; by ensuring that all children feel included, secure and valued and by building on what children already know, understand and can do. How are children with English as an additional language supported in your setting? Do you have access to qualified bilingual staff to support such children? Recent evidence (Ofsted 2001) highlights the changes in funding through the Ethnic Minority Achievement Grant (EMAG) in April 1999 and the subsequent passing of the Race Relations (Amendment) Act in 2000. Recommendations for effective support places the emphasis on the role of the LEA to recruit and train specialist staff. The conditions under which nursery education providers and LEAs receive the nursery education grant are laid down. Broadly, local authorities have a duty to secure the provision for the early education of children, initially all four-year-olds and more recently all three-year-olds. It is interesting to study the requirements of the Nursery Education Grant in relation to what Early Years Development and Childcare Partnerships (EYDCP) (DfEE 2000) are required to produce in order to secure funding. There is no reference to requiring the providers (i.e. those settings which have agreed to provide free early education places) with any data on a quota of minority ethnic children. The reason I raise this as an issue is the anomaly I recently found in a preschool operating in a community centre in a culturally diverse urban area of North London. Both staff were of a minority ethnic culture, but none of the children were. Why, I asked myself, knowing that the setting was by no means full, were there no minority ethnic children attending? Do early years settings have a quota to meet or is it as required by the legislation a case of places being allocated on the basis of children's social needs? Is this specific enough? I leave you the reader to ponder this question. The requirements for the grant are more specific when it comes to what LEAs must put in their Early Years Development and Childcare Plan ('Plan') with regard to children with statements of special educational need. All settings have a legal duty to have regard to the *Code of Practice on the Identification and Assessment of Special Educational Needs*. See later in the chapter for more information.

Curricular guidance (QCA 2000:16) acknowledges that a proportion of children in early years settings will have a home language other than English. Practitioners will need to value this linguistic diversity and provide opportunities for children to use their home language in their play and learning. The Ofsted report *Raising the Attainment of Minority Ethnic Pupils* (Ofsted 1999) identified Traveller children as those most at risk of underachievement. My own, albeit limited, experience tends to support the view that there is a lack of support specifically targeted at Traveller children. Is this because they are usually well-adjusted to nursery or school and also rather quiet and not very noticeable. The situation is very different where there are children from other minority ethnic cultures. The following case study highlights the way in which a reception class in an inner city school in Manchester encouraged talk between two children from the same cultural background.

> Nasreen and Ranjit are exploring the 'cave' (role play for the duration of the homes topic) with torches. They discover a collection of books, about bears as it so happens. Nasreen has been in school longer than Ranjit, who lacks confidence and is very quiet, choosing to watch what goes on and remain quite impassive as he sits with the rest of the class on the carpet 'listening' to a story. He has been encouraged to play with Nasreen. Nasreen opens *Peace at Last* and starts to read to Ranjit, who points to the baby bear and says 'bear' in a very self-assured tone. She carries on telling the story to Ranjit. He listens enraptured as he gazes at Nasreen.

One can see that, although Ranjit was assessed by his teacher as a new pupil with very limited understanding of English, he was more knowledgeable than he had been given credit for. As with many such classes, the support for Ranjit was provided by the classteacher, with occasional classroom assistant support.

Children with English as an additional language make best progress when helped by practitioners who:

- build on children's experience of language at home and in the wider community, so that their developing use of English and other languages support one another;

- provide a range of opportunities for children to engage in speaking and listening activities in English with peers and adults;

- provide bilingual support in particular to extend vocabulary;

- provide a variety of writing in the children's home languages as well as in English, including, books, notices and labels;

- provide opportunities for children to hear home languages as well as English, for example through the use of audio and video materials.

(DfEE 1999d:17)

Combating racism in the early years

> Racism in general terms consists of conduct or words or practices which disadvantage or advantage people because of their colour, culture or ethnic origin. In its more subtle form it is as damaging as in its overt form.
>
> (Macpherson 1999)

At a very young age, children begin to identify physical and other differences and use them as a basis for identification and categorization. The prejudices and attitudes manifest by children are not inborn, but learned from the whole environment – language, books, toys, posters, adults, other children and the media. Children need to be provided with specific opportunities to unlearn any negative attitudes and behaviours towards people who are different from themselves. It should not be assumed that just because no obvious racial incidents occur, young children may not already be prejudiced or learning to be so. Racial harassment may be hidden under apparently acceptable behaviour. Sometimes it is only careful vigilance that identifies what is really going on in an apparently 'happy' play situation.

Celebration of the diversity of cultures can be tackled by exploring the similarities between children. Bruce (1987:146) focuses on developing a sense of self-worth through helping children understand that differences are acceptable. The following example, from a reception class in eastern England, follows a discussion and demonstration about how to make fruit juice. A group of four-year-olds familiar with Coca-Cola and orange juice learned that Thomas's favourite drink was mango juice, because that is what he drank in Jamaica when visiting his grandparents. This small difference compared to his peers was used sensitively by Thomas's teacher to explore other aspects of his culture with the indigenous white children in his class. They showed pictures of his parents' traditional dress and discussed hair, skin and eye colour in a matter of fact way.

In guidance on promoting an anti-bias curriculum, the NAEYC (1989) recommends the following as starting points.

- Connect cultural activities to individual children and their families.
- Remember that while cultural patterns are real and affect members of an ethnic group, families live their culture in their own individual way.
- Connect cultural activities to concrete, daily life.
- Explore cultural diversity with the principle that everyone has a culture.
- Have cultural diversity permeate the daily life of the classroom, through frequent, concrete, hands-on experiences relating to young children's interests.
- Avoid the editorial 'we' when talking to children.
- Explore the similarities among people through their differences.
- Begin with the cultural diversity among the children and staff in your classroom.

(Teacher Training Agency 2000)

Learning for All: Standards for Racial Equality in Schools (Commission for Racial Equality 2000) provides guidance on effective practices to support English language acquisition. Longitudinal research studies (Thomas and Collier 1997) have shown that children who are given the opportunity to switch languages and have instruction in both home language and English and work with minority language speakers and English pupils achieved more highly than children who were taught away from the rest of their peers, learning the sounds and structures of English in withdrawal classes. Children with EAL need to be encouraged also to be independent in their use of a range of learning strategies. Repeatedly research shows that EAL children make more progress when engaged with English-speaking children in mainstream classes. This is what happens in good early years settings. Those of you working with bilingual children will know that using stories such as *Peace at Last* and *Not Now Bernard* with a lot of repetition can often be the stimulus for the first English words spoken. Puppets, too, can provide a necessary stimulus for all children.

Provision for children with special educational needs in early years settings

Adaptations need especially to be made in settings where there are children with limited mobility. The example below shows the innovative and simple way equipment was modified in a nursery school.

> The water trays have been raised by the caretaker to allow children in their wheelchairs to reach them and so help them to learn about emptying and filling containers using their own easily accessible supply of water.
>
> Grosvenor Nursery School, Bolton

Practice must recognise that there needs to be compensation for the senses that are impaired, by providing enriching kineasthetic (tactile), auditory (hearing) or visual (seeing) activities depending on the child's specific need. All children have preferred learning styles. Some children nevertheless have strongly preferred styles, especially those with special educational needs.

> The sensory stimuli are outstanding in some parts of the nursery; for example, in the space centre the impact of the flashing lights, well-resourced launch pad and evocative strains of space music helped the children to develop their sensory skills. They listened to a range of sounds and observed the actions of other children as they prepared for the lunar landing, well equipped with their survival bags and dressed in their sparkling, reflective space suits. The improvement in the communication skills of some children as they tried to verbalise their sense of delight was very evident. On another occasion, the children were encouraged to explore the lunar landscape using their hands to move the space people over the frozen jelly, large blocks of scented soap and a myriad of coloured stones. Again tactile skills were effectively developed which helped the children begin to articulate experiences they were

exploring. All children, but especially the children with special educational needs, enjoyed such exploratory activities as they discovered how to attribute a word to a sensation that was new to them.

Grosvenor Nursery School, Bolton

A setting in receipt of government funding for early education and maintained nursery schools must have a written SEN policy. The implementation of the policy is the responsibility of the headteacher or manager and the governors in maintained settings. Parents must be updated annually on the effectiveness of the policy and on any changes to be made. The important role of the Foundation Stage in identifying and supporting pupils with SEN is given a much higher status in the revised *Code of Practice* (DfES 2001b). The statutory duties are clear and can be summarised as follows.

Roles and responsibilities in Early Education Settings

- *The settings management group* should work with practitioners to determine the setting's general policy and approach to provision for children with SEN.

- *The head of the setting* has responsibility for the day-to-day *management* of all aspects of the setting's work, including provision for children with SEN. The head of the setting should keep the management group fully informed and also work closely with the special educational needs co-ordinator (SENCO).

- *All practitioners* should be involved in the development of the SEN policy and be fully aware of the procedures for identifying, assessing and making provision for children with special educational needs.

- *The SENCO* working closely with the head of the setting and colleagues has responsibility for the day-to-day *operation* of the setting's SEN policy and for co-ordinating provision for children with SEN, particularly through *Early Years Action* and *Early Years Action Plus*.

(DfES 2001b:17)

The *Code of Practice* assumes that a child's special educational needs fall within a number of broad areas, including:

- communication and interaction;

- cognition and learning;

- behavioural, emotional and social development;

- sensory and/or physical.

An area that warrants further exemplification in the early years is that of arrangements made to identify children with special educational needs. I say this because there are some settings which would claim not to have children with special educational needs because they do not have the systems in place to identify specific learning, language or social difficulties. This part of the book will deal in general terms with how provision takes account of the individual needs of children. Chapter 4 will give examples of the assessment systems used for children with special educational needs and the procedures which need to be followed once a child has been identified as having special educational needs.

In all types of settings it is crucial to involve parents from their child's very first days in the setting. This applies to all children of course, but is doubly important for children who may manifest signs of having particular needs. The dilemma for practitioners is that of distinguishing the child who is making slower progress than others because of specific difficulties, from those who have clearly defined reasons for their slower progress. However, both categories of children will be given closer attention to decide what appropriate intervention is required. In more and more settings, there are language-screening arrangements. For example, a small group of children were identified for targeted support as a result of very low scores on a language assessment programme. I know some of you will throw up your hands in horror at the implications of this procedure, preferring the sustained observational assessments as a more accurate measure of a child's needs. From the experience of seeing both methods in use: from targeting a small group of children with language delays early and regularly to try and compensate for, perhaps, a language-impoverished home environment; to the *laissez-faire* approach where small numbers of children are observed not communicating with other children or being targeted for one-to-one support by an appropriate adult and falling further and further behind socially and intellectually. A key message from the *Code of Practice* is early intervention. 'The younger the child is when intervention begins, the more chance there will be of making optimum progress – so long as the programme devised is appropriate for her developmental age and suitable for her needs' (Roffey 2001: 6).

It is impossible to prescribe one particular form of provision or teaching method, because what is needed varies so much. The *Code of Practice* recognises this and suggests a combination of:

- allocating extra adult time to plan and monitor the programmes of intervention;

- providing different learning materials and equipment;

- offering individual or group support, or staff development and training to introduce more effective teaching strategies;

- creating small groups within the ordinary classroom or setting, which receive extra attention from the practitioner, or other adult;

- creating small groups which work outside the classroom for short periods of time, with a practitioner or other adult.

Defining the early years curriculum: a theoretical perspective

In a philosophical debate about how we decide what to teach, Eisner (1996) reminds us that our capacity to create symbols is an inherent part of our species via the differentiated sensory system we possess which enables us to learn to 'read' the qualities of the environment to which the components of the system are responsive.

> The visual world is made conscious through the exercise of sight, the auditory world through the capacity to hear, the tactile world through the ability to feel what we touch. These biologically given capacities are the resources we use to adapt to the demands of the environment and, for humans, the resources that we employ to alter it. Our sensory system is . . . a kind of information pick-up system. We literally get in touch with the world through our increasingly refined ability to experience the qualities of the world we inhabit.
>
> (Eisner 1996:17)

Bruner (1990) refers to 'technologies of mind' as the means of extending our biological limits. This is critical for education. Eisner, quoting Bruner, states that while our biological endowment gives us the capacity to experience the environment, it is through culture that these capacities are extended. As humans we have created a variety of forms of representation which allow us to recreate or record an experience which memory alone cannot sustain. We are able to enter, psychologically speaking, into worlds through story, poetry, painting, music, mathematics and sciences, and each has their own special content. They perform unique epistemic functions if we are able to read their content. The curriculum, therefore, must enable children to become multi-literate and offer the opportunity to understand and experience the special and unique meanings that different forms of representation make possible. For the early years of education there are clear indications here of the need to ensure that experiences provided for children allow them to represent in a variety of ways and to avoid a narrow concentration on what is easily measurable. There may be echoes here of the Reggio Emilia approach to early learning, which is founded on a 'distinct, coherent, evolving set of assumptions and perspectives drawn from three important intellectual traditions: European and American strands of *progressive education*, Piagetian and

Vygotskian *constructivist psychologies*, and Italian postwar *left-reform politics'* (Edwards *et al.* 1998:5). In their approach to learning children are involved in extended in-depth investigations. This project approach to early learning has always been a characteristic of early childhood curricula in the UK. However, it has not been adopted as *the* way of working in the early years.

Balance and distribution of time should also be considered. Cognitive development, a prime educational goal, defined as the child's ability to understand the world, to deal effectively with problems, and to acquire wide varieties of meanings from interactions with it (Eisner 1996:20), contrasts with the more generally held view of cognition as essentially dealing with thought mediated by language (Anderson 1975). The contrast between the cognitive and affective domains points clearly to the different perspectives attached to each. Affect is said to deal with feeling and not with knowing, while cognition deals with knowing and not with feeling. This has implications for the priority given to each of these domains within a nursery context. Cognitive studies, mathematics, reading and science may be given prime time. When areas of learning are taught is as important as for how long. The early learning goals (QCA 2000) have a strong focus on cognition. Concerns are rightly expressed about the marginalisation of the affective domains within recent government initiatives. A range of strategies to embed the dimensions of creativity into everyday practices in the preschool environment are outlined in Chapter 11. Priority to communication, language and literacy and mathematical development alongside that of personal, social and emotional development are the hallmarks of the English curriculum framework for the early years as we start the twenty-first century. Eisner and others (Brierley 1987) would claim that the curriculum needs to take equal account of the cognitive and affective domains, as the two are interdependent, 'they are part of the same reality in human experience'. This view contrasts strongly with the current orthodoxy of distribution of curriculum time. The recently published early learning goals give scant attention to creative and physical development when compared to the other four areas of learning: personal, social and emotional development; language and literacy; mathematics and knowledge and understanding of the world. It is perhaps the focus which is being given to the cognitive domain, or rather the way in which cognition is defined by central government, which is causing the greatest angst amongst early years educators (Blenkin and Kelly 1997, Ghouri 1999a, Scott 1998). Evidence from a survey carried out by Ofsted (1993) may be contributing to the new reality in the early years (see Figure 2.1). The Report identified factors contributing to high quality provision and good standards of work. Increased attention to language and literacy was a major recommendation.

Is it appropriate to divide an early years curriculum into discrete areas of learning and focusing on the outcomes of that learning? Or should we, as claimed by

- The recruitment of staff, well-qualified by training and/or experience for work with reception class pupils: professional support which fully recognises the complex and demanding task of providing a suitable curriculum for the age group which dovetails successfully into the National Curriculum.
- Enlisting the help of parents with a focus upon involving them in supporting their children's learning.
- The length of time children spend on the reception class. This suggests that wherever possible three terms in the reception class, i.e. early entry, is to be preferred. This is particularly important for summer-born children who as a group are the most likely to have the shortest time in the reception class and in primary school. However, they should have a pattern of admission suited to their needs.
- The provision of a broad and balanced programme for the reception year and attention paid to planning the curriculum at all levels – classteacher, year group and whole school.
- Priority given to teaching the skills of literacy and numeracy. This is not to say that the most effective schools focus narrowly on these aspects of the work; rather that they provide a rich and varied but manageable programme of work which secures ample opportunities for pupils to listen carefully to good models of language, speak clearly and confidently, increase and use their vocabulary imaginatively, and make a sound start on the road to reading and writing.
- A high degree of attention to establishing standards of behaviour reinforced by praise and understanding by such strategies as stories depicting human relationships and values.
- The assessment of children's progress and attainment as an integral part of the programme of work. Much of this is achieved by the close observation of children's responses but some schools also use diagnostic tests successfully.
- Meeting the demands of combining a prolonged reception period, caused by early entry, with those of the National Curriculum as pupils reach statutory age.

FIGURE 2.1   Factors contributing to high quality provision in reception classes (Ofsted 1993:14)

Pascal and Bertram (1997), exercise caution in promoting a curriculum defined by 'dominant power bases which exist in society at a particular point in time'? Should definitions of an early years curriculum be as narrow as the early learning goals imply? Research provides a range of possible answers to these questions, which are included in subsequent chapters and in the next section.

An appropriate curriculum for the early years: the English version

A definition of curriculum cited in recent publications (Rodger 1994, Early Years Curriculum Group 1989, and adapted from Drummond *et al.* 1989:11) states the curriculum for young children should include:

- all the opportunities for learning and development that are made available to young children;

- the activities, attitudes and behaviour that are planned, encouraged, tolerated or ignored;
- the way the room is organised and the routines followed by adults and children;
- the part adults take in organising, directing, influencing and joining in what the children do;
- the extent to which parents are involved in each of the above.

David *et al.* (1993) stated that effective early education is characterised by:

- practical, experiential learning;
- the significance of the social context;
- the vital role of adult intervention;
- dangers of introducing them [the children] to too formal a curriculum too soon.

These are all-embracing definitions inclusive of all activities in the nursery setting and ones which recognise the part played by adults. But does this go far enough in defining what form activities should take? The title for this publication has undergone several changes before the current one was finally decided upon. What counts, surely, must be the appropriateness of the experiences on offer to children. Should an early years curriculum be definable by the characteristics of the activities contained within it? Are the activities appropriate? Is the balance between the cognitive and the affective domains equitable? What is an appropriate activity for children under five? Is there a consensus view on this? Bruce (1987:51) considers three aspects: the child; the knowledge; and the environment in which the child is educated. The environment is the means of linking the child and knowledge. It is made up, first, and most importantly, of people, but also of objects (material provisions), places and events. David (1996:85) recalls the seminal work of Curtis (1986:3) who significantly maintained that there is a recognisable curriculum for children under statutory school age based on skills and competences which can be developed in a flexible, child-centred environment, and that there is ample material with which to challenge and extend children without offering them a watered-down reception class programme. Do the six areas of learning do this? At long last the areas of learning framework for the curriculum acknowledges that children in reception classes are entitled to their own curriculum (Scott 1999). Many children enter nursery schools with very limited social and language skills. Unlike our European neighbours (Mills and Mills 1997) the English tradition of creating a child-centred play-based environment, which values and supports child-initiated learning at the expense of the development of speaking and listening and personal and social skills, could be said to be disadvantaging the English child under five (Tizard and Hughes 1984). Selective use of the limited research evidence perpetuates these myths of the value of the child-centred, play-based environment. What is known from the work of psychologists such as Vygotsky and Bruner is that children need to engage in play to promote their personal and social skills and with the *support and involvement* of a knowledgeable adult intellectual development can be enhanced. Observations of nursery workers (Munn and Schaffer 1993) and young learners in educationally focused nurseries in the Strathclyde region of Scotland showed how adults carefully supported and sustained children's experiences. Children engaged in the challenges of literacy and numeracy within a familiar and goal-directed context.

There is a lack of research about what constitutes successful practice, and the early years ideology continues. The belief that children learn through their play is well grounded in the ideologies derived from the work of Montessori and Isaacs (Bruce 1987). However, although ideologically the case for play may be strong (Bennett *et al.* 1997) there is a distinct lack of research evidence to substantiate the claim that play is the educationally powerful process it is claimed to be historically. Anning (1998) also supports this view regarding the lack of empirical evidence in this area to inform politicians, who in her view do not understand how children learn and who deride the value of play as an appropriate way of learning effectively. Their counter-argument emphasises the extent to which pre-school education should be seen as a means of preparation for 'proper' school (Anning 1998:30). Can one blame the politicians, given the lack of evidence or indeed critical analysis of the nature of an appropriate curriculum for the early years by those with responsibility for it? The slogan 'children learn through their play' has gained an almost universal status in the early years arena. Caution is needed in taking this too literally. Some of the most extensive evidence (Ofsted 1993, DES 1989) expressed concern at the lack of purpose to play in reception classes and at the aimlessness of some activities purporting to be play.

In the previous edition, reference was made at this point to the outcomes of the *Effective Provision for Pre-school Education Project* (Sylva *et al.* 1999) which was a DfEE project funded for five years to look at the most effective pre-school provision in England. The questions raised then were:

- Are some pre-school settings more effective than others?

- What does effective mean in terms of academic, social and emotional outcomes?

- What is the contribution of the *de facto* curriculum to effective learning?

The findings of the research project (Siraj-Blatchford *et al.* 2002) can now be reported. In their Report *Researching Effective Pedagogy in the Early Years* a key finding based on an analysis of qualitative and quantitative data is the key role of the involvement of both the adult and a child for learning to be worthwhile. The content of learning should in some way be instructive, requiring some element of shared thinking. In terms of pedagogy (defined as instructional techniques and strategies that enable learning to take place), effective settings encourage sustained shared thinking. This is characterised by staff extending child-initiated interactions. In the settings surveyed, half of the child-initiated episodes contained intellectual challenge, including intervention from a staff member to extend children's thinking. The project also found that open-ended questioning was generally associated with better cognitive achievement. The good practice cited below to illustrate the research findings took place in a North London playgroup serving an ethnically diverse local authority housing estate.

Delivering flowers

A well-resourced outdoor area comprising a flower shop and a garden centre role play areas along with a truck with carrying capacity were the resources available outside. Inside, children could make paper flowers with the assistance of a nursery nurse using sticks, sellotape and coloured tissue paper. An adult was on hand to extend the children's learning at all times. Making the flowers was straightforward, but the three-year-olds struggled to make the links with the flower shop and the truck until they had this explained to them. Firstly, it was decided to make the truck look like a delivery van with appropriate signs, scribed by the adult with some emergent writing and flower patterns made by the children. The children showed confidence in going to purchase flowers at the shop. The next problem to be solved was how to carry them, then how to deliver them. The children wrestled successfully with counting five flowers and making 'bouquets' which were then delivered by the driver.

At one level this was a child-initiated learning experience as a consequence of the props available, but at another level it was a carefully planned adult-led learning experience because of the planned outcomes. However, whatever it was, it was successful in helping children see the consequences of their actions and to take part in role play, develop co-operative skills and sustain interest and concentration. This activity was particularly effective for a Polish child with very limited English. He saw the purpose of delivering flowers to the home corner inside the playgroup and did this with great gusto. This was an excellent opportunity to build on children's developing understanding and encapsulates the free flow between the indoor and outdoor curriculum.

Implementing the Foundation Stage curriculum

The Qualifications and Curriculum Authority have defined a curriculum for children under five in their guidance to practitioners (QCA 2000) as one which should underpin all future learning by supporting, fostering, promoting and developing children's

- personal, social and emotional well-being;
- positive attitudes and dispositions towards their learning;
- social skills;
- attention skills and persistence;
- language and communication;
- reading and writing;
- mathematics;
- knowledge and understanding of the world;
- physical development;
- creative development.

This, at the present time, is the statutory definition of an early years curriculum and places a clear focus on what is on offer for children to do in their pre-school environments. A view stated earlier is that one of the defining characteristics of high quality experiences in the nursery is the way in which activities support and extend children's learning. Settings are also expected to provide opportunities to address important aspects of children's spiritual, moral, social and cultural development. The plans that settings produce are at various levels, for example, long-term (across a year), medium-term (across a term), and short-term (day-to-day) (see Chapter 3 for more information). QCA guidance recognises the crucial role of parents as children's 'first and most enduring educators'. (QCA 2000:9) It advises that each setting should seek to develop an effective partnership with parents characterised by the following common features:

- practitioners show respect and understanding for the role of the parent in their child's education;
- the past and the future part played by parents in the education of their children are recognised and explicitly encouraged;
- practitioners listen to parents' accounts of their child's development and any concerns they have;

- arrangements for settling in are flexible enough to give time for children to become secure and for practitioners and parents to discuss each child's circumstances, interests, skills and needs;

- all parents are made to feel welcome, valued and necessary through a range of different opportunities for collaboration between children, parents and practitioners;

- the knowledge and expertise of parents and other family adults are used to support the learning opportunities provided by the setting;

- practitioners use a variety of ways to keep parents fully informed about the curriculum, such as brochures, displays and videos which are available in the home languages of the parents and through informal discussion;

- parents and practitioners talk about and record information about the child's progress and achievements, for example through meetings or making a book about the child;

- relevant learning and play activities, such as reading and sharing books, are continued at home. Similarly, experiences at home are used to develop learning in the setting, for example visits and celebrations.

Organisation and management in the Foundation Stage

Most effective settings combine the provision of open-framework free-play opportunities with more focused group work involving some direct instruction. Children's successful achievement is directly related to the quality and quantity of

---

- Split the elements of the literacy and numeracy strategies and teach throughout the day.
- Give a high priority to personal, social and emotional development, communication, language and literacy and mathematical development.
- Always include classroom assistant or nursery nurse in focused teaching activities.
- Nursery class and reception class may be combined as an early years unit.
- Do not differentiate between work and play.
- Include planned opportunities for learning in the outdoor environment for all areas of learning.
- Identify a specific learning intention in your planning for adult-focused activities and indicate the role of adults on your plans.
- Check how often you expect your children to sit all together on the carpet.
- What strategies have you introduced to involve parents?

FIGURE 2.2 Checklist for working towards good practice in the reception class

the teaching (Siraj-Blatchford *et al.* 2002). The adult-planned and initiated focused group work is crucial to successful learning. Effective settings achieve a balance between the opportunities for children to benefit from teacher intensive group work and the provision of freely chosen yet potentially instructive play activities. In reception classes, high intellectual challenge tended to occur in teacher-initiated episodes. This was not the case in pre-school settings.

Guidance on the Foundation Stage curriculum (QCA 2000) emphasises an 'emergent, cognitively orientated approach' to learning. They state that effective practitioners assess the child's performance to ensure the provision of challenging yet achievable experiences, model appropriate language, values and practices, encourage socio-dramatic play, praise and encourage, ask questions and interact verbally with children to encourage *sustained shared thinking*.

A curriculum for three-year-olds

Government has provided extensive sums of money to increase opportunities for childcare and extend the universal provision for four-year-olds to three-year-olds. By 2004, £6 million will have been provided for three-year-olds. There has been concern expressed in the past that many preschools will need significant support to achieve the quality levels demonstrated by other sectors (DfEE 1999f:48). This situation is being remedied through the introduction of a new arm of Ofsted which brought together the regulation of education and day care. In addition, a national training strategy is in place to guarantee that settings are appropriately staffed. A career structure exists for all practitioners whatever their level of initial training. One significant area of improvement has been the increase in graduates with early years as their main subject. The pre-school case study cited earlier in this chapter was led by an early years graduate.

Three-year-olds' patterns of behaviour

Needs and priorities for young three-year-olds should reflect their behaviours. An approach which, in my opinion, offers considerable scope for practitioners is cited by Athey (1990). She maintains that children notice elements from their surroundings, depending on their interest at the time, and that they have their own intrinsic motivation which must be facilitated by materials and support from adults. Each pattern of behaviour is called a 'schema', which she defines as 'a pattern of repeatable behaviour into which experiences are assimilated and are gradually coordinated' (Athey 1990:37). An appropriate curriculum therefore needs to ensure that the schemas are enriched and supported. There are many schemas, but some of the easily identifiable ones are:

- connection (joining) – a child may enjoy playing with train tracks, construction sets, string or Sellotape;

- enveloping (covering and surrounding) – a child may enjoy playing with dens, things in boxes and envelopes and may spend a lot of time dressing up and wrapping 'presents';

- rotation (circles) – a child may enjoy circle games and be fascinated by wheels, roundabouts, spinning tops or kaleidoscopes;

- trajectory (straight lines) – a child may enjoy throwing games, woodwork, percussion, football or playing with running water;

- transporting (moving things) – a child may enjoy using shopping bags, buggies or trailers.

(National Primary Centre and Oxfordshire Education Department 1995)

To illustrate this more practically one needs to observe a three-year-old to note his or her patterns of repeated behaviour and the points at which adult intervention contributes to progression from the form of the schema to the curriculum content required to ensure there is progression in learning. Nutbrown (1994) provides a stimulating and rich account of the ways in which children's learning is facilitated in an active, dynamic and creative way.

This chapter has aimed to raise questions about the form of an appropriate curriculum for the early years and to consider the diverse ways of regarding the constituents of an appropriate early years curriculum.

Further reading

Bennett, N., Wood, L., and Rogers, S. (1997) *Teaching Through Play: Teachers' Thinking and Classroom Practice*. Buckingham: Open University Press.

Bredecamp, S. (ed.) (1997) *Developmentally Appropriate Practice in Early Childhood Programs Serving Children From Birth Through Age 8*, 2nd edn. Washington DC: National Association for the Education of Young Children.

Edwards, C., Gandini, L., and Forman, G. (eds) (1998) *The Hundred Languages of Children: The Reggio Emilia Approach – Advanced Reflections*. London: JAI Press.

Hohmann, M., Banet, B., and Weikart, D. P. (1979) *Young Children in Action*. Ypsilanti, Michigan: The High/Scope Press.

Nutbrown, C. (1994) *Threads of Thinking*. London: Paul Chapman Publishing.

Writing an early years policy and curriculum planning

Introduction

This chapter provides guidance, to leaders and practitioners in the early years, on writing an early years policy and the most effective methods of curriculum planning. Exemplar material from a range of authorities and settings (Bolton, Lincolnshire, Wandsworth 2000) will be included in order to show how the statutory requirements have been interpreted to provide practitioners with guidance. Account is also taken of the planning guidance provided by QCA (2001). At the heart of a policy must be what will most effectively meet the needs of children

What is an effective Foundation Stage policy?

A policy for the Foundation Stage may not exist as a single statement, but comprise various elements: induction arrangements; partnership with parents; curricular guidance for staff and parents; assessment policy; equal opportunities policy; special educational needs policy; gifted and talented policy; and a continuing professional development (CPD) policy. Practitioners working in the maintained sector in a nursery and/or reception class may be expected to have their policies for the aforementioned areas included as a part of whole school policies. Whatever the arrangements, it is important to ensure that the curriculum statement identifies the distinctiveness of the Foundation Stage. At long last there are now statutory requirements for the vital first stage of education. I make no apologies for sharing practices from those settings that have the highest of expectations and have publicly demonstrated this either through outstanding inspection reports or through their status as an Early Excellence centre or a Beacon nursery school. Adams (1994) described the steps taken to produce an equal opportunities policy by the staff of a combined nursery centre in Stockport. I recommend reading her chapter to see how skilfully the manager of the centre involved a range of stakeholders in the policy-writing process. The curricular guidance provided by QCA (2000) provides a comprehensive outline as to what headteachers and managers need to take account of when defining their curriculum through well formed principles, aims and objectives, opportunities to meet the wide range of diversity and the role of parents and carers.

Who is the early years policy for?

As well as meeting statutory requirements with regard to information which needs to be provided for parents, an early years policy should outline the aims and philosophy of the setting to inform staff working in it what its priorities are with regard to the quality of education and care provided for the children. What are the beliefs which underpin the practices in your under fives setting? In this section of the chapter examples of early years policies are shared with you. What are the aims of your setting? Can you conjure up an image of the setting whose aims are listed below?

Statement of aims

The centre is committed to providing:

- a high quality teaching and learning environment which is purposeful, efficient and effective;
- a value for money integrated service, which meets the needs of the local community and enables families to access new opportunities and support in a lifetime of learning;
- a wide range of choice in education and care (the Early Years) through a working partnership with families, carers and agencies, both in-house and outreach;
- clearly defined policies, plans and strategic objectives which are constantly reviewed, monitored and evaluated;
- an Early Years setting of 'Best Practice' to share with other professionals through a programme of training and development.

Above all it is child-centred and child-focused based on a network of play.

(Donnelly 2003)

An earlier section of the chapter has outlined the statutory requirements with regard to providing information for outsiders and officials from the local authority. While vital for the continued survival of your setting it is also important that issues relating to quality are reviewed and examined. As I have maintained throughout this book the highest level of quality lies in the learning experiences and activities you provide for your children. Are they appropriate for the needs of your children? Are they enjoyable? Do they hold the attention of your children?

Sometimes you will enhance what the children are learning, but at other times the resources and resourcefulness of the children will be sufficient. Children under five need many opportunities to learn through their play. How do you justify this to your parents who see play as something to be done after work? More importantly, if you work in a school how do you justify play to your colleagues? How do you raise the status of play in your setting? It is wise to recall at this point the outcomes of the most significant research into effective early years practices that there has been for several years. Siraj-Blatchford's (2002) case study analysis shows that while effective settings strike a balance between adult-led and child-initiated activities, in excellent settings adults extended about half of the child-initiated activities. To be effective, play activities were found to need to be potentially instructive. This sends a strong and clear message to practitioners to be able to articulate the purposes of free choice activities.

Effective early years policies

An early years policy is a statement of the aims and objectives of your early years practice. It may be very short and be supported by more detailed policies on specific aspects of your provision, for example, special educational needs, racial equality, equal opportunities or involvement with parents and carers. As stated earlier, it is important that the policy is an accurate reflection of what happens in your setting. Does it inform and guide your staff? Do you have a different statement of intent for parents? Generally settings do, but there is inevitably some overlap. Typically an early years policy will contain:

- a statement of principles which are fundamental to good early years practice;
- a statement of general aims which frequently cover all areas of development: social, cultural, emotional and intellectual; and physical and aesthetic;
- information about the role of the early years staff: who they are, what their responsibilities are;
- details about classroom management: the purposes of each area and a justification for this; the routine of the day and what times the sessions are held;
- information about the role of parents and carers;
- a statement about the identification of children with special educational needs and indication of the range of outside agencies involved regularly in the setting;
- curriculum information: planning methods; and assessment and recording systems;
- transfer arrangements;

- indication of various booklets that are available to parents;
- examples of report forms;
- admission criteria;
- staff development procedures;
- performance management arrangements.

What are the characteristics of effective curriculum planning?

Traditionally, teachers in the maintained sector, i.e. in nursery schools and classes and in reception classes, have been involved with whole school curriculum planning. The idea is not new and certainly one which is a major feature in the initial training of teachers. Staff working in playgroups on the other hand may have less experience of curriculum planning. Consequently the introduction of the six areas of learning as a framework for the planning of a curriculum for children under five has posed greater problems: staff have little time to plan, as they may only work part-time or even be working on a voluntary basis; they may lack understanding of the process and purpose of educational planning. Indeed, the principle that activities are planned with specific learning goals in mind may be an anathema to many small voluntary groups working with children under five. This gap in the experience of two very diverse groups of educators is one which the *Early Years Development Partnership and Plans* (DfEE 1997) is seeking to overcome through the involvement of qualified teachers in the work of all providers of early education.

> The strategic principles indicate that a qualified teacher (early years specialist) should be involved in any setting providing early education in a plan. This is intended to raise standards, not to impose the same philosophy on all providers, or even to be a device to exclude certain providers from participating in a plan. The evidence from inspections indicates that the planning of activities and the assessment of children often need attention: qualified teachers could help with development of these areas.
>
> (DfEE 1997:16)

Everything that children do in your setting will need to be documented to show what you want children to learn and what they have learned. Planning and assessment are very closely linked, but for clarity each is given their own chapter. QCA (2001) have recognised the importance of successful planning by providing additional guidance to settings following the exemplification of the early learning goals in their guidance document. A key to effective planning is that it builds on what children already know, understand and can do. I do not propose to repeat the examples provided in the document, which are readily available to all settings, but to include completed exemplars from a range of settings. The purpose of planning is to provide practitioners with an overview of what children are going to learn based on their prior experiences and to make sure that resources are available.

- What are the children's learning needs?
- What are the children going to learn?
- What are they going to do and experience?
- How will different needs be met?
- What will you need?
- What adult support will be needed?

(Nicholson 2000)

Following the requirement that all settings providing educational experiences for four-year-olds need to plan a curriculum based on the six areas of learning, many more groups are needing support and guidance in this area. Sources of support for the private, voluntary and independent sectors are the inspection process (Ofsted 1996b), guidelines from the Pre-school Learning Alliance (PLA) and QCA (1997, 1998a, 2001). Ofsted have provided guidelines for their own inspectors on what to look for when inspecting the Foundation Stage. It is recommended that inspectors will look for:

- planning which covers a range of experiences to cover the six areas of learning;
- various layers of planning: short, medium and long term;
- clear learning objectives and focused teaching by all adults working with children;
- a focus on children's personal development, e.g. confidence, independence, co-operation;
- breadth and balance but with a strong emphasis given to the development of language and literacy and mathematics;
- use of baseline assessments;
- shared planning with all adults working regularly with the children;
- continuity and progression with the next stage;
- effective use of assessment and recording.

(Ofsted 1996a)

Some providers in the private and voluntary sectors are concerned that they are unable to match the rigour with which schools plan the early years curriculum. Ofsted too (1999b) recognise that expectations for planning in the voluntary sector are likely to be more informal than in other settings. QCA have provided guidance to providers in the form of various explanatory documents and guidelines for good practice (QCA 1997, 1998a). An important factor in effective curriculum planning is that it needs to be seen as part of a 'continuous cycle involving planning, observing, recording, assessing and returning to planning in the light of the intermediate' (DES 1990:10).

Effective planning will cover *long-*, *medium-* and *short-term* periods of time. This may mean a year or term for long-term plans, the length of a topic or half a term for medium-term, or a week or day for short-term plans.

Long-term

As stated in Chapter 1 settings are expected to plan at three levels: long-, medium- and short-term. Long-term planning should reflect the aims of the setting and be a record of when and where children will have experience of each area of learning. The long-term plan may also be the scheme of work for each area of learning. Those authorities that have produced curricular frameworks or schemes of work (Stockport 1996, Field and Lally 1996) are able to provide settings with a progressive list of experiences on which to base their curriculum. Examples from the planning guidance in the two authorities mentioned are included in several chapters following. Continuity and progression in children's learning needs to be considered when planning in the long term, especially where there is a wide age range in the setting. Sylva (1994) defines continuity and progression in the following way:

> continuity and progression are interlinked concepts relating to the nature and quality of children's learning experiences over time. Progression is essentially the sequence built into children's learning through curriculum policies and schemes of work so that later learning builds on knowledge, skills, understanding and attitudes learned previously. Continuity refers to the nature of the curriculum experienced by children as they transfer from one setting to another, be it from home to playgroup, from playgroup to school, from class to class within a school or from one school to another. Continuity occurs when there is an acceptable match of curriculum and approach, allowing appropriate progression in children's learning. Effective assessment and record keeping are the key to these ends.
>
> (Sylva 1994)

You should personalise your plan to reflect the resources you have. In a reception class you will need to include the requirements of the National Literacy and Numeracy Strategies. You may wish to cut and paste from the guidance document and check off what you have planned for the medium term from this. Another strategy that can be used for assessment purposes is to map out the *stepping-stones* for each area of learning. Figure 4.5 (p. 57) is an example of this for personal, social and emotional development and the activities and experiences you expect to plan to enable the children to make progress. Throughout the book the *stepping-stones* for each area of learning are presented in this form. A starting point for planning could be a theme or a topic. Figure 3.1 adopts that approach. On the other hand, you may wish to look at the *stepping-stones* and decide how children's learning needs can be met in various parts of your setting.

Spring Term – Journeys

7 Jan	Journey to the nursery
14 Jan	Trains (train trip)
21 Jan	Trains
28 Jan	Buses (bus depot trip)
4 Feb	Space
Half Term	
18 Feb	Space
25 Feb	Water journeys
4 March	Journeys through stories
11 March	What journeys do I make?
	Where do I go?
18 March	Easter activities

FIGURE 3.1   Long-term plan, Grosvenor Nursery School

Medium-term

This plan will be in more detail and show what children are to learn in a block of time. This may be the time for a topic/theme and therefore may vary according to the topic. It may be for a period of time, such as half a term, although generally this is too long for a topic to last unless it has sub-topics. For example, a theme of fairy stories could take a different story each week or fortnight. A transport theme might look at land, sea and air transports as separate mini-topics. I would recommend a theme-based approach as it has the scope to provide a context for children's learning. It is often advocated that learning should build on what children already know. However, there can be limitations to this if a number of your children have very restricted pre-nursery experiences. It will require ingenuity and creativity on the part of the setting to recreate meaningful situations to help children have first-hand experience. Some children will not know what a florist is for example, or know that bouquets of flowers can be delivered. Have the children been to the countryside, or visited a castle or a farm? A first-hand topic for young three-year-olds such as gardening will need to have a range of first-hand experiences in the

TRAIN/BUS STATION

Communication, language and literacy
- To develop and extend vocabulary – station, waiting room, timetable, tickets, journey, passenger.
- To develop speaking and listening skills by recreating a range of interactions between passengers/ticket sellers, ticket collector, driver, station guard.
- To develop awareness of environmental print and number within the bus or train station – tickets, timetables, routes, signs, directions (writing for a purpose).
- To use a widening range of words to express or elaborate ideas.
- Use language for an increasing range of purposes – role play of a passenger, ticket collector, driver.

Personal, social and emotional development
- To work as part of a group, sharing and taking turns – queuing, waiting.
- To show care and concern for others.
- To seek out others to share experiences – going on a journey, buying tickets.
- To develop self- confidence and competence which aids a positive disposition to learn.

Physical development
- To show respect for other children's personal space when playing among them.

LEARNING OBJECTIVES

Mathematical development
- To develop counting skills and language such as add one more, take one away, how many now? Counting buses, engines, carriages, passengers.
- Ordering numbers – first in the queue, carriage.
- Recognise some numerals – bus nos, platform nos, timetables, ticket prices.
- To observe and use positional language – next to, behind, in front of, on top.
- Use shapes appropriately for tasks – making train/bus pictures using circle, rectangle, triangle, square.
- To develop problem-solving/estimation skills – how many people can get on the train/bus, how many in the waiting room? Have we got enough tickets?

Creative development
- To notice the role of adults.
- Use available resources to create props to support role-play in the station area.
- To engage in imaginative role-play based on first-hand experiences of train and bus journeys.
- To make constructions – trains/buses.
- Develop story line in role play.

Knowledge and understanding of the world
- To talk about what is seen and what is happening.
- To remember and talk about significant things that happened to them – experiences of journeys.
- To talk about people who work on trains and buses.
- To describe features of an event.
- Describe a simple journey – train ride, journey to school.

FIGURE 3.2 Medium-term plan, Grosvenor Nursery School

setting to bring it alive and provide children with the opportunity to use all their senses. Figure 3.1 shows a long-term plan for one area in a nursery school resourced for special educational needs, and Figure 3.2 part of the medium-term plan to show the detail for the week beginning 14 January.

Each setting will need to decide on the detail of its planning at various levels, for example, long-term (across a year), medium-term (across a term), and short-term (day-to-day). These plans together with the setting's overall aims, values and priorities should:

- build on the children's prior experiences and their skills and knowledge;
- give an outline of what is to be taught and learned in each area of learning and how the teaching and learning will take place;
- show major links across aspects of the areas of learning;
- indicate opportunities to foster children's spiritual, moral, social and cultural development through the six areas of learning;
- place an emphasis on personal and social development, language and literacy and mathematical development;
- identify planning for those children with special educational needs or English as an additional language.

FIGURE 3.3   QCA curriculum planning requirements (QCA 1997)

Medium-term planning addresses aspects of the curriculum in more detail, and will usually cover half a term or a term. The emphasis will usually be on adult-directed learning, although self-initiated experiences will be indicated and may have intended outcomes attached to them. A sequence of activities may be identified, resources needed, expected learning outcomes and assessment opportunities indicated. It is important that there is no duplication with other levels of planning, which is counter-productive. Medium-term planning may follow half-termly reviews of what has been achieved by children. The starting point will be the assessment of children's learning alongside intentions identified in the long-term plan. Figure 3.3 outlines the requirements for planning

Short-term

There are many variations in short-term plans. Figures 3.4 and 3.5 provide examples of focused plans for different areas of a nursery. Opportunties for learning outside and the balance between adult-directed and child-initiated learning should be clear on plans. Outdoor activities should be identified explicitly, the deployment of adults should be clear, especially for focused activities which are used as assessment opportunities. Planning may also differ according to what children are doing. For example, weekly circle time plans, small group plans, area plans, story plans and outdoor plans are sometimes seen in nursery schools.

Short-term planning is carried out weekly or daily, depending on the system adopted in the setting. It is important at this level that activities are planned according to the needs of the individual or group of children and that the planning recognises that children have very different learning needs. How will the children

Week beginning: *7 May*   Area: *Maths development*

Learning objective: *To recognize the properties of 2D shapes — corners and sides*

Materials   *2D shapes — 0, TRIANGLES, SQUARE, RECTANGLE, HEXAGON*

Activity
- *Adults to describe a shape in the bag eg 3 corners, 3 sides*
- *Child to take shape if correct.*
- *Sing and draw shape in the air*

Evaluation
KC and JP do not know the difference between the shapes.
All others recognize shapes — can move to 3D next time we look at shapes
Assess yellow group in small group time

FIGURE 3.4   Circle time planning sheet

Date: Area of learning: *communication, language and literacy*

Learning objective/s:
- *to build up vocabulary;*
- *to extend vocabulary, especially by grouping and naming*

Activity (beginning, middle and end):
B As a group discuss the animals and encourage children to name them if possible. Discuss their individual characteristics — stripes, long neck etc (note those children who name them). Discuss 'pair' as you introduce the second matching animal.

M Put six boxes in a row in front of you. Allow individual children to select, name and place animal in box encouraging them to say which box . Model what you want them to say: 'I'll put mine in the brown hexagon box.' Support those who cannot name and put the lid on. Ask different children to remember what went into each box and then name if possible — if not allow child to find a matching animal to support their thoughts.

E when all boxes are open, put pairs together and remind children about the Noah song or teach them the Noah song.

Evaluation:

FIGURE 3.5   Small group planning sheet

be grouped? How will you know what the children need to do next. Outcomes for learning may be differentiated to take account of the range of abilities: the least or more able. In some settings you may find the children work in groups of similar ability, as they do in Pennywell Early Excellence Centre for some of their time.

When planning activities staff need to be clear about:

- how each activity builds on the children's previous experiences, interests and achievements;
- the purpose of each activity;
- which aspects within the area of learning provide the focus for the activity;
- the nature of the evidence of children's learning that would be expected to result from each activity;
- their own role and that of other staff both in the activity itself and in gathering evidence of children's learning;
- how they will communicate to the children the purpose of each activity and their expectations;
- the resources and equipment that will be needed;
- the number of children that could take part in each activity and how they will manage this group of children in the context of a larger group or class;
- the balance of adult-directed and child-initiated activities.

Evaluations of the success of a topic, theme, the role play area or management of the indoor/outdoor learning will need to take place alongside planned assessments of children's learning. This may occur half-termly or at the end of a topic. Figure 3.6 raises some of the questions you may need to ask. The planned curriculum and the received curriculum may be very much at odds with each other for some children. However, this is where the skill of the educator is paramount in responding to the needs and interests of the children in their care. Detailed plans mean that resources to extend learning are more likely to be available, staff have planned the questions they need to ask to scaffold the children's learning either in a group setting or with individual children. Throughout this section of the chapter I have avoided prescribing planning which takes account of children's learning holistically or learning goal by learning goal. It is sensible to plan a limited range of outcomes in the knowledge that what children learn may be very different from what is taught. Specific outcomes are to ensure that your questions, instructions and demonstrations ensure that the knowledge, skills and concepts you wish to convey are understood by the children. The planning framework is a tool for the educator, not a straightjacket for children's learning. The rest of the book includes examples of planned activities, sometimes covering one learning goal, but nevertheless providing children with a worthwhile experience.

Refer to forecast and refer to the following questions to help evaluate the half-term programme.

Activities

- Were planned activities covered? – if not why not? Are there future plans to carry out these activities at another time?
- Which activities were successful? Why?
- Which activities were unsuccessful? Why?
- Which activities can be continued, extended or enhanced?
- Which activities did the children enjoy? – Why?
- Which activities lacked challenge? – Why?
- Which activities were unstimulating? – Why?
- Which activities were disruptive? – Why? Were they still valuable? – Could improvements be made to lessen disruption?
- Were there any different spontaneous activities?
- Could specific activites be improved?
- Other questions related to the children, resources used, assessment opportunities, use of the outdoor environment and targeting of children with learning and social difficulties.

FIGURE 3.6 Half-termly evaluation of learning: questions to guide discussion (Rodger *et al.* 1995)

Further reading

Nicholson, R. (2000) *Planning for Foundation Stage Learning.* London: Wandsworth Council.

Qualifications and Curriculum Authority (2000) *Curriculum Guidance for the Foundation Stage.* London: DfES.

Qualifications and Curriculum Authority (2001) *Planning for Learning in the Foundation Stage.*

www.foundation-stage.info/articles/pracstate.php plan

www.hants.gov.uk/childcare/trainingpublications.htm/

www.cornwallearlyyears.org.uk/tlam/2-curriculum.htm/

Assessment and record keeping

The profile . . . will not be a test that children pass or fail but will represent a valuable tool for teachers and help them build up knowledge of each child's capabilities throughout the year.

Ashton (September 2001)

Introduction

Views of the profession suggest that perhaps the value of the newly introduced baseline assessment scheme referred to in the above quotation may not be as positive as was hoped prior to its introduction in January 2003. As always, teacher unions put their own spin on national initiatives, but in relation to the one recently reported (Ward *TES* January 2003) they may have a valid point as it echoes some concerns I had in the consultation process, prior to the introduction of the previous baseline scheme. I came away from the day and indeed stated on the day that the government ought to make their intentions for a baseline more transparent. If headteachers want an on-entry assessment system that enables them to show how much value is added, then let that be the purpose of the national scheme. Instead of trying to introduce a scheme that, as stated by John Bangs, head of education at the NUT, 'attempts to ride two horses, to provide information for value-added scores and to be diagnostic'. The pressure on practitioners to assess every child against the 117 measures is excessive and is likely to be used to gather a summative assessment of achievement and be less useful for formative assessment which is at the heart of the teaching and learning process. Lists of ticked boxes are the most worthless form of assessment as any practitioner knows. A practice criticised in the past by Dearing as part of the review of the National Curriculum in the mid-1990s. Three-quarters of practitioners surveyed in a recent survey by Warwick University said that the assessment profile would increase their workload significantly. Two-thirds of the 803 practitioners polled said they were carrying on with their existing baseline scheme which was more helpful and used to assist with planning and to gain information about pupils. It will be important that practitioners stand firm in their beliefs and principles when using assessment as a tool to improve learning for young children. Make no mistake, the statutory national scheme is a tool to assist in the calculation of value-added as children progress through the education system. Wise practitioners have cottoned on to this and are maintaining their current practices.

Effective assessment in the early years

Assessment takes many forms and is used for a variety of purposes in early years education. Fundamentally, assessment is at the heart of the teaching and learning process (Figure 4.1). Practitioners assess children on entry to the nursery school, sometimes with the involvement of parents. This form of assessment, known as formative assessment, and usually involving the observation of children, is part of the teaching and learning cycle mentioned earlier. It is regarded as educationally valid and widely accepted and practiced by practitioners. The value of ongoing formative assessment was a key finding of the five year funded DfES project (Siraj-Blatchford *et al.* 2002) identifying the effectiveness of different forms of early years provision. In recent years another dimension to assessment has

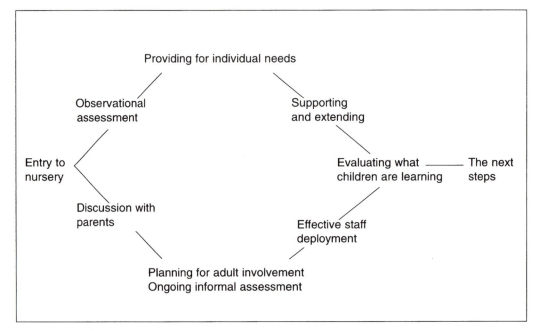

FIGURE 4.1   The teaching and learning cycle

emerged that is less popular, although the pragmatic early years professional can articulate and justify why they feel the need to quantify the progress their children make through the nursery or reception class. I refer, of course, to those assessment schemes, of which there are many – PIPS (Performance Indicators in Primary Schools) (Tymms and Merrill 1996), Flying Start (Durham County Council 1999), Infant Index (Desforges and Lindsay 1995), Signposts (Birmingham County Council 1997) – to name but a few, that measure children's knowledge, understanding, abilities and skills at the beginning of their formal education. The assessment information is used formatively in many settings to group children in similar ability / developmental groups for some aspects of learning.

Until September 2002, an assessment on entry to the reception class was a statutory requirement for all children. Although a national scheme was available (SCAA 1997), authorities were allowed to accredit their own schemes with the result there were 90 or so schemes in existence across the country. In September 2002, a single national scheme was introduced as a result of research that found that teachers wanted a nationally comparable assessment to use as evidence for threshold assessment applications and inspection. A change as a result of this was the shifting of the assessment point to the end of the Foundation Stage, that is the end of the reception year. One might want to question the justification for the new scheme. Are the reasons quoted educationally viable? Excellent practitioners currently produce detailed numerical scores to show how well or otherwise their children achieve on a range of measures: language; literacy; communication skills; numeracy; personal and social skills. However, there are reception class teachers who struggle to understand the detailed analysis which accompanies some baseline assessment data and which is frequently left languishing in a cupboard. The summative data is used most effectively as a tool for school improvement, to identify trends over time or to highlight priorities for improvement in nursery or Foundation Stage development plans. In addition, the numerical data provides robust evidence to show how much progress children make over a period of time. This information can be used as evidence to meet the pupil progress standard as part of threshold assessment requirements.

The Qualifications and Curriculum Authority introduced the Foundation Stage profile in January 2003. In essence, it enables early years practitioners to record children's achievements in the year before they start compulsory schooling. Achievements are in the following categories: personal, social and emotional development; communication, language and literacy; mathematical development; knowledge and understanding of the world; and physical and creative development. It has been stressed that the numerical results will not be used to draw up league tables, although schools will be able to compare their results to the national picture (Ward *TES* March 2003).

What is the purpose of assessment in the early years?

A distinction needs to be made between ongoing formative assessment that informs what children need to do next and the use of summative assessment data to provide a measure of performance. The latter assessment type which characterises the new national scheme analyses the achievements of groups of children, makes comparisons between different cohorts of children, different genders and ethnicities. In their analysis of current assessment schemes Wilkinson *et al.* (1998) came up with the following purposes for assessment:

- to record aspects of a child's knowledge, abilities etc.;
- to assist pedagogy, including diagnosis of learning difficulties;
- to identify children with special needs;
- to provide a common frame of reference for staff;
- to promote home and school continuity/dialogue;
- to assist with school planning;
- to provide value-added information;
- to assist with school inspections;
- to assist with LEA planning;
- to inform the LEA evaluation.

To gather this information early years practitioners will complete checklists, scales or narrative descriptions. Do early years settings need to go to such lengths to check how well their children are progressing? I can only show you, the reader, what happens in the best settings, which generally have the performance data to demonstrate how well their children achieve over time. This data is also used to highlight aspects of the areas of learning that are less well understood by children. Equally important is the use made of assessment data to identify key priorities in school improvement planning. The assessment methods used by practitioners are diverse, but the criticism that is made most regularly concerns the time-consuming nature of the unmanageable expectations practitioners frequently make of themselves. Can you recall the boxes of annotated examples of work waiting to be assembled into the individual profile for each child? Or the pages of notes of significant achievement waiting to be transferred to individual folders? How can this onerous task be made more efficient? Figure 4.2 is an example of the comprehensive assessment strategies used in a nursery unit.

As educators of young children you must not underestimate the importance of assessment of their learning. As Drummond (1993a:10) says, 'the process of

---

Quality in Action – Assessment and Record Keeping

Nursery record
- Individual folders containing stickers of significant achievement (red – Autumn, green – Spring, blue – Summer) and annotated work samples, including home visit pictures and a record of the home visit
- Focus groups assessment sheets
- Individual reading records
- Critical incident file cards – recording possible patterns of behaviour, concerns and changes while at the nursery
- Class matrix of mark making and name writing samples, updated termly and kept in planning and assessment folder
- Class matrix of individual learning priorities and targets set for social skills, language and physical development. Targets shared with parents informally at the end of sessions as required and formally at parents' open evenings in the spring and summer terms
- SEN file

FIGURE 4.2   An example of a nursery assessment scheme

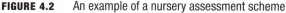

assessing children's learning – by looking closely at it and striving to understand it – is the only certain safeguard against children's failure, the only guarantee of children's progress and development'. In the years since leaving academia, I have spent considerably more time working with practitioners and being privileged to see excellent practices in many settings. The warnings about the emphasis on assessment as an end in itself rather than a tool to improve teaching and learning are less evident in practice than one has been led to believe, because experienced early years leaders and managers make statutory requirements work for them. The Foundation Stage Profile encourages observational assessment.

The Foundation Stage Profile

The statutory requirement is that practitioners have a method of assessing each child's development in relation to the early learning goals. This assessment is made on the 'basis of the practitioner's accumulated knowledge of the whole child' (QCA 2002:4). The intention of the profile is that it can be completed termly throughout the reception year, although it is not a requirement to do so, as long as it is completed in the summer term. At that point, practitioners can transfer records from other systems. Many settings and schools have already developed quite sophisticated assessment systems; however, there are those that abandoned previous systems to wait for the *Foundation Stage Profile*. It is likely that as a result of delays to training for staff on the use of the newly introduced system it will only start in earnest in September 2003. The assessment system is simplistic and looks relatively straightforward. However, it does have a tick list approach, which has limitations as a tool for informing the next steps, but is valid as a means of quantifying progress. The *Handbook* provides plenty of exemplification and case study examples. Practitioners are required to make a yes–no judgement based on their existing knowledge of the child. The intention is that this information is then transferred to the individual profile for each child. It is at this point that practitioners need to discuss the management of assessment in their setting, especially if there are many children. Do you work in a combined setting or just a nursery setting? How will you work the statutory requirements alongside the formative assessment arrangements already in place for your younger children?

At this stage in the implementation of the scheme, there are no intentions of using the data to provide numerical data. It is unlikely that this will remain the situation as there is scope in the system to record assessments electronically. Indeed, there are many nursery and reception classes making extensive use of existing assessment schemes that provide numerical data.

At the end of the Foundation Stage, practitioners need to assess each child's development in relation to the early learning goals that form part of the *Curriculum Guidance for the Foundation Stage.* This assessment is made on the basis of the practitioner's accumulated knowledge of the whole child. The Foundation Stage Profile provides a way of summing up that knowledge once the child reaches the end of the Foundation Stage. The expectation is that the profile will only be used in the final year of the Foundation Stage, when children are in the reception class. It will be used to record achievement of particular early learning goals as they are observed. The profile recording system relates to the three terms of the year, for practitioners who wish to make ongoing records or to track progress. It must be completed in the summer term, summarising each child's development at that point. Practitioners can transfer their records from other systems onto the profile during the summer term.

Using assessment information to plan future work

Intuitive formative assessment, such as the example below, is at the heart of assessment in the early years and is an integral part of good teaching. When headteachers or inspectors assess teaching they look for examples of how 'assessment is used to inform their planning and target-setting to meet the needs of individual pupils and groups' (Ofsted 2003:30). The criterion stated above is generic to all pupils whatever their age. Is this also appropriate for children in the Foundation Stage?

Mercedes sits pressing the keys on the computer key board desperately trying to move the little man on the screen, which she had observed an older boy doing only moments earlier. In sequence she pressed every letter key, humming the alphabet rhyme she had sung earlier in the session during group time. Nothing happened on the screen. Resolutely, Mercedes persisted until at last the figure on the screen moved. She was unaware that she had pressed one of the arrow keys. Somewhat disconsolately she shuffles her chair back and looks around trying to attract someone's attention to help her. Mercedes has only been in the nursery for three weeks. To venture to the computer trolley is a big achievement for her, but to ask for help? She is not confident enough to do this. Time to get ready for lunch. The lunchtime passes and once again afternoon activities begin, but what happens? Earlier observation by a member of staff of Mercedes' difficulty had not gone unnoticed. With gentle encouragement Mercedes is persuaded to return to the computer and with the help of her teacher is guided to the arrow keys and the space bar and has a demonstration of the directions followed by the man in the maze depending upon the arrow key pressed. Complete delight and concentration follow as Mercedes confidently directs the man on the screen home. The adult makes a note of her achievement in the small notebook she effortlessly produces from the pocket of her jacket.

Speaking with the adult later we discuss the event in detail. Mercedes is one of the children in this adult's personal group. She had noticed her in difficulty earlier in the day, but because she was working on her adult-directed (teacher-focused activity) with a small group of children on another computer she was unable to come to her support, but knew that later in the day would be free to do so. The entry in her notebook would be transferred into Mercedes' record of achievement. Such an example endorses several of the principles of assessment stated by Blenkin and Kelly (1992:ix):

- assessments made by practitioners themselves have highest value;
- continuous observation, rather than one off testing, is to be encouraged;
- focus on what the children can, rather than cannot, do.

Analysis of that experience demonstrates the effectiveness of the highly skilled and experienced professional at work. 'Assessment is the most professional area of a teacher's work' (Hurst and Lally 1992:46). A mental observation was made that the child was in difficulty and an opportunity created later in the day to follow up the difficulty and provide sustained support and encouragement to help the child master the complexities of the computer programme and thus achieve a greater understanding of information technology. Would this have occurred without adult intervention? Mastery may have come later, because another child may have shown her how, but cognitively Mercedes was ready at that point to begin to understand the association between the keys and the figure on the screen. A possible step in her learning may have been missed completely, but for the vigilance of the member of staff responsible for that area. An unplanned example of the way in which an early years practioner used her intuitive observational assessment to extend the learning of a child at an appropriate moment. This is an important reminder of the value of everyday, informal, intuitive assessment which forms the basis of understanding what children know, understand and can do and which is fundamental to good teaching. Edgington (1998:3) reinforces the need for practitioners to use an approach to baseline assessment which fits with the needs of their children:

> It will be the responsibility of early years staff to ensure that their schools select an approach which has the best interests of the children at heart, which is consistent with what we know to be effective practice in early years assessment.

Baseline assessment data must not be used as the total evidence base of the assessment information required to plan the next step in a child's learning – a fact emphasised by SCAA (1997a:7). 'A child's response during a single activity is not always an accurate or reliable guide to underlying competence . . . evidence collected over time from a large range of activities is always necessary in establishing what a child knows, understands and can do.' The case study below highlights a drawback to a one-off assessment.

Ahmed is distressed. He cries and points to the telephone in the nursery in a very agitated manner. It is Ahmed's second week at the nursery. Every day he cries and asks the nursery teacher to ring for his father to come and take him home. Some weeks later I visit the nursery again, just at the time the staff are rushing to complete the baseline assessments on all children as they have all been in the nursery for almost half a term. Ahmed has stopped crying, but he is very quiet and drifts around the nursery in a desultory manner, flicking construction material to the floor as he passes by tables in the nursery. No one goes to him. Previously he spoke very animatedly in Arabic. But now he is silent and clearly very unhappy, but unhappy with a quiet resignation, that this is what it is like to be in the nursery. Soon it is Ahmed's turn to be assessed. Fortunately for him his teacher also speaks Arabic and she encourages him to sit down and talk about the pictures on the photocopied sheet she places in front of him. His responses are minimal. He is distracted by the movement of other children around the room and pays little attention to the teacher. The aim of the test, which is what this is, is to assess his speaking and listening on a five point scale (Figure 4.3).

Using an outline line drawing of a boy, the adult, in Arabic, asks Ahmed to name various parts of the body. He is distracted and inattentive and fails to see the purpose of the task. Consequently, his responses are graded 'no observable evidence', thus placing him very clearly at the bottom end of the five point scale. As these are the responses expected by the teacher she makes no comment and distractedly moves on to the next name on her list. Meanwhile, Ahmed wanders outside and goes to stand by the railings. Pointing along the road he launches

Listed below are the criteria for the baseline performance descriptions. A score has been assigned to each of the criteria for statistical purposes.

Code	Level of Performance	Score
C	Competence Typical at Level 1	5
E	Emerging Competence (Working within Level 1)	4
D	Developing Competence (Working within Level 1)	3
B	Barely Developed Competence (Working within Level 1)	2
N	No observable evidence of competence in this area	1

Baseline assessment requires judgements of children's performance in relation to performance descriptions in language and literacy and mathematics. These judgements should be based on evidence gathered over a period of time from a range of different learning contexts.

(Manchester City Council 1997)

Performance Descriptions

Language and Literacy

	Speaking and Listening	Reading	Writing
C	Children talk about matters of immediate interest. They listen to others and usually respond appropriately. They convey simple meanings to a range of listeners, speaking audibly, and begin to extend their ideas or accounts by providing some detail.	Children recognise familiar words in simple texts. They use their knowledge of letter and sound–symbol relationships in order to read words and to establish meaning when reading aloud. In these activities they sometimes require support. They express their responses to poems, stories and non-fiction by identifying aspects they like. (Level 1)	Children's writing communicates meaning through simple words and phrases. In their reading or their writing, children begin to show awareness of how full stops are used. Letters are usually clearly shaped and correctly orientated. (Level 1)
E	Children listen attentively in one-to-one and group situations, respond appropriately and know some songs, stories and rhymes by heart.	Children are able to follow print in the appropriate direction, recognise letters and symbols in their own name and some familiar words.	Children write their name and can arrange recognisable letters into groups and patterns to communicate meaning.
D	Children listen attentively and talk about their experiences using sentences.	Children understand that words and pictures convey meaning in a variety of contexts and can recognise their name.	Children use pictures, some recognisable letters and symbols to communicate meaning and have begun to write their own name.
B	Children listen and respond using single words and actions.	Children show an interest in books and enjoy sharing a book with an adult.	Children make random marks using a variety of implements and resources.
N	No observable evidence.	No observable evidence.	No observable evidence.

FIGURE 4.3 Baseline performance descriptions (Manchester City Council 1997)

into a torrent of Arabic, which, with the help of another adult nearby, is translated as a description of his father's car, where he lives and that later in the day his father will come and collect him from the nursery.

Ahmed scored 'N' on his assessment for speaking and listening. I leave you to judge how accurate this judgment is of his capability. In this particular school the baseline assessment is used with children from their entry to nursery, whereas other schemes are introduced as children enter the reception class.

Is the baseline assessment of this pupil a true reflection of his competence in speaking and listening? The guiding principles which should be observed when carrying out baseline assessment are explicit:

- recognise the vital contribution of parents and carers to the process;
- take account of learning in a variety of contexts;
- include observation as a key element;
- take account of the variety of cultures and languages;
- take account of all aspects of a child's early development.

(Manchester City Council Education Department 1997)

The example of Ahmed illustrates how the baseline assessment is misused. Can one begin to speculate that for children in their first half term of reception class this may be the way in which the baseline assessment is carried out? Is this a pragmatic solution to a practical problem? Observational assessment takes time and human resources. Large classes of 40 children will cause some teachers to do just what Ahmed's nursery teacher did. How can this be avoided? Reception class teachers are usually organised, efficient and creative in their use of time. Daily targeting of one or more children as they carry out a range of activities is the way many teachers respond to this requirement. The observational assessment is carried out in a natural way and followed up by a discussion with the parent at the end of the school day. By the end of the first half term in school a baseline profile is complete. Those reception and nursery classes which stagger entry to school (Cleave and Brown 1991: 24) are at an advantage as they have fewer children to get to know over a larger period of time. Staggered entry is a phased starting date which allows children to be admitted to school singly or in small groups.

Measuring children's attainment using baseline scores

This section gives examples of the use of performance data in nursery schools. Increasingly, early years practitioners have become more skilled in the use of calculating assessment scores and making use of the data analysis to improve teaching and learning in their settings. Generally, scores are calculated and then analysed to give each child a predicted level of attainment by age seven (Tymms 1999). The results may be compared to previous years, especially if the cohorts of children are similar in terms of ability, gender and ethnicity. Scores are usually sent to the LEA for analysis, and in some they will be compared to a national average (i.e. the average of all the schools/settings using that assessment scheme). It is better to rely on the analysis carried out as soon as the assessments are complete, especially if you do this when the children first start in the nursery or reception class, because the delays in getting analysed data back to schools can be quite long in relation to the time spent by children in a nursery school. There is a brief synopsis of some existing assessment schemes at the end of the chapter.

Figure 4.4 shows the percentage of children achieving each statement in reading, writing and speaking and listening in a class of children in a Liverpool school. Almost four-fifths of the children in this particular example have experience of nursery education. To analyse the reading competence of the children it is interesting to note the high proportion of children who can:

- hold a book appropriately and turn pages one at a time;
- respond appropriately when choosing or reading a book;
- understand that print conveys meaning.

How might a reception class teacher begin to assess the needs of his or her class with this pattern of achievement? One interpretation may be that the children have been read to frequently, that they enjoy stories and know their favourites. Perhaps the nursery involved parents in their early reading experiences. Possibly the nursery serves an area where parents are well-informed of their role in their child's early learning experiences. When combined with the overall percentages for speaking and listening a pattern begins to emerge which could act as a trigger to the staff that more emphasis needs to be given to speaking. Whilst attitudes towards books are very positive, relatively fewer children talk about the pictures in the books they read. A much higher proportion of children are unable to make up their own stories or ask appropriate questions and listen to the response. Could this lead to a series of planned activities to develop children's confidence and enjoyment in talking to each other or to small or large groups? Chapter 7 outlines some of the planned ways in which practitioners can include speaking and listening activities in their overall curriculum plan.

Common practice in the nursery schools in one authority is that there is an 'on entry' and 'on exit' assessment made of the children based on a commercially available assessment scheme from a neighbouring LEA. There are three strands to the 'on entry' assessment: home visit; induction meetings; and continuous practitioner assessment. The assessment information is gathered from a variety of sources and is consequently reliable. The data is not generated from a single activity, such as the

Baseline Checklist
One mark is awarded for attainment of each criterion

Name: (Student First)(Student Last)　　　　　　　　**School:** (School)

　　　　　　　　　　　　　　　　　　　　　　　　　　　Admin.No.: (Admin No.)

Reading

[92.0%]	1	Holds book appropriately and turns pages one at a time
[72.0%]	2	Talks accurately about the pictures in a familiar book
[89.3%]	3	Responds appropriately when choosing or reading a book
[72.0%]	4	Comments on aspects enjoyed or found interesting (supported)
[80.0%]	5	Understands that print conveys meaning
[57.3%]	6	Reads from left to right and knows where text starts and ends
[53.3%]	7	Recognises 3+ words from the familiar environment
[4.0%]	8	Recognises 10+ words from familiar contexts
[1.3%]	9	Recognises 25 words
[37.3%]	10	Recognises 9 letters (sounds) including the initial letter of own name
[30.7%]	11	Recognises 10 – 18 letters
[18.7%]	12	Recognises 19+ letters
[28.0%]	13	Gives rhyme for monosyllabic words
[16.0%]	14	Gives words with same initial sound
[6.7%]	15	Decodes words C-V-C
	/15	Total

Writing

[97.3%]	16	Recognises the difference between writing and drawing
[84.0%]	17	Makes purposeful marks on paper and assigns meaning to them
[10.7%]	18	Reads back own emergent writing consistently
[17.3%]	19	Uses groups of letters to represent meaningful words or phrases
[2.7%]	20	Writing communicates meaning through single words and phrases
[44.0%]	21	Writes own name using correct upper and lower case letters
[36.0%]	22	Has some control over the size and shape of letters
[21.3%]	23	Letters are usually correctly shaped and oriented
[0.0%]	24	Writes more than one sentence and attempts to spell unfamiliar words
[2.7%]	25	Writes letters in response to the sounds in words
	/10	Total

Speaking and Listening

[86.7%]	26	Listens attentively to a story and can retell a story
[22.7%]	27	Makes up own story
[89.3%]	28	Listens and responds to instructions
[81.3%]	29	Can recount an event or experience
[86.7%]	30	Speaks in sentences of 5+ words
[96.0%]	31	Joins in with rhymes
[73.3%]	32	Uses speech appropriately during role play
[60.0%]	33	Adapts speech and language for different purposes
[60.0%]	34	Asks appropriate questions and listens to the response
[84.0%]	35	Speech is generally fluent and understandable
	/10	Total

FIGURE 4.4　Baseline assessment of Language and Literacy skills. Percentage of children attaining each criterion in a sample class (Liverpool LEA 1997)

Case Study – Early Excellence Centre

Language and Literacy (on entry and on exit average scores)

	Sp&L entry	Sp&L exit	Writing entry	Writing exit	Reading entry	Reading exit	Subtotal E&F entry	Subtotal E&F exit	Subtotal D+ entry	Subtotal D+ exit
Girls	3.76	7.85	3.9	7.05	3.37	6.65	10.6	11.98	2	9.58
Boys	3.91	7.81	3.94	6.84	3.94	5.91	11.78	11.63	1.5	8.84
All children	3.7	7.83	3.7	6.95	3.1	6.28	10.6	11.81	1.75	9.21

Interpretation of the data

- on entry boys appear to be achieving higher than girls. On exit girls achieve higher than boys – not significant.
- D+ profile on entry has an average score of 1.75. Exit results show that all children make excellent progress.
- From the on entry results, seven children were targeted for small group time with a specific focus on speaking and listening activities. The majority of those children were offered extension to the usual nursery entitlement. This had a significant impact on the 'on exit' results of those children and the overall cohort. All achieved in the D+ profile on exit.

The data is collated and analysed for mathematical and for personal, social and emotional development.

Pennywell Early Excellence Centre

example cited earlier. The induction and on entry results inform the groupings of all children according to their individual needs. For example, this may range from a very low achieving group with specific language delays to able and very able groups of children. Scores achieved by individual children using this particular assessment scheme are averaged. The scores could range from A to F (A is high achievement and F is low). The numerical score is averaged within the level and compared with the exit score. Scores on exit are compared, especially in relation to the differences in the achievement of boys and girls. F scores trigger focused support. An analysis of the results as the children leave the nursery, in this example, highlighted the low achievement of boys in writing. The following term, actions introduced to increase opportunities to write were put in place; an interactive whiteboard was strategically sited to require children to climb to use it; a great motivator for boys, and all writing activity was linked to a role play or practical activity. For example, as part of a nursery rhyme theme, children made the characters for Humpty Dumpty and labelled each one with adult support. Another strand to the data analysis was to compare the on-entry results analysed by the provider with other settings. The centre's data was significantly different for communication, language and literacy and for personal, social and emotional development. This led to moderation of assessments to ensure that they were an accurate assessment of the children on entry. The view of the staff was that they were being too generous and inflating the baseline assessments on entry.

The case study setting below has not yet reached the stage of having numerical data against which to measure progress. You could usefully compare the two strategies and consider the strengths and weaknesses of each for your own practices. Those of you who are teachers, however, may wish to bear in mind the following from *Guidance to the Threshold Process* (DfES 2001c)

3. Pupil progress
This standard requires evidence that, **as a result of the teacher's teaching**:
Their pupils achieve well in relation to the pupils' prior attainment, making progress as good as or better than similar pupils nationally. This should be shown in . . . <u>school based assessment for pupils where national tests are not taken.</u>

(DfES 2001c)

Case Study – Nursery Class attached to a Primary School

The nursery class has children speaking several languages and about ten children with particular special educational needs. An issue referred to earlier is that of making assessment manageable. The system used in this setting achieved this through the use of strips of self-adhesive labels to record specific examples of achievement against each of the areas of learning. This information was transferred to each child's portfolio of achievement against each area of learning. In addition, the staff used red labels to record critical behaviour incidents, for example, if a child was particularly good, polite, angry or aggressive. Figure 4.2 lists the range of assessments gathered in this setting. A summary report is prepared for each child along with the completed portfolio of achievement, so that when the children leave to go to school there is a summative document to show what each child has achieved.

A common system of recording progress towards the early learning goals is to break the goals into the 'stepping-stones'. These steps are not expected to be progressive. Children may achieve some before others. However, they do provide a sense of progression from entry to a nursery to the end of the Foundation Stage and have a key role to play in planning specific assessment activities. A common picture in settings is to track individual children's progress towards the early learning goals term by term, highlighting achievement in a different colour for each term and dating achievement. Practitioners may use a checklist when carrying out focused observational assessments or planned assessment activities. The tables that follow include all the *stepping-stones* for each area of learning.

Yellow	Blue	Green	Grey	Grey (cont)
1. Show curiosity 2. Have a strong exploratory impulse 3. Have a positive approach to new experiences 4. Separate from main carer with support 5. Feel safe and secure and demonstrate a sense of trust 6. Seek out others to share experiences 7. Relate and make attachments to members of their group 8. Begin to accept the needs of others with support 9. Show willingness to tackle problems and enjoy self-chosen challenges 10. Demonstrate a sense of pride in their own achievement 11. Make connections between different parts of their life experiences	12. Show increasing independence in selecting and carrying out activities 13. Show confidence in linking up with others for support and guidance 14. Separate from main carer with confidence 15. Have a sense of belonging 16. Show care and concern for self 17. Talk freely about their home and community 18. Demonstrate flexibility and adapt their behaviour to different events, social situations and changes in routine 19. Show care and concern for others, for living things and their environment 20. Take initiatives and manage developmentally appropriate tasks 21. Show a strong sense of self as a member of different communities, such as their family or setting	22. Display high levels of involvement in activities 23. Persist for extended periods of time at an activity of their choosing 24. Take risks and explore within the environment 25. Have a sense of self as a member of different communities 26. Express needs and feelings in appropriate ways 27. Initiate actions with other people 28. Value and contribute to own well-being and self-control 29. show confidence and the ability to stand up for own rights 30. Have an awareness of the boundaries set and behavioural expectations within the setting 31. Operate independently within the environment and show confidence in linking up with others for support and guidance 32. Have an awareness of, and show interest and enjoyment in, cultural and religious differences 33. Have a positive self-image and show that they are comfortable with themselves	34. Continue to be interested, excited and motivated to learn 35. Be confident to try new activities, initiate ideas and speak in a familiar group 36. Maintain attention, concentrate, and sit quietly when appropriate 37. Respond to significant experiences, showing a range of feelings when appropriate 38. Have a developing awareness of their own needs, views and feelings of others 39. Have a developing respect for their own cultures and beliefs and those of other people 40. Form good relationships with adults and peers 41. Work as part of a group or a class, taking turns and sharing fairly, understanding that there needs to be agreed values and codes of behaviour for groups of people, including adults and children, to work together harmoniously	42. Understand what is right, what is wrong and why 43. Consider the consequences of their words and actions for themselves and others 44. Dress and undress independently and manage their own personal hygiene 45. Select and use resources and activities independently 46. Understand that people have different needs, views, cultures and beliefs that need to be treated with respect 47. Understand that they can expect others to treat their needs, views, cultures and beliefs with respect

FIGURE 4.5   Personal, social and emotional development

Yellow	Blue	Green
Communication 1. Use words and/or gestures, including body language such as eye contact and facial expression to communicate 2. Listen to favourite nursery rhymes, stories and songs. Join in with repeated refrains, anticipating key events and important phrases 3. Respond to simple instructions 4. Listen to others in one-to-one/small groups when conversation interests them 5. Use familiar words, often in isolation, to identify what they do and do not want 6. Use vocabulary focused on objects and people who are of particular importance to them 7. Use isolated words and phrases and/or gestures to communicate with those well known to them 8. Use action, sometimes with limited talk, that is largely concerned with the 'here and now' **Reading** 9. Enjoy rhyming and rhythmic activities 10. Distinguish one sound from another 11. Listen to and join in with stories and poems, one-to-one and also in small groups 12. Show interest in illustrations and print in books and print in the environment 13. Begin to be aware of the way stories are structured **Writing** 14. Draw and paint, sometimes giving meanings to marks 15. Engage in activities requiring hand-eye coordination 16. Use one-handled tools and equipment	**Communication** 17. Use simple statements and questions often linked to gestures 18. Use intonation, rhythm and phrasing to make their meaning clear to others 19. Listen to stories with increasing attention and recall 20. Describe main story settings, events and principal characters 21. Question why things happen, and give explanations 22. Build up vocabulary that reflects the breadth of their experiences 23. Begin to experiment with language describing possession 24. Begin to use more complex sentences 25. Use a widening range of words to express or elaborate ideas 26. Talk activities through, reflecting on and modifying what they are doing 27. Use talk to connect ideas 28. Explain what is happening and anticipate what might happen next 29. Use talk, actions and objects to recall and relive past experiences **Reading** 30. Show awareness of rhyme and alliteration 31. Recognise rhythm in spoken words 32. Have favourite books 33. Handle books carefully 34. Suggest how the story might end 35. Know that information can be relayed in the form of print 36. Hold books the correct way up and turn pages 37. Understand the concept of a word **Writing** 38. Ascribe meanings to marks 39. Draw lines and circles using gross motor movements 40. Manipulate objects with increasing control	**Communication** 41. Have emerging self-confidence to speak to others about wants and interests 42. Use simple grammatical structures 43. Ask simple questions, often in the form of 'where?' or 'what?' 44. Talk alongside others, rather than with them. Use talk to gain attention and initiate changes. Use action rather than talk to demonstrate or explain to others 45. Initiate conversation, attend to and take account of what others say, and use talk to resolve disagreements 46. Initiate a conversation, negotiate positions, pay attention to and take account of others' views 47. Extend vocabulary, especially by grouping and naming 48. Use vocabulary and forms of speech that are increasingly influenced by experience of books 49. Link statements and stick to a main theme or intention 50. Consistently develop a simple story, explanation or line of questioning 51. Use language for an increasing range of purposes 52. Confidently talk to people other than those who are well known to them 53. to sequence and know how events lead into one another 54. Begin to make patterns in their experience through linking cause and effect, sequencing, ordering and grouping 55. Begin to use talk to pretend imaginary situations 56. Begin to use talk instead of action to rehearse, reorder and reflect on past experience, linking significant events from own experience and from stories, paying attention to sequence and how events lead into one another **Reading** 57. Continue a rhyming string 58. Hear and say initial sound in words and know which letters represent some of the sounds 59. Enjoy an increasing range of books 60. Begin to recognise some familiar words 61. Know what information can be retrieved from books and computers 62. Begin to break the flow of speech into words **Writing** 63. Use writing as a means of recording and communicating 64. Begin to use anticlockwise movement and retrace vertical lines 65. Begin to form recognisable letters

FIGURE 4.6   Communication, Language and Literacy

Yellow	Blue	Green	Grey
1. Show an interest in numbers and counting 2. Use some number names and number language spontaneously 3. Enjoy joining in with number rhymes and songs 4. Use mathematical language in play 5. Compare two groups of objects saying when they have the same number 6. Show an interest in shape and space by playing with shapes or making arrangements with objects 7. Show awareness of similarities in shapes in the environment 8. Observe and use positional language 9. Use size language such as big and little	10. Show curiosity about numbers by offering comments or asking questions 11. Use some number names accurately in play 12. Willingly attempt to count, with some numbers in the correct order 13. Recognise groups with one, two or three objects 14. Show an interest in number problems 15. Separate a group of three or four objects in different ways, beginning to recognize that the total is still the same 16. Show interest by sustained construction activity or talking about shapes or arrangements 17. Use shapes appropriately for tasks 18. Begin to talk about the shapes of everyday objects 19. Show curiosity about numbers	20. Show confidence with numbers by initiating or requesting number activities 21. Count up to three or four objects by saying one number name for each item 22. Recognise some numerals of personal significance 23. Begin to represent numbers using fingers, marks on paper or pictures 24. Recognise numerals 1 to 5, then 1 to 9 25. Count up to six objects from a larger group 26. Count actions or objects that cannot be moved 27. Select the correct numeral to represent 1 to 5, then 1 to 9, objects 28. Show increased confidence with numbers by spotting errors 29. Count an irregular arrangement of up to 10 objects 30. Say the number after any number up to nine 31. Begin to count beyond ten 32. Sometimes show confidence and offer solutions to problems 33. Find the total number of items in two groups by counting all of them 34. Use own methods to solve a problem 35. Say with confidence the number that is one more than a given number 36. Sustain interest for a length of time on a pre-decided construction or arrangement 37. Match some shapes by recognizing similarities and orientation 38. Use appropriate shapes to make representational models or more elaborate pictures 39. Show curiosity and observation by talking about shapes, how they are the same or why some are different 40. Find items from positional/directional cues 41. Describe a simple journey 42. Order two items by length or height 43. Choose suitable components to make a particular model 44. Adapt shapes or cut material to size 45. Select a particular named shape 46. Begin to use mathematical names for 'solid' 3D shapes and 'flat' 2D shapes 47. Show awareness of symmetry 48. Order two or three items by length 49. Order two items by weight or capacity 50. Instruct a programmable toy	51. Say and use number names in order in familiar contexts 52. Count reliably up to 10 everyday objects 53. Recognise numbers 1 to 9 54. Use developing mathematical ideas and methods to solve practical problems 55. In practical activities and discussion begin to use the vocabulary involved in adding and subtracting 56. Use language such as 'more' or 'less than' to compare two numbers 57. Find one more or one less than a number from one to 10 58. Begin to relate addition to combining two groups of objects and subtraction to 'taking away' 59. Use language such as 'greater', 'smaller', 'heavier' or 'lighter' to compare quantities 60. Talk about, recognize and recreate simple patterns 61. Use language such as 'circle' or 'bigger' to describe the shape and size of solids and flat shapes 62. Use everyday words to describe position 63. Use developing mathematical ideas and methods to solve practical problems **Refer to NNS objectives for more detail**

FIGURE 4.7   Mathematical Development

Yellow	Blue	Green	Grey
1. Show curiosity and interest by facial expression, movement or sound 2. Explore objects 3. Show interest in why things happen and how things work 4. Investigate construction materials 5. Realise tools can be used for a purpose 6. Show an interest in ICT 7. Remember and talk about significant things that have happened to them 8. Show an interest in the world in which they live 9. Express feelings about a significant personal event	10. Show curiosity, observe and manipulate objects 11. Describe simple features of objects and events 12. Sort objects by one function 13. Talk about what is seen and what is happening 14. Join construction pieces together to build and balance 15. Begin to try out a range of tools and techniques safely 16. Know how to operate simple equipment 17. Show interest in the lives of people familiar to them 18. Begin to differentiate between the past and present 19. Comment and ask questions about where they live and the natural world 20. Notice differences between features of the local environment 21. Describe significant events for families or friends	22. Examine objects and living things and find out more about them 23. Notice and comment on patterns 24. Show an awareness of change 25. Construct with a purpose in mind, using a variety of resources 26. Use simple tools and techniques competently and appropriately 27. Complete a simple program on the computer and/or perform simple on ICT apparatus 28. Gain an awareness of the culture and beliefs of others	29. Investigate objects and materials by using all of their senses as appropriate 30. Find out about, and identify, some of the features of living things, objects and events they observe 31. Look closely at similarities, differences, patterns and change 32. Ask questions about why things happen and how things work 33. Build and construct with a wide range of objects, selecting appropriate resources, and adapting their work where necessary 34. Select the tools and techniques they need to shape, assemble and join materials they are using 35. Find out about and identify the uses of everyday technology and use information and communication technology and programmable toys to support their learning 36. Find out about past and present events in their own lives, and in those of their families and other people they know 37. Observe, find out about and identify features in the place they live and the natural world 38. Find out about their environment and talk about those features they like and dislike 39. Begin to know about their own cultures and beliefs and those of other people
NC Level 1 Science • Describe or respond appropriately to simple features of objects, living things and the events they observe, communicating their findings in simple ways • Recognise and name external parts of the body and of plants. Communicate observations of a range of animals and plants in terms of features. Recognise and identify a range of common animals • Know about a range of properties and communicate observations of materials in terms of these properties • Communicate observations of changes in light, sound or movement that result from actions. Recognise that sound and light come from a variety of sources and name some of these	**NC Level 1 Design and technology** • Generate ideas and recognize characteristics of familiar products. Plans show that with help children can put their ideas into practice • Use pictures and words to describe what they do • Explain what they are making and the tools they are using • Use tools and materials with help, where needed • Talk about their own and other people's work in simple terms and describe how a product works	**NC Level 1 ICT** • Explore information from various sources, showing how they know that information exists in different forms **NC Level 1 History** • Recognise the distinction between present and past in their own and other people's lives • Show an emerging sense of chronology by placing a few events and objects in order, and by using everyday terms about the passing of time **NC Level 1 Geography** • Recognise and make observations about physical and human features of localities • Express their views on features of the environment • Respond to questions about places and the environment	
National Curriculum Level 1			

FIGURE 4.8   Knowledge and understanding of the world

Yellow	Blue	Green	Grey
1. Move spontaneously within available space 2. Respond to rhythm, music and story by means of gesture and movement 3. Can stop 4. Manage body to create intended movements 5. Combine and repeat a range of movements 6. Negotiate an appropriate pathway when walking, running or using a wheelchair or other mobility aids, both indoors and outdoors 7. Show awareness of own needs with regard to eating, sleeping and hygiene 8. Often need adult support to meet those needs 9. Operate equipment by means of pushing and pulling movements 10. Engage in activities requiring hand-eye coordination	11. Move freely with pleasure and confidence 12. Move in a range of ways, such as slithering, shuffling, rolling, crawling, walking, running, jumping, skipping, sliding and hopping 13. Use movement to express feelings 14. Adjust speed or change direction to avoid obstacles 15. Negotiate space successfully when playing racing and chasing games with other children 16. Sit up, stand up and balance on various parts of the body 17. Demonstrate the control necessary to hold a shape or fixed position 18. Mount stairs, steps or climbing equipment using alternate feet 19. Show respect for other children's personal space when playing among them 20. Persevere in repeating some actions/attempts when developing a new skill 21. Collaborate in devising and sharing tasks, including those which involve accepting rules 22. Show awareness of a range of healthy practices with regard to eating, sleeping and hygiene 23. Observe the effect of activity on their bodies 24. Construct with large materials such as cartons, long lengths of fabric and planks 25. Show increasing control in using equipment for climbing, scrambling, sliding and swinging 26. Demonstrate increasing skill and control in the use of mark-making implements, blocks, construction sets and 'small world' activities	27. Go backwards and sideways as well as forwards 28. Experiment with different ways of moving 29. Initiate new combinations of movement and gesture in order to express and respond to feelings, ideas and experiences 30. Jump off an object and land appropriately 31. Manipulate materials and objects by picking up, releasing, arranging, threading and posting them 32. Show increasing control over clothing and fastenings 33. Move body position as necessary 34. Show a clear and consistent preference for the left or right hand 35. Show some understanding that good practices with regard to exercise, eating, sleeping and hygiene can contribute to good health 36. Use increasing control over an object by touching, pushing, patting, throwing, catching or kicking it 37. Retrieve, collect and catch objects 38. Explore malleable materials by patting, stroking, poking, squeezing, pinching and twisting them 39. Manipulate materials to achieve a planned effect 40. Use simple tools to effect changes to the material 41. Show understanding of how to transport and store equipment safely 42. Practice some appropriate safety measures without direct supervision	43. Move with confidence, imagination and in safety 44. Move with control and coordination 45. Travel around, under, over and through balancing and climbing equipment 46. Show awareness of space, of themselves and of others 47. Recognise the importance of keeping healthy and those things which contribute to this 48. Recognise the changes that happen to their bodies when they are active 49. Use a range of small and large equipment 50. Handle tools, objects, construction and malleable materials safely and with increasing control

FIGURE 4.9   Physical development

Yellow	Blue	Blue	Green	Green	Grey	Grey/NC 1
– Begin to differentiate colours. – Use their bodies to explore texture and space. – Make three-dimensional structures. – Join in favourite songs. – Show an interest in the way musical instruments sound. – Respond to sound with body movement. – Enjoy joining in with dancing and ring games. – Pretend that one object represents another, especially when objects have characteristics in common. – Notice what adults do, imitating what is observed and doing it spontaneously when the adult is not there. – Show an interest in what they see, hear, smell, touch and feel. – Use body language, gestures, facial expression or words to indicate personal satisfaction or frustration	– Differentiate marks and movements on paper. – Begin to describe the texture of things Use lines to enclose a space, then begin to use these shapes to represent objects. – Begin to construct, stacking blocks vertically and horizontally and making enclosures and creating spaces – Sing a few simple familiar songs – Sing to themselves and make up simple songs. – Tap out simple repeated rhythms and make some up – Explore and learn how sounds can be changed – Imitate and create movement in response to music – Use one object to represent another, even when objects have few characteristics in common	– Use available resources to create props to support role play. – Develop a repertoire of actions by putting a sequence of movements together. – Enjoy stories based on themselves and people and places they know well. – Engage in imaginative and role play based on first hand experience. – Further explore an experience with a range of senses. – Begin to use representation as a means of communication. – Describe experiences and past actions, using a widening range of materials.	– Explore what happens when they mix colours – Understand that different media can be combined. – Make constructions, collages, paintings, drawings and dances. – Use ideas involving fitting, overlapping, in, out, enclosure, grids and sun-like shapes. – Choose particular colours to use for a purpose – Experiment to create different textures. – Work creatively on a large or small scale. Begin to build a repertoire of songs – Explore the different sounds of instruments Begin to move rhythmically.	– Introduce a story line or narrative into their play – Play alongside other children who are engaged in the same theme – Play co-operatively as part of a group to act out a narrative – Try to capture experiences and responses with music, dance, paint and other materials or words. – Develop preferences for forms of expression – Talk about personal intentions, describing what they were trying to do. – Respond to comments and questions, entering into dialogue about their creations. – Make comparisons	– Explore colour, texture, shape, form and space in two or three dimensions – Recognise and explore how sounds can be changed, sing simple songs from memory, recognize repeated sounds and sound patterns and match environments to music – Use their imagination in art and design, music, dance and imaginative role play and stories – Respond in a variety of ways to what they see, hear, smell, touch and feel. – Express and communicate their ideas, thoughts and feelings by using a widening range of materials, suitable tools, imaginative and role play,	– Movement, designing and making, and a variety of songs and musical instruments **Art and Design** – Respond to ideas. Use a variety of materials and processes to communicate their ideas and meanings. – Design and make images and artifacts – Describe what they think and feel about their own and others' work. **Music** – Recognise and explore how sounds can be made and changed – Use their voices in different ways such as speaking, singing and chanting and perform with awareness of others – Repeat short rhythmic and melodic patterns. Create and choose sounds in response to given starting points – Respond to different moods in music and recognise well-defined changes in sounds, identify simple repeated patterns and take account of musical instruction

FIGURE 4.10   Creative development

Early Years Assessment Schemes

Performance Indicators in Primary schools (Tymms and Merrill 1996) and ASPECTs for nursery

The **PIPs** scheme uses a modified psychometric approach to assess children's competence in personal and social development, literacy and numeracy. Literacy is broken down into speaking and listening, reading and writing. Children are assessed individually with each assessment taking about 20 minutes. The aim of **ASPECTs (Assessment Profile on Entry for Children and Toddlers)** is to enable practitioners to monitor the progress of children aged three and four years during their time in nurseries or playgroups. There are four separate components to the assessment, and teachers may choose to assess using any or all of them. As with other schemes, parents are encouraged to be involved by completing a 'Starting Nursery' questionnaire with their child before they start in the nursery. The questionnaire gives parents and the child the chance to say what they like and dislike. This is not seeen as part of the assessment, but a record for staff to refer to in the first few months children are in the setting. The scheme encourages assessment in one or more of three areas: personal and social development; motor development; and language and mathematical development. Feedback can be provided on an analysis of children's understanding of literacy, writing, vocabulary, concepts about print and phonological awareness, ideas about mathematics, shape recognition, counting and problem-solving. Evidence of skills in the former areas is gathered via observational assessments and in the latter using a pair of illustrated stories and takes about 10 minutes per child. An advantage of ASPECTs is that it feeds into PIPs, so it can be used to calculate value-added throughout the Foundation Stage. A disadvantage is that it requires an available adult to work with one child for a set amount of time on a task which may be alien to a three-year-old, and the results may not be such an accurate predictor of level of attainment.

Signposts – baseline assessment for the primary phase (Birmingham City Council 1997)

The Signposts scheme relies on scales. Statements for each designated area are specified for the person undertaking the assessment. The assessor then assigns a code on a four-point scale. Personal, social and emotional development are given a central role. Birmingham devised the national Foundation Stage Profile with QCA.

Flying Start (Durham County Council 1999)

This assessment scheme is the one used by the nursery school case studies in this chapter. This scheme has been revised to be compatible with the six areas of learning. The two key purposes are:

- to provide information to help teachers plan effectively to meet children's individual learning needs;

- to measure children's attainment using numerical outcomes which can be used in value-added analyses of children's progress.

Assessment covers communication, language and literacy; mathematics; and personal, social and emotional development.

Assessment of children with special educational needs

The prime purpose of early assessment or screening in the recent past was to identify those children with special educational needs. All children need to be screened in order to identify those children with special educational needs. To follow up the initial screening or baseline assessment to identify a child with a special educational need may involve the SEN co-ordinator from a school or a support worker. A combined nursery centre in Stockport devised their own checklist for staff to use prior to alerting the SEN co-ordinator that they had a concern about a child (Figure 4.11). Leading on from this will be the requirement to assess the extent of a

---

WORRY LIST

Literacy

Poor listening skills
Poor communication – verbal/non-verbal
Speech delay/language delay
Problems with general recall
Poor manipulative skills/clumsy
Withdrawn/limited eye-contact
Inability to follow simple instructions
Reluctance to draw or make marks
Hearing/sight problems
Lack of imaginative play
Uses language inappropriately

Numeracy

Lack of spatial awareness
Inability to sequence
Cannot sort or match
Unable to complete a simple jigsaw
Unable to differentiate

Behaviour/emotional/social

Doesn't form relationships with peers/
  adults
Solitary play
Excessive awareness of bodily functions
Aggressive behaviour towards peers/
  adults
Lack of self-esteem
Over-compliant behaviour
Constant need for re-assurance/
  attention
Lethargy
Constant temper tantrums – no regard
  for own safety
Limited eye-contact
Hyperactive
Compulsive eater
Inappropriate behaviour
Adverse family relationships – rejection
  within family.

FIGURE 4.11   How to identify a problem (Grennan 1996)

child's special needs in accordance with the approach taken in the *Special Educational Needs Code of Practice* (DfES 2001b).

For those of you working in settings with children under five and registered to provide education as part of an Early Years Development Plan there is additional guidance (DfEE 1998d) outlining the requirements for the identification and assessment of children with special educational needs in settings in the private, voluntary and independent sectors. In summary this guidance recommends that providers should have a staff development programme in place to help staff to observe early signs of special educational needs, to take early action to meet those needs within the normal work of the setting, to set up appropriate monitoring and recording of a child's progress and to know where to get further advice from.

It may be inappropriate for children with special educational needs to be assessed using the *stepping stones*. Practitioners are increasingly making use of performance criteria or as they are more commonly referred to 'P' scales. (DfEE 1998f). Use of these scales means that small steps of progress can be measured. There are early development scales for communication, language and literacy and personal, social and emotional development. In my experience they are not widely used in mainstream provision. Some of the scales are identified in the chapters for the three areas of learning to which they apply.

Record keeping

Careful assessment and record keeping underpin all good educational practice. They are essential elements in securing effective continuity and progression; as the ESAC report on Achievement in Primary Schools made clear, the skills of diagnosing success and difficulties are fundamental to educators' work and vital to children's progress.

(DES 1990:16)

Early years practitioners are frequently prolific record keepers. How much information about children's progress is it manageable to keep? Who is the information gathered for? How is the information to be used to improve the quality of education for children either during their pre-school experience or on transfer to the reception class of an infant or primary school?

Listed below are the basic requirements used most frequently by experienced educators.

Essential record keeping for the early years

- Recorded assessments in each area of learning based upon regular observation.
- Records of progress in reading and mathematical understanding completed by

parents and diagnostically annotated by teachers or other staff in the nursery or reception class.

- Entries to be made at least twice a term, more often for children exhibiting learning, social/emotional or physical difficulties.

- Initial record of child's family circumstances and health related information.

- Assessments kept in an individual profile, accessible to children and parents.

Early years portfolios

A frequent practice in nursery schools and classes is that of keeping portfolios of children's achievements. This practice can be extended through to infant schools. An informative account of the way in which this was achieved in an infant school is described by Ackers (1994: 55) in Abbott and Rodger (1994). The name given to the portfolio may vary between schools. Sometimes it is called a record of achievement. An important part of the portfolio is the information gathered on entry to a setting. The principles on which to base an entry profile are listed below.

- The process should begin with the child and his or her needs.

- The major partners in compiling the record should be the child, the parent(s) and the teacher.

- Records should be of facts, and avoid judgements which lead to stereotyping and lower expectations.

- Records should stress positive achievements and record what a child can do.

- An entry profile should be the first foundation of a record of achievement and not an end in itself.

- Entry profiles and subsequent assessments and achievements should inform reporting.

- Entry profiles should address equal opportunities issues.

- Outside agencies should be involved where necessary.

A portfolio is described by Pollard (1997:303) as a

. . . simple durable file which can act as a method of retaining and recording evidence of a child's learning. To maximise the educational value, each child should be closely involved in the selection of evidence for inclusion in his or her portfolio, and in review of the contents. Portfolios should thus be accessible to the pupils in the classroom and, in that the portfolio is an attempt to represent their achievements, the pupils should have a sense of ownership of the contents. Portfolios can move with children as they progress through school, thus providing information for successive teachers and facilitating continuity and progression.

The case study below describes how a record of achievement was compiled in a nursery school with a four-year-old boy called Josh.

Josh climbed into the quiet area clutching his 'special book' and sat down beside Joan his key worker. Joan took out a number of photographs of Josh and other children building with the blocks outside earlier in the term. 'Which one would you like to put inside your "special book" Josh?' Josh glanced at the pictures and then seeing one with a clear picture of himself balancing a cylindrical brick on top of a tower of rectangular blocks pointed to the blocks and uttered a few unintelligible words. Carefully supported by Joan, who rephrased what she thought he had said, Josh tried again, 'big tower'. He examines other photographs and sees himself sharing *Peace at Last* with Ella. 'Bears in garden,' he ventures, and disappears from the quiet area, returning moments later with *Peace at Last*. Joan has another intention. She reassures Josh she will read the story after they have decided which photograph to put in the 'special' book. Leafing through the completed pages Josh looks at the drawing of himself completed when he entered the nursery after Easter, six months earlier. He stops and counts the balloons coloured red, takes out and opens the little story book he has completed as part of one of his planned early writing tasks and very methodically arranges the photograph of Ella and himself reading a story.

A daily occurrence in this nursery, where children attend full-time: every afternoon between 1.30 and 2.00 p.m. the nursery officer or nursery teacher target one or two children to provide intensive one-to-one support and to review each child's 'special book', the name given in this setting to the portfolio of achievements. Complete ownership of the book by the child is assured through the consideration which is given to the selection of items contained in it. Alongside this purpose, Joan uses this as a chance to listen carefully to Josh's responses. He spoke very little when he entered the nursery six months earlier. Now he is able to string two or three words together and initiates conversations sometimes, but still has problems with some key sounds, no 's' on the ends of words for example. A note of his progress is made by Joan, to be discussed at the weekly review meeting held every Friday lunchtime.

In another setting the staff handbook outlines detailed guidance to staff on record keeping strategies for writing activities (Figure 4.12).

The guidance goes on to provide information on gathering data from focused observations, outlines time-sampling and lists items for recording during a PE session.

Discussion

Those of you reading this book who plan to teach or who work in some other capacity with young children will spend a lot of time in nursery or school settings

Before starting writing with a child, staff should discuss the child's picture with him/her.

Records should include:
- whether the child can discuss their picture and answer questions asked of them about their work;
- which hand the child uses;
- grip;
- does the child use L ~ R; T ~ B orientation?
- can the child 'read' work back?
- record of exactly what the child wants to communicate;
- can the child discriminate sounds?
  if yes: can they write sounds from memory?

   can they find sounds on the alphabet sheet?

   can they find sounds on a colour line (how many times does it take?)

   can they discriminate further sounds in one word?

FIGURE 4.12   Guidance for record keeping on writing activities

- What assessment procedures does the setting use?
- Which baseline assessment scheme is used?
- What use is made of this information?
- Ask if you can see an analysis of the baseline assessments
- How often are assessments carried out?
- Are there agreed assessment criteria?
- What are the procedures for the early identification of children with special educational needs?
- Ask to see the assessment policy and to speak with the assessment coordinator.
- Does the setting have examples of recorded pupils' writing and/or first marks on paper?
- Find out how expectations for three- and four-year-olds differ.

FIGURE 4.13   Finding out about assessment in your training placement

working with different groups of children. Assessment and record keeping are one of the most difficult areas for trainee teachers to understand. In preparation for this you will need to gather information from the settings in which you are training. The checklist (Figure 4.13) shows some of the questions you need to ask and the investigations you need to make.

An important dimension to baseline assessment is that relating to children with special educational needs. In 1998 QCA produced a baseline scheme for children with special educational needs (QCA 1998c). There have been some criticisms of the scheme in that it does not compare too favourably with the nationally accredited baseline scheme for all other pupils in school. Nutbrown (1998) has analysed the differences, and in particular cites as a comparison the two scales for personal and social development. She does this, she claims, because the scales for SEN children in this area of learning are much more detailed and helpful to practitioners than for mainstream children. She argues that very young children who are just four in reception class may have special needs and should be considered appropriately. All practitioners would benefit from further information especially in relation to personal, social, and emotional development. Use the information in Figure 4.14 to provide yourself with exemplification of personal and social development.

An important point to remember at all times is your role in your informal ongoing assessment in your day-to-day interactions with children. Time needs to be found in a busy nursery day to do this. In one nursery, for example, targeted children were observed and informally assessed ready for a meeting at the end of the week to discuss aspects of their learning. The importance of observation as a tool for assessment was succinctly captured by Chris Athey (1997) in a lecture given at the Museum of Childhood in connection with the 'Hundred Languages of Children' exhibition at which she said:

If we taught less we could listen more carefully to what children are saying. If we taught less and observed more we would be in a better position to learn how children conceptualise events. We could then make significant aspects of early learning and thinking more visible than they are at present.

Further criticisms have been voiced that suggest that teachers will prepare children for the baseline by focusing activities on the assessment items to encourage children to do better. Munn (1998) told the British Psychological Society developmental conference that pupils' mental arithmetic may suffer as a result of the introduction of baseline assessment. Reception class teachers, she cited, are focusing on teaching four- and five-year-olds to recognise numbers and to count because these skills are tested. This is leading to less time spent playing games which enable children to develop an understanding that numbers are made up of other numbers, which is a fundamental concept in mental mathematics.

Baseline assessment has not received universal acclaim. A well-voiced criticism is the range of accredited schemes in place and the difficulties this will pose when comparing school with school, where each school uses a different scheme. Professor Geoff Lindsay (Ghouri 1998) identified the lack of quality control as a problem. He claims that very few schemes have been thoroughly researched and

	QCA Baseline Scales (SCAA 1997a)		QCA Baseline Scales *Special Educational Needs* (QCA 1998c)
	Personal and Social		**Personal and Social Development A: Attention skills**
		1	Attends to a sensory source
		2	Engages in an activity with adult support
		3	Concentrates on an activity for 10 minutes with intermittent supervision
3	Concentrates without supervision for 10 minutes	4	Concentrates without supervision for 10 minutes
			Personal and Social Development B: Expressing needs and opinions
		1	Expresses a like or dislike
		2	Makes a choice
		3	Attracts the attention of a familiar adult to communicate needs and preferences
4	Expresses own opinions with a range of adults	4	Expresses own opinions with a range of adults
			Personal and Social Development C: From dependence to independence
		1	Takes part (adult led activity)
		2	Able to anticipate
		3	Follows routines
2	Is independent and keen to contribute	4	Is independent and keen to contribute
			Personal and Social Development D: Interaction and collaboration with peers
		1	Experiences activities led by others
		2	Becoming an active participant
		3	Interactive participant
1	Plays collaboratively	4	Plays collaboratively

FIGURE 4.14   Comparison of QCA baseline scales with special educational needs baseline scales (Nutbrown 1998)

evaluated. The consequence of this may lead to invalid assessments of the children's current stage of development. A wider concern expressed relates to the negative labels which may be attributed to children. It was ever thus. Children, irrespective of their age, deserve the right to be provided for appropriately. Assessment of what they can and cannot do on entry to school is part of a process by which effective teachers achieve a good match between the needs of individual children and the activities provided for them. Headteachers of primary schools have fought a long battle to have a baseline system in place which will enable them to show the value-added by their school at the end of Key Stage 1, when children are seven. However, one thing is clear. The multiplicity of schemes will not deliver the straightforward value-added data on children's progress and school performance many politicians would like.

Further reading

Ackers, J. (1994) '"Why involve me?" Encouraging children and their parents to participate in the assessment process', in Abbott, L. and Rodger, R. (eds), *Quality Education in the Early Years*. Buckingham: Open University Press.

Drummond, M. J. (1993) *Assessing Children's Learning*. London: David Fulton Publishers.

Drummond, M. J., Rouse, D., Pugh, G. (1992) *Making Assessment Work: Values and Principles in Assessing Young Children's Learning*. London: NES Arnold in association with the National Children's Bureau.

DfEE (1998) *Supporting the Target Setting Process*. Nottingham: DfEE.

Lindsay, G. and Desforges, M. (1998) *Baseline Assessment: Practice, Problems and Possibilities*. London: David Fulton Publishers.

Norwich, B. and Lindsay, G. (eds) (1998) *Baseline Assessment*. Tamworth: NASEN.

Leadership and management in the early years

Introduction

This chapter looks at the impact of the requirements of the Foundation Stage curriculum in the past two years on leadership and management in early years settings, and shows how different settings have adapted their practices and restructured roles and responsibilities to meet the ever increasing demands on the headteacher's or manager's time. In recent years, there has been a significant increase in the range of responsibilities now part of the headteacher's role in early years centres, Early Excellence centres and nursery schools. The change that is most pertinent to this book is the statutory requirement to implement the Foundation Stage curriculum. However, there are several other changes which have an impact on the leadership and management roles of headteachers and managers. These include: financial management; performance management; extending the nature and range of provision; and training. A tier of super headteachers are emerging via Early Excellence centres, Beacon nursery schools and from the increasing number of headteachers who have very successful Ofsted inspections each year as listed in HMCI's Annual Report to Schools (Ofsted 2003). There is a career path for recently qualified early years practitioners and for those who may not have qualified with a degree in early years but who wish to pursue a career and ultimately aspire to leadership in this area. Changes to the requirements of the SEN Code of Practice now rightly give greater responsibilities to early years settings to identify and support children with special educational needs. There are specific roles and responsibilities for the headteacher and/or teacher with this area as their responsibility which will be discussed.

The chapter is premised on the view that there will be someone with responsibility for the Foundation Stage in maintained primary schools. This is a fundamental requirement for the senior management structure in primary, infant or first schools in the maintained sector. There may be more children in the Foundation Stage than in Years 1 and 2. This has major implications for the status, roles and responsibilities of the Foundation Stage leader, who should be a member of the senior management team. This responsibility could be given to someone who is teaching in the Foundation Stage and not added to the responsibilities of the Key Stage 1 co-ordinator, except perhaps in a very small school. The roles and responsibilities of such a position are discussed later. I have added to this edition a section on the ways in which small schools tackle the resource, staffing and curricular implications of the Foundation Stage. The key sections of this chapter are:

- Effective leadership and management in the early years
- The roles and responsibilities of the Foundation Stage leader in maintained sector primary schools
- Roles and responsibilties for the special educational needs co-ordinator
- Managing the introduction of the Foundation Stage in a small school
- Improvement through inspection in the private and voluntary sectors

Leadership and management in the early years

An effective early years headteacher, manager or leader will have the following characteristics:

- lead by example;
- take responsibility;
- add value to the children's development as a result of high quality provision;
- create a strong, self-motivated team of staff;
- share responsibilities and delegate appropriately to enable the strengths of everyone to be recognized and valued;
- build a strong team and give opportunities for institutional and personal development;
- include all stakeholders in strategic development of the setting: parents; other professionals; governors; staff;
- be innovative, ingenious, creative, optimistic and efficient.

There are several published lists of the characteristics of effective leaders, but few that relate specifically to the head of an early years setting. The above list comes from my own perceptions of the qualities of the outstanding headteachers with whom I have worked in recent years. Government initiatives have placed considerable additional pressures on headteachers to enable them to expand their provision and to have the same rights and responsibilities as their counterparts in primary schools.

Financial responsibilities

Current legislation requires all maintained schools to have governing bodies. At present this does not apply to maintained nursery schools. However, the government has proposed that nursery schools should be required to have their own legally constituted governing body. The Governance Consultation document states that the government is set to introduce provision to enable schools to federate under a single governing body. This would allow a nursery school and infant or primary school to be run as separate schools by a single governing body or separate governing bodies to take joint decisions on specific issues. Funding mechanisms for nursery schools are under review, but in some areas they are working towards having a fully delegated budget stage by stage, with the LEA taking some responsibilities. The LEAs are obliged to ensure that those who deliver early education meet all the requirements of good practice irrespective of how the funding is delivered. The requirements are:

- Meeting the early learning goals;
- Registration;
- Special educational needs;
- The Foundation Stage Profile;
- A ban on corporal punishment;
- The elimination of unlawful racial discrimination;
- The promotion of equal opportunities.

Many settings are taking on several initiatives that are enabling them to expand their provision to include care for children before and after the normal two and a half hour daily session. The headteacher may have responsibility for management of all the services on her site, but individual providers may be the responsibility of another organization under the overall management of the headteacher.

Development planning

On what is the strategic direction of a nursery school based? I ask this question deliberately as I want to show that excellent practitioners use the evidence of how well children achieve or don't achieve to set their priorities alongside external initiatives over which headteachers may have less control; for example, to manage the change in status of a setting. How rigorous are your monitoring and evaluation systems to enable you to know exactly what goes well and what needs to be improved in your school? Do you use the self-evaluation model suggested by Ofsted (2000)? Or you may work in an LEA which has their own model of self-review via *Headfirst*. Basically, development planning is about analysing regularly what you do and making judgements about the effectiveness of your actions. The four questions at the heart of evaluating everything you do are:

■ Are the children in my setting achieving as well as they are capable?

■ What can I do to find this out?

■ How do I know that the answer to this question is right?

■ What am I going to do about it when I have the answer?

To ensure that self-evaluation has the maximum impact on the work of your setting you need to be able to take an objective look at your children's achievements and know the areas in which your children may be underachieving. You will also need to have a clear view of the strengths and weaknesses in the teaching, before you look at what else you do to support children's learning. This information can then be used to devise your School Improvement Plan.

Case Study

The example below shows how an Early Excellence centre developed their Plan for one aspect of raising attainment in communication, language and literacy. Actions not included in the example below included raising the profile of the area of learning across the centre, improving the quality of teaching and learning and extending language and literacy between home and the centre.

Priority 1   To raise attainment in communication, language and literacy

Action to be taken	Personnel	Planned programme and outcome	Success criteria	Monitoring and evaluation	Costing
To improve opportunities for all children to learn through improved teaching strategies.	All staff	Organise provision and resources in all rooms. Enhance play provision. Provide ideas, prompts and questions – photos, written word and pictures. Produce big book file on reading and writing. Develop observational skills to inform better planning.	More time spent reading, writing, role-play and drama. Increased resources, easy access and better organisation. Raised levels of speaking and listening/ communication.	Monitoring. Tracking records. Evaluation. Weekly check by teacher responsible for curriculum in one room and by headteacher through the rest of the centre. Feedback from children. Increased scores on the on exit baseline.	

The completion of an evaluation at the end of the school improvement cycle is important as this is where some of the priorities for the following year will come from. The actions in the Plan above were evaluated against the 'on entry' and 'on exit' baseline scores for communication, language and literacy. As a result of significant movement of the children between one building and another because of new building works, it was felt that some children did not make the progress expected and the priority was continued the following year. There were also some issues to do with staff knowledge of the early learning goals and the best ways to promote effective learning, which were then identified as performance management targets for the staff concerned and led to training courses being provided.

Inspection expectations

The new *Framework for Inspecting Schools* (Ofsted 2003: 40) is unequivocal: 'the leadership and management at all levels . . . should be judged by their [headteacher's and senior staff's] effect on quality and standards of the school. Leadership should provide the drive and direction for raising achievement, while management should make best use of resources and processes to enable this to happen. Management includes effective evaluation, planning, performance management and staff development.' Inspectors should consider the extent to which leadership is embedded throughout the school and vested solely in the most senior staff. They should explore how well the leadership team creates a climate for learning.

How well is your setting led and managed?

The checklist below may help you review your current systems and ensure that all stakeholders are involved in the improvement process.

- **The governance of the setting**
  - How well do your governors help to shape the vision and direction of the setting?
  - Do they ensure that the setting fulfils its statutory duties, including promoting inclusive policies in relation to SEN, race equality, disability and sex?
  - Have they a good understanding of the strengths and weaknesses of your setting?
  - Do they challenge and support the management team?

- **The quality of leadership of the setting**
  - Is there a clear vision, a sense of purpose and high aspirations for the setting, with a relentless focus on children's achievement?
  - Does strategic planning reflect and promote the setting's ambitions and goals?
  - Does your leadership inspire, motivate and influence staff and pupils?
  - Do you create effective teams?
  - Is there knowledgeable leadership of areas of learning and teaching?
  - Are leaders committed to running an equitable and inclusive setting, in which each individual matters?
  - Do leaders provide good role models for other staff and the children?

■ **The effectiveness of management**
  ● Do you undertake rigorous self-evaluation and use the findings effectively?
  ● Do you monitor performance data, review patterns and take action?
  ● Are your arrangements for performance management, including support staff, thorough and effective in bringing about improvement?
  ● Is your commitment to staff development reflected in effective induction and professional development strategies, and where possible, the setting's contribution to initial teacher training?
  ● Does your approach to financial and resource management help the setting to achieve its educational priorities?
  ● Are the principles of best value central to the setting's management and use of resources?

Adapted from *Framework for Inspecting Schools* (Ofsted 2003)

Managers of settings inspected under the requirements of the nursery education inspections have until the new inspection regulations come out not been inspected on leadership and management. In the revised inspection requirements child care inspectors will be making judgements on how well the setting is led and managed. The criteria are broadly similar to the categories listed above which would be equally useful to a setting manager in the private and voluntary sectors. The main difference is that now inspections in those settings are combined there is a need to consider the quality of childcare as well as education.

Monitoring and evaluation

A key aspect of the role of leaders in the early years is monitoring and evaluating the work of your setting. In particular you will be expected to check the quality of teaching by observing staff and giving them feedback, both written and oral, on the strengths and weaknesses of their performance. The checklist below (Figure 5.1) (is based on the Ofsted criteria for monitoring teaching, but has been adapted to reflect the early years.

Individual headteachers will have their own methods of checking planning also. The example in Figure 5.2 is one used by a headteacher of a large nursery school.

The roles and responsibilities of the Foundation Stage leader in maintained sector primary schools

The role of the Foundation Stage leader in primary schools is probably the most difficult in the early years because of conflicting demands, especially if you work in

The quality of teaching in the foundation stage

When evaluating the quality of teaching in the foundation stage, consider the extent to which staff:

- Show a good knowledge and understanding in the way they present the foundation curriculum and the early learning goals;
- Are technically competent in teaching phonics and other basic skills, (*especially through talk*);
- Plan effectively, setting clear objectives (*to promote the six areas of learning, giving priority to personal, social and emotional development; communication, language and literacy; and mathematical development. The focus should be on what children should learn, how they will be organised, the deployment of staff and the resources needed*);
- Meet the needs of all children (*by taking account of the different rates of child development*);
- Challenge and inspire children, expecting the most of them (*to attain the early learning goals by the end of the reception year and for some to go beyond*);
- Use methods which enable children to learn effectively (*including effective interaction in children's play and building trusting relationships*);
- Manage children well and have high standards for behaviour;
- Use time, support staff and other resources effectively (*including accommodation so that the environment is well organised to help children become self-sufficient*); and

Assess children's work thoroughly (*using regular observations to assess children's progress towards the early learning goals*).

FIGURE 5.1   Evaluating the quality of teaching in the early years

a small school with only one reception class (more about this later in the chapter). You need to be reassured in this case that the statutory requirements are to plan your curriculum to meet the early learning goals (elgs) in all areas of learning by the time your children start in Year 1. Undoubtedly, you will know that once your children have achieved the early learning goals, you will use National Curriculum programmes of study as a basis for planning. Difficulties may arise at the start of the term in which the children start school. It is not usually appropriate for reception class children to attend whole school assemblies in the first term at least, or for them to play outside with the rest of the children at playtime. A very small school may be an exception to this. The organisation and management of the classroom will need to differ markedly from the way the children will work when they go into Year 1. As Foundation Stage Co-ordinator your role will comprise the following responsibilities (see Figure 5.3). A survey raises the questions, 'What is a reasonable and productive concentration span for a six-year-old? What are the implications for the way we structure lessons and pace teaching?' (Ofsted 2003b: 41).

Date:_____ Teacher:_____ Year:_____

Checklist

- Timetable enclosed
- Group lists
- Learning objectives
- Early learning goals/*stepping-stones*. National Curriculum levels
- Activities
- Differentiation
- Extra resources needed
- Groups to be assessed
- Time
- Assessment/development

Any other comments

Please address the above points as soon as possible. Thank you.

Signed _____

FIGURE 5.2   Example of a short-term monitoring record

The roles and responsibilities of the special educational needs co-ordinator (SENCO)

The *Code of Practice* (DfES 2001) makes very clear what needs to happen in the early years as far as SEN arrangements are concerned. The *Code of Practice* was effective from 1 January 2002. Early years settings must have regard for it.

Changes from the original Code of Practice

- A stronger right for children to be educated at a mainstream school.
- New duties on LEAs to arrange for parents of children with SEN to be provided with services offering advice and information and a means of resolving disputes.

1. Writing a policy for the Foundation Stage or contributing to school-wide policies – especially inclusion and racial equality.
2. Admission arrangements – involvement of parents, home visiting, preparation sessions for parents and children, when? how often?
3. Point of entry to nursery, staggered entry, provision for playtimes in the reception class, lunchtimes and whole school assemblies – where practice is good, children should have own area for outdoor play, not be expected to attend whole school assemblies, and have lunch separately from the rest of the school.
4. Routines and organisation of the sessions.
5. Assessment – baseline on entry to nursery, how is this recorded, should be against each area of learning. Arrangements for identification of SEN children.
6. Planning – long, medium and short term, continuity between nursery and reception class and to Key Stage 1.
7. The contribution of the outdoor environment? It should include more than physical development.
8. Plans for the week should indicate adult-focused activities. Often they will have detailed learning objectives and assessment opportunities identified. Ask if more time is allocated to communication, language and literacy and mathematical development because the QCA guidance does not recommend that it should be. Ofsted generally expect it.
9. Contribution of performance management, lesson observations, monitoring progress, feedback to staff (oral and written)
10. Are you a team leader for performance management? Staff other than teachers may be involved in performance management.
11. Involvement in whole school developments.
12. Training provided and received.
13. Priorities for the Foundation Stage and involvement in SIP.
14. Involvement of parents – day by day.
15. Involvement with outside agencies – educational psychologist, speech and language therapists.
16. Involvement in other initiatives – Sure Start, Early Excellence, Education Action Zones and Excellence in Cities may have implications for involvement in parenting programmes.

FIGURE 5.3   Roles and responsibilities of the Foundation Stage Co-ordinator

- A new duty on schools and relevant nursery education providers to tell parents when they are making special educational needs provision for their child.

- A new right for schools and relevant nursery education providers to request a statutory assessment of a child.

The Disability Rights Code of Practice for Schools

- Schools are prohibited from discriminating against disabled children in their admission arrangements.

- From September 2002 schools were required not to treat disabled pupils less favourably for a reason relating to their disability and to take reasonable steps to ensure they are not placed at a substantial disadvantage to those that are not disabled.

The role of the SENCO – what to look for

- Liaison with parents and other professionals.
- Advising and supporting other practitioners in the setting.
- Ensuring that appropriate individual education plans (IEPs) are in place (see below).
- Ensuring that relevant background information about individual children with special educational needs is collected, recorded and updated.

The SENCO should also

- Take a lead in planning future support for the child in discussions with colleagues.
- Monitor and review the actions taken.
- Keep appropriate records which include a record of children at EARLY YEARS ACTION and EARLY YEARS ACTION PLUS and those with statements.
- Keep parents informed.
- Be a member of the senior management team.
- Ensure that the SEN policy is updated.
- Ensure the governors publish the school's policy for SEN and review the effectiveness of it on a yearly basis.

Early Years Action

Interventions that are additional to or different from those provided as part of the setting's usual curriculum provision. The triggers that a child needs Early Years Action are:

- little or no progress even when approaches are targeted on the child;
- continuing to work at levels significantly below other children the same age;
- presenting persistent emotional and/or behavioural difficulties;
- having sensory or physical problems;
- having communication or interaction difficulties.

Actions required include:

- Child needs to learn and progress, therefore the arrangements for learning and teaching need to be individualised.
- Resources may be additional staff, extra staff or LEA support.
- IEP for the child – include short-term targets, teaching strategies and the provision, when the plan is to be reviewed and the outcomes of the actions – only record what is additional and different.
- IEPs should be crisply written and only focus on 3 or 4 targets.
- Review termly with the parents if possible – review meetings to be informal.

Early Years Action Plus

- Involvement of outside agencies/external support services.
- Triggers to request external help taken at the review meetings.
- Parents' views to be sought.

Triggers for statutory assessment for the over-twos

- Physical health and functioning
- Communication skills
- Perceptual and motor skills
- Self help skills
- Social skills
- Emotional and behavioural development
- Responses to learning experiences
- Views of parents.

Provision

Portage

Home teaching

Services of a peripatetic teacher for hearing or visually impaired

Access to an educational psychologist for emotional and behavioural difficulties

Specialist provision if required/or available.

The responsibility for children with special educational needs in pre-schools lies with the LEA not the setting. Schools and settings should consider whether the SENCO should be on the senior management team.

Managing the Foundation Stage in a small school

Examples of some of the ways in which small rural primary schools provide effectively for children in the Foundation Stage where they share their education with pupils in Years 1 and 2 are outlined in this section of the chapter. The limitations of outdoor space can make provision for daily activities in the outdoor environment difficult. Nevertheless, there are schools all over the country taking good account of the recommendations of the guidance provided by QCA (QCA 2000).

How do headteachers and staff of small schools provide an appropriate curriculum for children aged between three and five years old? How do they organise and manage the demands of teaching Year 1 and 2 pupils the literacy hour and the daily mathematics lesson and provide the reception class children with a high quality experience? Is outdoor play possible? Generally, the children will be four years old and may have spent time in a pre-school attached to the school or elsewhere or attended a private nursery. Some children may have older siblings in school and be reasonably familiar with the school environment. One challenging recommendation for an effective early years curriculum is that it is carefully structured to provide opportunities for teaching and learning both indoors and outdoors.

Organising and managing the mixed age classroom

Provision cannot be as effective if there are no additional staff to support a teacher working with reception-aged children and other age groups in the same room. In reality, the additional support may be a trained caretaker, a parent or a classroom assistant. Small schools do not generally have the good fortune to employ a qualified nursery nurse. While skilled teaching can adjust the levels of questions for the younger children in a whole group session so they are included, there are times when the youngest children need to be working as a discrete group, especially when they are learning to recognise the initial, final and medial sounds of words in literacy activities which need to be matched to meet their developmental needs. Detailed planning can show how the activities are differentiated to meet the needs of a wide age range. How does the lone teacher in such a situation 'observe and respond appropriately to the younger children' or 'intervene to help children make progress in their learning'? It would seem that it is impossible to do this, although the other teacher in a two-teacher school may find herself (it usually is a woman) in this position.

Where there is only one teacher for the Foundation Stage and Key Stage 1, the following teaching methods can be used:

■ The environment of the classroom has been adapted to meet the needs of younger pupils through the designation of an area for their use only – it may be an annexe area, part of a corridor or a section of the main classroom, but it will be personalised and reflective of a nursery environment.

■ Parent helpers are briefed and deployed to work with a group of younger children for some of the time.

■ Reception-aged children take part in self-initiated learning in a section of the classroom dedicated to their needs. The activities available have been planned by the staff and have a clear purpose.

■ The teacher moves from the Year 1 group to the reception group of pupils to give them the attention they may need to extend their learning in their self-initiated play.

To provide access to a wide range of activities, the classroom needs to contain:

Role play area, which can be resourced to meet the needs of older and younger children

Sand and water play area

Construction area

Writing area

Book corner

Creative area.

The number of areas can be changed if space is limited. Sand can be alternated with water play, and the construction area can be used to play floor games or complete jigsaws. Use of the space outside the classroom should be considered as long as safety measures are followed and the children are clear what the rules and expectations of their play are in the area.

More usually, there will be a full- or a part-time nursery nurse or classroom assistant who, in my experience, takes the role of teaching either Year 1 or 2 or the reception class. It is important that the reception children are taught by a teacher as well as a classroom assistant or nursery nurse. The children may be part of a whole group for the first part of the day, for registration and collective worship requirements for those children of five for whom this is a statutory requirement. Personal, social and emotional development can be effectively fostered during a whole group session once the children have settled into the routines of the school.

Curriculum planning in mixed age classes

The most efficiently managed planning is the differentiation within a subject-based topic to meet the needs of all age groups. The activities for older children are planned using the National Curriculum programme of study, usually following the national guidance provided by QCA, and the activities for reception aged children are planned using the *stepping stones* for each area of learning. Planning is completed for the Foundation Stage and Key Stage 1 together. By the summer term reception aged children may have met or exceeded the early learning goals. Consequently, the transition to National Curriculum programmes of study is straightforward because the teacher may already be planning work for older pupils in the class using the same material.

Case study

The topic was materials, and the reception-aged children were investigating the properties of various fabrics to help them decide which material would be the most suitable to make an umbrella. At all times the children were supported by a teaching assistant. When the investigation was carried out they moved to their dedicated area to test different fabrics for porosity.

Providing for literacy and numeracy in mixed age classes

Practically, there are times when reception aged pupils will be together with the rest of the class: for whole class shared text and word level work, and possibly for the plenary in schools which do not have additional support. This practice is appropriate when the needs of the younger pupils are considered. If a shared text is too difficult, the reception aged children will need to have a text they can cope with at another time of the day or after the rest of the class have completed their whole class work. In such situations it is likely that the time for text and word level work is split so the younger children are not sitting for too long. The daily mathematics lesson recommended for children in Key Stage 1 generally takes place with the reception aged children taking part in the whole class session. Good teachers know how to differentiate their questions and tasks to meet the needs of a wider age range and include the youngest children.

Providing for outdoor play

This is a more difficult aspect of the curricular provision for the youngest children because access to an outdoor environment must be staffed, and the space available to provide a dedicated area for a very small number of reception aged children may not be the most cost effective use of the school budget, even if the school has the surplus finances needed. Schools have various ways of overcoming this. They may have a small dedicated area which is used at playtime and lunchtime by the reception aged children as an area for self-initiated learning, exploration and moving around freely. Remember that children in the Foundation Stage need time to:

- Play

- Talk

- Observe

- Plan

- Question

- Experiment

- Test

- Repeat

- Reflect.

However, my experience is that if the school is restricted for space the youngest children may get no more than their twice-weekly physical development sessions in a hall. Schools compensate by taking the children further afield – a walk along a contrasting street, to the woods or to examine the buildings in the village. The opportunities are endless when the teaching staff acknowledges that young children learn effectively through purposeful first-hand experiences. Half-termly topics should have clearly planned opportunities for learning in the outdoor environment beyond the school. While this may not be a daily event, the children are enhancing their learning through the outdoor experiences. They are developing observational and investigative skills from first-hand experiences, albeit on a less regular basis than if the children had their own outdoor area.

Other factors contributing to success

The following is a list of other ways in which schools cope with too few staff and limited resources.

- Contact the local Early Years Development and Childcare Partnership to borrow play materials for short-term loans.

- Use the expertise of development workers employed to support aspects of the early years, such as helping to establish pre-schools and supporting children with special educational needs.

- Create a small schools federation with a Foundation Stage focus to share practices and exchange staff.

- Make links with other providers such as the Pre-School Learning Alliance who are well experienced in creating vibrant early years environments in the most unlikely places.

- Provide time for the Foundation Stage children to work away from Key Stage 1 under the direction of a nursery nurse or classroom assistant some of the time, but also to spend time with their teacher.

There are many well-experienced and well-trained classroom assistants who are doing a magnificent job of supporting classteachers. However, they should not be given total responsibility for the Foundation Stage children.

The picture I have painted is a positive one of the practices I have seen in schools up and down the country. There are three main factors in determining the quality of the provision for the Foundation Stage in small schools. First, the support provided for the teacher by the headteacher, who may also be teaching several year groups in a classroom; this is most likely to be in providing additional staffing and funding to improve the provision, especially outside. Secondly, the knowledge the teacher has of the principles of a Foundation Stage curriculum, so that the children are provided with a broad and balanced curriculum covering all areas of learning. Finally, but by no means least, the impact of Section 10 inspections on the Foundation Stage curriculum. All inspection teams are now required to have an inspector who has been trained to inspect the Foundation Stage. Registered inspectors are required to give the inspection of the Foundation Stage a high priority. They have been provided with extensive guidance on what needs to be in place to judge that the provision is at least satisfactory. To give readers a flavour of this the following guidance was given to registered inspectors in September 2001:

> Judgements on standards, teaching and learning must give clear judgements for all six areas of learning . . . Evaluate how schools include the outdoor environment in their planning as well as what is in evidence during the inspection.

In the Foundation Stage briefing attended by inspectors prior to the implementation of the new recommendations they were alerted to the fact that the 'Foundation Stage was a distinctive phase in its own right' and that 'learning through play initiated by children, was highlighted as important'.

Improvement through inspection on the private and voluntary sectors

The actions settings need to take in preparing themselves for a combined inspection are listed below.

Improving the quality of education for all (Hopkins 1994:103)

- establishment of priorities, via an audit of strengths and weaknesses, in existing practices (completion of the Self-appraisal Schedule);

- the creation of internal conditions that will underpin and sustain the change process, existence of a stable staffing base and completion of curriculum policies and guidelines for staff on a range of nursery matters);

- a strategy, or set of strategies, designed to achieve the priorities and to establish the internal conditions to support these (the action plan identified at the last Ofsted inspection).

Effectiveness, on the other hand, is concerned with observation, analysis and evaluation in order to judge schools, usually, and occasionally to illuminate how their effectiveness or lack of it was achieved. The use of the word 'usually' is intentional as studies of school effectiveness have generally focused on the primary and secondary sectors of education. (Scheerens 1992, Ofsted and Coopers and Lybrand 1994, Sammons *et al.* 1995). School effectiveness research has progressed considerably since the sixties to reveal a more accurate picture of the many factors in schools which determine standards among pupils. Figure 5.4 lists those factors contributing to effectiveness in the school sector. Can these factors be applied with regard to the education of children under five? Reynolds *et al.* (1990:1) state that 'schools matter, that schools do have major effects upon children's development and that, to put it simply, schools do make a difference'. Early years professionals have, in the main, been slow to accept that what children know, understand and can do when they are under five is also of vital importance and matters just as highly as for provision for older children. A national agenda to raise standards for all children has affected what happens to children under five in their settings. How practices can be improved in the early years was one of the aims of inspection. The days of saying that 'quality is an elusive concept in the early years' are long past. Early years practitioners everywhere are accountable for what they provide for the children in their care, precisely because what happens in the pre-school has an impact on later learning (Sylva 1994).

Statutory requirements

As mentioned in the first chapter, recent changes to the funding of nursery education for four-year-olds has introduced a very strong element of accountability into early years provision. All providers registered in the local education authority's Early Years Development Plan (EYDP) must agree, as a condition of registration, to have their educational provision inspected regularly by a registered nursery inspector, who will report on the quality and standards of the education funded under the

1. Professional leadership	Firm and purposeful A participative approach The leading professionals
2. Shared vision and goals	Unity of purpose Consistency of practice Collegiality and collaboration
3. A learning environment	An orderly atmosphere An attractive working environment
4. Concentration on teaching and learning	Maximisation of learning time Academic emphasis Focus on achievement
5. Purposeful teaching	Efficient organisation Clarity of purpose Structured lessons Adaptive practice
6. High expectations	High expectations all round Communicating expectations Providing intellectual challenge
7. Positive reinforcement	Clear and fair discipline Feedback
8. Monitoring progress	Monitoring pupil performance Evaluating school performance
9. Pupil rights and responsibilities	Raising pupils' self-esteem Positions of responsibility Control of work
10. Home-school partnership	Parental involvement in their children's learning
11. A learning organisation	School-based staff development

FIGURE 5.4   Eleven factors for effective schools (DfE and OFSTED 1995)

arrangements for EYDPs (Ofsted 1998a:6). Schools with nursery classes and four-year-old children in reception classes are also inspected, but not under the same system at the moment. Four-year-olds in schools are included in the inspection of the whole school under the requirements of a Section 10 inspection. They are inspected as 'Under Fives' within that inspection process. The inspection criteria against which the school inspection of four-year-olds is carried out has some similarities to that of the nursery education scheme inspections, although the process of carrying out the inspection differs in the following ways. Both systems are reporting on the strengths and weaknesses of the quality of education offered to the children in order to help them achieve the standards expected by the time they complete their first year in statutory education, that is, by the time the children reach the end of reception year. Those standards are defined by government as the early learning goals (QCA 2000). Nursery education scheme inspections are carried out over one full day or two half days by one registered nursery inspector and school inspections are carried out by a team of people over several days and to a very different Framework for Inspection. Consequently, making comparisons between the outcomes of the two types of inspection need to be treated with some caution. Similarities in what the schools and the settings have to do following the inspection are broadly similar, in that both inspection reports contain a set of key issues which are expected to form the basis of an action plan. Key issues in a Section 10 inspection focus on a wide range of aspects and subjects taught in the primary school. It is unlikely that a key issue relating to provision for under fives will occur unless it is a serious weakness in that phase.

What is an action plan?

When a setting has been inspected by a registered nursery inspector the provider must prepare an action plan to deal with the key issues identified in the inspection. An action plan:

- is a written framework for improving some aspects of educational practice, usually within a 12 month time span;
- should focus on the key issues for action identified by the inspector in the inspection report;
- sets out the way the manager and colleagues plan to address each of the key issues;
- should be concise and set out clearly what intends to be done.

(DfEE 1997:2)

The purpose of an action plan in a nursery setting is to:

- focus attention on each of the key issues;
- build on areas of strength and ensure there are targets set for improving the educational practice in the setting;
- provide a step by step plan to take the setting from where it is now to where it wants to be in 12 months time;
- helps to map out how the required changes will be brought about;
- shows how the setting is actively responding to the inspection report, which will be used at the next inspection as part of the evaluation.

(DfEE 1997:2)

The above description of an action plan is taken from guidance for the private, voluntary and independent sectors of nursery education. When registered nursery inspectors see the action plan before a reinspection there are several key features they are looking for. These include:

- dealing with each of the key issues mentioned in the report;
- ensuring that the actions taken are realistic, clear and specific;
- working out a clear timescale and order of priority which reflects the order of the key issues;
- the identification of appropriate resources, including time and costs;
- showing who is responsible for carrying out the planned action;
- setting appropriate targets;
- determining the ways in which achievement of the targets will be measured;
- the setting having ways to monitor and evaluate its success.

(Ofsted 1998a:84)

The findings of another report (Ofsted 1995) are much more explicit about what purpose an action plan serves. It is worth considering the differences and exploring the views of colleagues as to their views on the Ofsted description of an action plan and how it matches the way you have structured your action plan.

Action plans are primarily concerned with raising achievement.

The best plans . . . incorporate:

- specific targets for raising standards or improving the quality of provision;
- practical strategies and programmes of development focused on these goals;
- arrangements for monitoring and evaluating the progress and the impact of the measures taken.

(Ofsted 1995:3)

The action plans produced by the managers of the children's centres in the north-west city in which the research mentioned earlier took place had the following structure to follow in compiling their action plans (Figure 5.5).

Schools and nursery settings all have the same time scale in which to draw up their action plans, that is, 40 working days following the publication of the inspection report.

Target	Action	Person Responsible	Dates	Resourcing	Monitoring	Success Criteria
1.						
2.						

FIGURE 5.5   Sample action plan

Improving practice through action planning

In the early stages of the action planning process there needs to be effective consultation with a range of staff involved in the setting to ensure that everyone concerned is familiar with the inspection findings:

■ Are the key issues in priority order?

■ Are there some key issues which will be easier to cope with than others?

■ Do there need to be short-, medium- and long-term targets set in the action plan?

■ How does the inspection action plan compare with the setting development plan?

■ Did the Self-appraisal Schedule identify the same weaknesses?

■ Do individual members of staff need support?

What is obvious here is the need for collaboration and consultation. Rodd (1997:126) would add diagnostic skills to the former two, i.e. the gap between the present situation and the former needs. As the team leader, manager or specialist early years teacher there will be a need to identify priorities and allocate responsibilities to staff, incorporate the key issues into the long-term development of the setting. A good action plan is described by Ofsted in the following terms.

Good plans:

■ address all the key issues in the inspection report and take account of other findings;

■ are concise;

■ show clearly written overviews;

- identify priorities and specific targets;
- have a clear focus on improvement in the classroom;
- list manageable steps towards raising standards of achievement;
- include reference to monitoring and evaluation of intended outcomes including the effects on pupils' achievements;
- give indicators and criteria by which improvement could be recognised;
- identify and quantify resources;
- are drawn up consultatively.

(Ofsted 1995:15)

There is little guidance to headteachers regarding what their priorities should be with regard to children under five in reception classes. Evidence from research is contradictory with regard to age of admission (Sharp 1998a). Factors which contributed to better conditions and more appropriate practices for under fives in reception classes in Salford LEA (Rodger *et al.* 1995) were: a senior management role for the early years coordinator; a spacious environment both indoors and outdoors; support of the headteacher in terms of additional staffing and resources; very detailed planning dovetailed to the National Curriculum where appropriate; direct teaching and highly motivated children. Figure 5.6 lists the principles which headteachers, senior managers and governors need to review when considering practices for the under fives.

Case study

A pilot research project was carried out in a large city in the north west of England to investigate the ways in which the children's centres constructed their action plans following a nursery inspection, and to evaluate the impact of the action plans on practice in the settings. The example cited is from a children's centre in the south of the city which had six key issues: one to extend written curriculum plans to identify more specifically what children are intended to learn as well as the activities that they will do; two – to implement plans to review the programme for physical outdoor play and plan more structured use of the outdoor area, as identified in the development plan; and thirdly to implement plans to train staff in the use of the computer so that it can be used more effectively with the children to support their learning. In addition this centre had minor weaknesses in provision for language and literacy, mathematics and knowledge and understanding of the world. The example included here (Figure 5.7) is of the actions planned for improving an aspect of language and literacy.

Another key issue required the children's centre to provide more time for mathematics, particularly counting activities (Figure 5.8).

- The recruitment of staff, well-qualified by training and/or experience for work with reception class pupils: professional support which fully recognises the complex and demanding task of providing a suitable curriculum for the age group which dovetails successfully into the National Curriculum.

- Enlisting the help of parents with a focus upon involving them in supporting their children's learning.

- The length of time children spend in the reception class. This suggests that wherever possible three terms in the reception class i.e. early entry, is to be preferred. This is particularly important for summer born children who as a group are most likely to have the shortest time in reception class and in primary school. They need however a pattern of admission suited to their needs.

- The provision of a broad and balanced programme for the reception year and attention paid to planning the curriculum for the reception year at all levels – classteacher, year group and whole school.

- Priority given to teaching the skills of literacy and numeracy. This is not to say that the most effective schools focus narrowly on these aspects of the work; rather that they provide a rich and varied but manageable programme of work which secures ample opportunities for pupils to listen carefully to good models of language, speak clearly and confidently, increase and use their vocabularly imaginatively, and make a sound start on the road to reading and writing;

- A high degree of attention to establish good standards of behaviour reinforced by praise and underpinned by such strategies as stories depicting human relationships and values.

- The assessment of children's progress and attainment as an integral part of the programme of work. Much of this is achieved by the close observation of children's responses but some schools also use diagnostic tests successfully.

- Meeting the demands of combining a prolonged reception period, caused by early entry, with those of the National Curriculum as pupils reach statutory age.

FIGURE 5.6 Principles for headteachers, governors and teachers to consider when reviewing practices for children under five in reception class (OFSTED 1993:14)

Discussion

There are considerable differences in the way the two settings have tackled their key issues. It would be useful for you to use these two examples as a basis for staff discussion to see how much priority is given by each setting to what the children know, understand and can do as a consequence of the actions. Refer back to the characteristics of effective action plans listed earlier and the early learning goals for each area of learning.

Target	Action	Responsibilities	Resources	Time Scale	Monitoring	Evidence/ Outcome
1. To encourage the productive use of the book corner.	1. All books and references divided into learning areas by colour and number. 2. Each child has his or her own library card, to be stamped when book correctly used and read.	Staff in room	Card Coloured paper Storage bag	Short-term – 1 month	1. Staff in room explain and encourage children to use resources correctly. 2. Observation and recording children's actions in book corner.	1. Children will use the book corner in a more productive way. 2. They will obtain pleasure from books.
2. To encourage children to concentrate on books and encourage reading and listening skills.	Divide children into smaller groups during the afternoon.	Staff in room adjust their planning for groups.	Tape recorder and head phones. Books with tapes	Medium-term	3. Staff feedback. Group reactions, observations and recordings should show improvements.	Recording observations. Senior staff to ensure group reading takes place and plans are altered.
3. Use of upper and lower case letters.	Buy upper/lower case set of alphabet for display.		Need set of letters	Short-term – 1 month	Make children aware; use during activities.	Display in room for all to see.
4. Ensure book area includes all areas of learning.	To re-examine our books and fill gaps in areas of learning.	Senior staff and staff in room.	New books	Long-term – initially £150 per room in financial year	Continue to repair, replace books as necessary.	Areas of learning clearly visible and simply referenced in the book corner.

FIGURE 5.7   Example of an action plan for language and literacy for analysis

The views of the managers of the children's centres with regard to the inspection process strengths and weaknesses were generally varied, but mainly positive. The majority of views about the completion of the Self-appraisal Schedule were positive because it provided settings with a means of linking the inspection requirements with their own institutional development plans and an agenda for action. The ways in which the inspection itself was carried out was commented on by managers, who stated that the following conditions reduced stress levels amongst staff:

- inspectors keeping to their plan for the day;
- inspectors who were approachable, well-organised and professional in their demeanour;
- staff in the centres prepared for the inspection.

(Rodger 1999)

Key issue To provide more time in the programme for mathematics, particularly counting activities and recognising numbers 1 to 10. As children become more confident they should be encouraged to explore when one or two objects are added to or taken away from a group.

Tasks (one example)
1. Expand on current planning for mathematics, to include number work daily and to explore the addition and subtraction of items from a group to ensure the recognition of numbers 1 to 10.
2. Expand the use of mathematical vocabulary in all activities and include in planning.
3. Create opportunities for using patterns, sorting and comparing objects.
4. Audit existing resources and activities to identify gaps.
5. Organise a training day to find out additional ways of teaching about numeracy.

Implications: finances, resources, training.

Success criteria *(This is clearly linked to provision and the children's mathematical learning.)*
Children recognise numbers 1 to 10.
Children understand the consequences of adding items to a group or taking them away.
Staff include mathematical vocabulary in all areas and in their plans.
A well-resourced mathematical area.

Time scale: 2 terms

FIGURE 5.8   Example of a target within an action plan

Personal, social and emotional development

This chapter shares a range of ways in which practitioners provide opportunities to support the personal, social and emotional development of the children in their care. Central to this will be a consideration of the role of a supportive adult and how different settings plan to ensure children's social and emotional development progresses. Examples of the ways in which other countries define this area of learning will be included. An interesting question to ponder as the chapter develops is how adults assist children to become personally and socially competent in a planned way. Are social and communicative skills taught in a systematic way? Do they need to be? Another important thread of the chapter is the relationship between the context in which personal, social and emotional development occurs and other areas of learning. Can attitudes to learning be taught? Is it possible to work with the child in isolation from his or her family to create effective relationships in a nursery setting? How is successful behaviour management achieved? How does the personal and social development of three-year-olds differ from that of older children? Answers to those questions using a wide range of evidence from research and practical examples from nursery settings are provided. The poem below reminds us of the important role model offered by adults to the children in their care.

Children live what they learn
If children live with criticism,
They learn to condemn.
If children live with hostility,
They learn to fight.
If children live with ridicule,
They learn to be shy.
If children live with shame,
They learn to feel guilty.
If children live with encouragement,
They learn confidence.
If children live with praise,

They learn to appreciate.
If children live with fairness,
They learn justice.
If children live with security,
They learn to have faith.
If children live with approval,
They learn to like themselves.
If children live with acceptance and friendship,
They learn to find love in the world.

Defining personal, social and emotional development

There are several ways in which early educators may define personal, social and emotional development. The definition with which most educators working with young children are likely to be most familiar is that defined by QCA (2000) (see Figure 6.1).

This definition of personal, social and emotional development covers almost every facet of children's relationships with others and with themselves. For all five-year-olds to have acquired this level of relationship and attitudes is a great achievement, and when in place lays a firm foundation for their future lives. But it could also be claimed that this is a very high expectation for children at the end of their reception year to have relationships as firmly embedded in their day-to-day lives as stated in the early learning goals. Do we as educators in the UK give enough attention to this area of learning in our day-to-day work? Is the attention intuitive? We comfort children who are upset, encourage co-operation and collaboration. Do we need to contrive situations in which children feel secure and so help to develop their confidence? Reception class teachers frequently proclaim that their pupils need the security of their own chair in the classroom. What do you think? What are the implications of the range of opportunities which need to be provided for the under fives in the reception class if this was the case?

The case study below captures the need for security in a small boy whose basic need for stability and familiarity is met in the nursery.

Jamie enjoyed nursery school. He loved the home corner, setting the table, putting the plates out and putting them away. He liked it best when he was on his own, because he could set the dolls and teddies out as he wanted. He talked to them all the time. Jamie had just returned following a long period of absence from the nursery school. His home was destroyed in a house fire some months earlier, along with the death of his two younger sisters and his mother. In his time away from the nursery Jamie was with a foster parent, but he was now back in the area living with his aunt. He spoke very little on his return but enjoyed the security and stability of the home corner as often as he could.

Can you as practitioners know how to cope with such grief and sadness in a young child's life? The home corner was the turning point for Jamie. Slowly, he began to regain his confidence as he welcomed playmates into his substitute home.

The official curriculum for Korean pre-school education comprises five main areas. The area which equates to the British personal and social development is social life. A component of this which is less explicit in British practice is a set of self-management and attitudinal skills, including comprehension monitoring, attention management and persistence. (French and Song 1998:414). Whilst holding many reservations about the *Despatches* television programme (Mills and Mills

---

This area of learning incorporates attitudes, skills and understanding and is a pre-condition for children's success in all other learning. The goals include children's personal, social, emotional, moral and spiritual development and the establishment of good attitudes to their learning.

By the end of reception year, most children should be:
• confident to try things, initiate ideas and speak in a group;
• able to maintain attention, concentrate and sit still;
• interested, excited and motivated to learn;
• aware of their own needs, views and feelings and sensitive to the needs, views and feelings of others;
• respectful of their own cultures and beliefs and those of other people;
• responsive to significant experiences, showing a range of feelings including joy, awe, wonder and sorrow.

They should be able to:
• form good relationships with adults and peers;
• work as part of a group or class, taking turns and sharing fairly, understanding that there need to be agreed values and codes of behaviour for groups of people, including adults and children, to work together harmoniously;
• understand what is right, what is wrong, and why;
• dress and undress independently and manage their own personal hygiene;
• select and use activities and resources independently;
• consider the consequences of their words and actions for themselves and others;
• understand that people have different needs, views, cultures and beliefs, which need to be treated with respect;
• understand that they can expect others to treat their needs, views, cultures and beliefs with respect.

FIGURE 6.1   Early learning goals for personal, social and emotional development (QCA 2000)

1997) one area which raises important issues for the British early years movement is that relating to the structured, formal ways in which children in Hungarian, Swiss and Belgian Flemish kindergartens are taught attention, listening and memory skills and appropriate group behaviour. The teaching is highly structured and places considerable emphasis on enabling children to master spoken language. *Language Development and the Disadvantaged Child* (Downes 1978) while being rather dated provides a wealth of suggestions for promoting oral language. Further discussion of this area can be found in Chapter 7.

Research by Broadhead (1997) conceives personal and social development in the context of play typologies. An important aspect of play development is the way in which children develop in their language and communication competence within a play situation. However, Broadhead's review of research (Bennett and Kell 1989, Slavin 1991, Galton and Williamson 1992, Schneider 1993) into promoting sociability and co-operation reveals that the educator must do much more 'than merely bring children together and must be prepared to take responsibility for promoting sociability and co-operation rather than leaving it at home or presuming it will occur merely because children are in close proximity' (Broadhead 1997:514). An appropriate note of caution precedes the claim that prescriptive teacher directed approaches for children following the early learning goals and baseline assessment may squeeze out the opportunity to develop social and co-operative skills. This is precisely the issue with the way in which practitioners interpret the areas of learning in their settings. Are there plans to develop social and co-operative skills in their own right, rather than always being an adjunct to the literacy or numeracy task? Where are the most worthwhile opportunities for developing sociability and co-operation? Large construction, scale version toys, home corner, sand and rough and tumble generated the most social interaction in Broadhead's study (Broadhead 1997:521)

What happens in English pre-school settings? Evidence from research and Ofsted

For children under five in reception classes and nursery classes the emphasis is usually on the promotion of good behaviour, co-operation and fairness, together with the promotion of self-discipline. It is cited by Ofsted that children complete tasks and follow the essential rules of the school day. Is it possible to detect expectations more in line with those required of children of statutory school age in this claim? A later section of the chapter outlines the practical guidance provided to settings to promote personal, social and emotional development. The evidence of another Ofsted survey (1997b:5) also claims a positive set of practices in relation to personal and social development. The survey indicates that this area of learning is indeed well catered for. A more recent analysis of a round of nursery inspection reports carried out during 1998–9 suggests that the concern expressed by some commentators on early years provision that an increased emphasis on a planned curriculum, giving priority to language and literacy and to mathematics, would be at the expense of children's personal and social development was ill-founded (Ofsted 1999c:7). There is some exemplification of statistical data from Ofsted on the quality of education in the Foundation Stage. The most recent Annual Report (Ofsted 2003a:89) shows that the provision for spiritual, social, emotional and cultural development was judged to be very good or excellent in 64 per cent of schools, which is an improvement on the previous year. The report on the survey of the quality of funded nursery education for three- and four-year olds (Ofsted 2001b), judged that 86 per cent of providers make good provision overall. Improvements have been significant, especially in playgroups, and 94 per cent of settings are effective in encouraging children to develop personally, socially and emotionally. Children behave well, relationships are warm and the children are prepared to share activities with their friends.

Critics sometimes allege that the early learning goals are too prescriptive and so closely bound to the National Curriculum that they impose an unacceptable pressure and a formality on the preschool curriculum which is damaging to four-year-olds. It is said too, that the 'caring' side of the provision often receives less attention than it deserves and too little consideration is given to the benefits of 'play' as an educational activity. These criticisms are not supported by the inspection findings. For example, the *personal and social development of children is judged considerably more favourably than any of the other desirable outcomes* irrespective of the type of institution inspected in both of the evaluations of inspections carried out by Registered Nursery Inspectors (RgNIs). In an earlier survey of the quality of education in the nursery voucher settings it was reported that 'in the majority of institutions the children's behaviour is generally good. Their self-confidence and respect for others and the environment are strongly fostered. They work well in groups and by themselves' (Ofsted 1997a).

A television programme *Despatches* which was based on research carried out by Clare and David Mills (1997) was very critical of the regime in British nurseries, particularly in relation to the development of social, cooperative and linguistic skills compared to the priorities in early years settings in Hungary, Switzerland, Belgium and to a certain extent in Japan, although no direct reference is made to the Japanese research. There are some fundamental differences in the way in which Korean kindergarten classrooms operate. Routinely, intellectual readiness is emphasised: four-year-old children were engaged and attentive during their lessons, which normally featured:

- some amount of information conveyed to the children;

- extensive use of questioning by the teacher;

- use of questioning by the children;

- specific cognitive demands placed on the children by the teacher's talk;

- refocusing the attention of unruly individuals and of an unruly group.

(French and Song 1998:418)

Attentiveness is taught through 'attentive-management songs' rather than by explicit criticism of the children.

Examination of curricular guidance and schemes of work developed by LEAs to support early years practitioners has attempted to flesh out the general statements in the early learning goals for personal, social and emotional development. The Foundation Stage Profile gives this area of learning the same status as all others. Since the introduction of the guidance document with exemplification, there is greater attention to personal, social and emotional development. Anecdotal evidence may suggest that some children in reception classes do not have as many opportunities to make choices as compared to their nursery class counterparts. Curriculum plans now include personal, social and emotional development. In the following section key aspects of personal, social and emotional development are outlined to indicate ways in which practitioners can include planned opportunities to develop the social, co-operative, independent and behavioural skills necessary to equip children to cope with the demands of statutory education. Planning guidance (QCA 2001) identifies each aspect of the personal, social and emotional area of learning to assist practitioners in their planning. They are: dispositions and attitudes; self-cofidence and self-esteem; making relationships; behaviour and self-control; self-care; and sense of community. Figure 6.2 shows the progression through the *stepping-stones* for each aspect. LEAs have also provided guidance to practitioners on pupils' achievements in personal, social and emotional development in the following way.

Does the child:

- show enthusiasm and pleasure in their work?

- show a range of feelings such as wonder, joy or sorrow in response to their experiences of the world?

- have a developing and positive self-image?

- show respect for the needs and feelings of others?

- show respect for materials, equipment, their work and the work of others?

- express their feelings in appropriate ways?

	Yellow	Blue	Green	Grey
Dispositions and attitudes	Show curiosity. Have a strong exploratory impulse. Have a positive approach to new experiences.	Show increasing independence in selecting and carrying out activities.	Display high levels of involvement in activities. Express needs and feelings in appropriate ways.	Continue to be interested, excited and motivated to learn. Maintain attention, concentrate and sit quietly when appropriate. Respond to significant experiences, showing a range of feelings when appropriate. Select and use activities and resources independently.
Self-confidence and self-esteem	Separate from main carer with support. Feel safe and secure and demonstrate a sense of trust. Demonstrate a sense of pride in own achievement.	Separate from main carer with confidence. Show confidence in linking up with others for support and guidance. Take initiatives and manage developmentally appropriate tasks.	Take risks and explore within the environment. Show confidence and the ability to stand up for own rights. Operate independently within the environment. Show confidence in linking up with others for support and guidance.	Be confident to try new ideas and speak in a familiar group.
Making relationships	Seek out others to share experiences. Relate and make attachments to members of their group.	Show care and concern for others, for living things and the environment.	Initiate interactions with other people.	Form good relationships with adults and peers. Have a developing awareness of their own needs, views and feelings and be sensitive to the needs, views and feelings of others.
Behaviour and self-control	Show a willingness to tackle problems and enjoy self-chosen challenges. Begin to accept the needs of others with support.	Demonstrate flexibility, and adapt their behaviour to different events, social situations and changes in routine.	Persist for extended periods of time at an activity of their choosing. Have an awareness of the boundaries set and behavioural expectations within the setting.	Work as part of a group or class, taking turns and sharing fairly, understanding that there need to be agreed values and codes of behaviour for groups of people, including adults and children, to work together harmoniously. Understand what is right and wrong, and why. Consider the consequences of their words and actions for themselves and others.

FIGURE 6.2 Early learning goals for personal, social and emotional development (QCA 2000)

	Yellow	Blue	Green	Grey
Self-care		Show care and concern for self.	Value and contribute to own well being and self-control.	Dress and undress independently and manage their own personal hygiene. Select and use activities and resources independently.
Sense of community	Make connections between different parts of their life experiences.	Have a sense of belonging. Talk freely about their home and community. Show a strong sense of self as a member of different communities, such as their family or setting.	Have a sense of self as a member of different communities.	Have a developing respect for their own cultures and beliefs of other people. Understand that people have different needs, views, cultures and beliefs, that need to be treated with respect.

FIGURE 6.2   (continued)

- respond to instruction with a developing sense of what is right, what is wrong and why?
- observe rather than participate?
- work alone/in parallel/in simple cooperative games?
- participate in group activities/work collaboratively?
- take turns and share with/without support?
- rely on adult support and reassurance?
- work confidently in known situations?
- accept change with explanations?
- work independently?
- concentrate in self-chosen activity for short/extended periods?
- sustain task involvement with support/in self-chosen activity?
- use language to meet personal needs/accept instruction?
- demonstrate independence and like to meet their own needs?
- have motivation and positive attitudes to learning?
- show enthusiasm and eagerness to learn?
- show an interest in activities and aspects of school/nursery life?
- respond to relevant cultural and religious events?
- develop positive images and show respect for people of other cultures and beliefs?

Developing independence

An important aspect of the educator's role is how the children are assisted in their development from total dependence towards self-care and how the adults who care for the children let the children learn to do things for themselves.

Snack time in the nursery

Regularly at the same time every day the children at Tiny Tots Playgroup cease their activities, everything is put away, mostly by the staff, with encouragement offered by staff to include the children in this chore. Tables are rearranged and all the children sit obediently in a circle and wait patiently, familiar as they are with this daily ritual. A tray is brought out containing the correct number of beakers of milk and a plate of carrot sticks. A member of staff gives out the drinks and snacks. Children are encouraged to say thank you and not to spill their milk.

So what is missing? Were the children encouraged to be independent? Did they help prepare the snack? What responsibility were they given? Were there too many lost opportunities to develop independence and to take responsibility? Too much of the children's attention was taken up with the snack-time routine to enable any worthwhile verbal interaction to take place between educators and the children. Opportunities for children to 'show and tell' are a frequent justification made for this session. Indeed it is frequently the only time in a session where personal, social and emotional development is planned to be promoted in a systematic way. What about the time spent clearing away all the activities available to the children in the nursery? Although this is likely to encourage children to take responsibility for clearing away their equipment it is frequently overshadowed by the speed with which this must happen to fit in with all the other activities planned during the session. Compare the example of daily snack time with Four Feathers Playgroup below.

On entry to the playgroup each child searches for their name and sticks it on the velcroed registration board. A table is laid in the corner of the room next to a jug of orange juice and a collection of differently coloured mugs. In the kitchen an adult and three children are buttering bread and spreading jam prior to cutting the squares of bread into four triangles. As the session progresses the children wander to their self-registration board, collect their name card and go to have their drink and snack, sometimes in pairs but very often on their own, secure in the knowledge that there will be someone sitting at the table eating their snack to talk to. Above the table, displayed on the wall is a menu illustrated with snack time foods and labels. The children's eyes wander to the notice and some of the children discuss the list and point to familiar letters. On finishing their snack the children return to their play. Some days an elderly pensioner sits with the children during snack time to share their talk and to help where needed. The older children encourage the younger ones to go for their snack sometime during the morning. Young Tommy went twice one morning because he missed his breakfast, but generally the children know they only have their snack once during the session.

The above example shows how successfully a group of children have been given responsibility and are developing independence. Of course, the jug of juice is occasionally spilt, but the children know where the mop stays and have become quite adept at clearing up when such accidents happen. It may take some weeks to achieve success when replacing your traditional whole group snack time with a cafeteria system, but the advantages are worthwhile. Children talk to each other and if it can be arranged for another adult to join the group during the informality of the cafeteria system conversations may be extended. Sometimes practitioners claim that the children miss the togetherness of the whole group session, and the staff are unable to share experiences with the children. Consequently, opportunities for developing speaking and listening skills are reduced. This may not be the case, especially where there are three-year-olds in the group. Too often children in all types of nursery provision spend too much time in large groups. This particularly disadvantages the shy children, the timid children and the insecure children who cannot identify with the whole group. Think about this in your own practice and observe your large group sessions, if you have them. Who talks?

Developing self-esteem and confidence

The decision to introduce this section with the 'survival skills' listed below was taken to illustrate the wide range of individual differences in children under five as they enter statutory school. Also, the increased emphasis in recent years on basic skills for young children and the future inclusion of three-year-olds in curricular frameworks for under fives settings increasingly requires practitioners to be ever vigilant as to the personal and social needs of very young children. Research shows no evidence to suggest that there is a neglect of this area of learning and particularly the ways in which practitioners ensure the effective development of self-esteem. However there are suggestions that some social skills are not systematically included within adult/child interactions as consistently in the UK as in other European countries. (Mills and Mills 1997). Children need to learn, know and use 'survival skills' to function confidently in a classroom. These include knowing:

- who they are and what they can do;
- that 'experience' has some meaning for them;

- that they have a right to their own interests and knowledge;

- what school is for, and what it is in physical terms;

- how to be with, consider and communicate with other adults and children when necessary;

- who teachers and other adults in school are and what they are for;

- how to help themselves in activities such as taking coats off, going to the lavatory or organising themselves in a chosen activity;

- how to cope with and overcome 'not knowing' things and the feelings this arouses.

(Barrett 1986:3)

The findings of the research by Barrett outlined above are no less evident now than 15 years ago when the research was undertaken in response to claims from the Assistant Masters and Mistresses Association (AMMA) that children in reception classes were becoming uncontrollable. One might be tempted to argue that, in response to the increased numbers of four-year-olds in reception classes, there may be an increase in disruptive behaviour. Nationally there may indeed be a lack of specific guidance as to how young children's self-esteem is developed to a degree which gives them confidence to talk in larger group settings and to know how to work in a co-operative situation. Many LEAs are well aware of the social and linguistic skills they need to introduce and teach to the children in their care. For example, the skills required to be taught to children to develop their self-esteem are made very explicit in a variety of curricular frameworks available to guide nursery and other early years settings. Tower Hamlets (Figure 6.3) and Stockport (Figure 6.4) are good examples.

Taylor (1999:11) emphasises the need for children to feel confident in doing, and outlines several strategies to help practitioners achieve this goal. These can be usefully applied to the way in which you interact with young children. As a result of the increase in the inclusion of children with special needs into mainstream nurseries and reception classes, staff need to ensure that each child is able to fulfil his/her potential so they too develop a higher self-esteem and positive attitudes to learning. For example, what steps are taken to ease access to the water tray by a child in a wheelchair? A simple tray was laid across the top of the water tray to enable the child to reach all the implements and play alongside peers. Chapter 9 in *Special Needs in Early Years Settings* (Drifte 2001:55) gives a good range of practical suggestions.

Learning self-worth			
Learning intention/ knowledge/skills/attitude	Areas and resources inside and out for spontaneous learning	Planned activities and experiences	Adult input and specific language input
To know that you will be listened to	• Listening area with pre-recorded and blank tapes • Role play area where children can create stories together	Opportunities for children to perform to others – rhymes, songs, storytelling . . . Group times where children take it in turns to talk – encourage others to ask relevant questions Small story groups that allow for discussion and sharing of experiences linked to the story Listening games, listening walks	• Listen and respond to all attempts at communication both verbal and non-verbal. • Give children time to finish sentences or to respond to questions • Make time to listen to children and to value what they say. • Model attentive listening – highlight the need to wait to talk. • Make it explicit that everyone is involved by referring to individuals by name and using their ideas. • Avoid negative compari-sons
To know others are as special as you are To be able to take responsibility for self/others/ environment with and without support To be self-disciplined	• Co-operative play – share wheeled toys, double bikes, turn-taking games . . . • Puppets and role play • Resources reflecting the ethnicity of the class and of the UK. • Children tidy up and show that they are aware they have a responsibility for the classroom and the outdoor area.	Co-operative games e.g. parachute games. Help children to know how to act responsibly by making group books about classroom activities e.g. *Alex is Painting* – use photos of getting paper, putting on an apron, painting, writing name and so on. Litter collections. Washing equipment – aprons, Lego, cars.	• Make explicit the value of everyone's contribution to the group. *'You've had your turn, now we'll listen to X.'* • Display work from all children. • Encourage responsible behaviour – *remind, praise, reward, challenge.* • Maintain resource-based classroom organisation which encourages independence and self-reliance.

FIGURE 6.3   Learning self-worth (3) (Field and Lally 1996)

Confidence in doing

■ New skills are best broken down into very small steps and each step cele-brated as though it were an end in itself. Children need time to be happy with each step before moving on.

■ When children master a skill, it boosts their confidence if we can acknowledge this by giving them responsibility.

■ The greatest confidence in doing comes from teaching others. We can look out for opportunities for children to pass on new skills – and see if they can also teach us something.

Personal, Social, Moral and Spiritual Development		
Areas of Learning	Learning Objectives	Attitudes/Ethos

3. Social	The development of:
	
	• ability to form effective relationships with
	  – children
	  – adults
	
	• ability to work co-operatively
	  – in pairs
	  – in small group
	
	• ability to take turns
	
	• ability to share fairly
	
	• ability to show appropriate behaviour
	
	• awareness of safety and hygiene
	
	• response to accepted social conventions
	
	• participation in acceptance and farewell rituals
	
	• ability to demonstrate a caring attitude to:
	  – others
	  – the environment (including resources)
	  – all living things
	
	• ability to communicate effectively
		Wide, varying experiences of working in a group of differing sizes and in different conditions.
		Adults – good role model
		
		Encouraging through games, turn-taking, looking after others.
		
		Card games, board games, circle time, etc.
		
		Understanding concepts that each can have a little – not fair for only a few to have a lot. Snack time, birthdays etc.
		
		Positive approach to inappropriate behaviour. Say what you would prefer to happen – don't be negative.
		
		Constant reinforcement of need to wash hands.
		
		Positive responses to socially acceptable behaviour.
		
		Give children a sense of responsibility by praising acceptable behaviour. Staff must lead by example – staff not to show dislike of some aspects, (e.g. spiders). Stress need to care for things

FIGURE 6.4   Extract from a scheme of work for personal, social, moral and spiritual development (Stockport LEA 1996)

Behaviour management

In effective settings there is planned promotion of positive behaviour which takes account of the needs of parents and teachers as well as children. The ethos, organisation and working policies in the setting make a significant difference to how children's behaviour is perceived and what is put in place to develop appropriate behaviours for groups and individuals. Problems arise where there is little consistency of approach among staff who may react to individual instances of difficult behaviour in different ways. The increase in the number of very young children being excluded from school is a great concern. There are several reasons for this: too many children in classrooms which are too small; inappropriate experiences offered to children in the educational setting; a mismatch between the home and school values due to lack of communication between home and school (Barrett 1986). Roffey and O'Reirdan (1997:11) claim that children who have few pre-school experiences may soon feel a failure if this isn't recognised and some steps taken to ensure that they achieve initial success. Success is more likely to be obtained if the following steps are taken.

- Children will focus better if they are offered a restricted choice of activity with variety over time.

- Opportunities to practise the same skill are valuable – e.g. a table with several different puzzles.

- Some children may need guidance to extend their play e.g. having an adult in the home corner for a while 'joining in' may encourage longer and more complex sequences of pretend play.

- Some children need to stand and watch before trying things out.

- Talking with children about what they are doing extends their vocabulary and their conceptual understanding.

- Some children may have problems initially with two-channel information. They can't do things and listen at the same time. Verbal input from adults needs to be brief and direct.

- If a child doesn't appear to understand, it is often helpful to relate what is being said to what is already familiar.

Other researchers have identified particular situations as problematic for very young children. Crowded spaces may lead to aggressive behaviour. For instance, lining up is generally inappropriate for very young children. The expectation that children sit for long periods of time may lead to inappropriate behaviour.

Developing relationships

Adults working with the children will need to make sure they speak to children who they have difficulty communicating with by speaking to them face to face. Children will then know they are expected to listen and have extra clues to what is being communicated by watching people's mouths and expressions as they speak.

Research carried out by Marsh (1997:27) identified the importance of the key worker system. The key worker is the person in the setting with responsibility for the induction of a child to the setting. He or she liaises with parents on day-to-day issues, keeps records, writes reports and generally spends some time with their particular key children during the day. She has identified features of good practice in the key worker system. These are:

- open, honest communication between educators and parents;
- the process of admitting children on a gradual basis and of operating the key worker system;
- flexibility in children's attendance;
- flexibility of response to children's needs and community needs;
- staff responding sensitively to children's non-verbal and verbal communications;
- opportunities for children to make friends with other children and spend time together on a regular basis;
- the need for appropriate personal qualities and professional qualifications for all staff;
- the curriculum is planned for each unit with the needs of individual children taken into account and incorporated into the programme.

(Marsh 1997:33)

As well as attention to children's own personal, social and emotional needs the setting itself can create systems and structures which promote personal, social and emotional well-being. Griffin (1997:46) in her research highlighted several important features present in settings which successfully created a sense of belonging within a group of children. These included: implementing a gradual admissions policy; employer support for working parents; a key worker system; adequate staff to work in teams and provide support for colleagues; an effective partnership with parents and ongoing exchange of information; personal space for the child, somewhere to keep their possessions to which they had regular access; and consistent behavioural expectations of the children.

Further reading

Drifte, C. (2001) *Special Needs in Early Years Settings*. London: David Fulton Publishers.

Roberts, R. (1995) *Self-Esteem and Successful Early Learning*. London: Hodder and Stoughton.

Roffey, S. and O'Reirdan, T. (1997) *Infant Classroom Behaviour*. London: David Fulton Publishers.

Communication, language and literacy

But although I know the alphabet inside out, back to front, and upside down, it makes absolutely no sense whatsoever.

(Atkinson 1995:116)

Introduction

This chapter provides an overview of the communication, language and literacy area of learning and describes some of the ways in which practitioners working in reception classes, nursery schools and classes and preschools are interpreting the requirements of the Foundation Stage curriculum. The *stepping stones* for the different aspects of this area of learning are included at the beginning of each section. As with the previous edition, the emphasis on communication skills is central to the early years of education and to this publication. In several other chapters references are made to communication skills, especially when introducing new vocabulary. This chapter takes each aspect of the area of learning in turn: language for communication and thinking; linking sounds and letters; reading; writing and handwriting. Consideration is given to the important role of the adult; planning methods used in a variety of settings; provision for children with special educational needs and children who have a mother tongue other than English. An overview of the theoretical ideas on which recent practices in supporting young children's early language development are based is included. Recent research and the outcomes of national surveys are considered alongside the ideas of Bruner (1983) and Vygotsky (1978). The implications of the National Literacy Strategy (NLS) for children under five are discussed along with the findings of the most recent HMI evaluation (Ofsted 2002) of the first four years of the NLS. The debate about the most effective method of teaching children to read is informed by consideration of the views of experts (Goswami and Bryant 1990, McGuinness 1997). The most effective strategies to promote early writing development are also outlined with case study examples. Each section will also include examples of planning taken from early childhood settings in the UK. Account is taken too of the most recent evidence from the Early Years Directorate (Ofsted 2001) which has evaluated the quality of provision for three- and four-year olds.

Language for communication and thinking

Language is the most powerful tool in the development of any human being. It is undeniably the greatest asset we possess. A good grasp of language is synonymous with a sound ability to think. In other words language and thought are inseparable.

(Vygotsky 1986)

This section intentionally covers more background information about the ways in which children acquire language because of the importance practitioners need to attach to it. Therefore, descriptions and examples of children's early language development and speech patterns are included to help inform readers of the developmental stages of their children. Strategies to inform practitioners of their role in supporting and extending language development are included. Adult–child interaction is a fundamental requirement for successful language development. Guidance to practitioners implementing the statutory *Foundation Stage curriculum* acknowledges the key role of language development and is an effective tool for practitioners. For those of you working with children with special educational needs some of the early development 'P' scales, as well as the *stepping stones* are included in this section (Figures 7.1 and 7.2)

Evidence from theory and research: language development

An understanding of the ways in which children acquire language helps to explain the focus on phonological awareness currently dominating early reading development. The process of learning to talk is fascinating. Somewhere around a child's first birthday, his [*sic*] first truly linguistic utterances, the first words, appear. The first words are distinctive in at least three respects: their pronunciations, or phonetic forms; their meanings; and the ways in which they are used. The words learned are names of articles that the child can act on easily. For example, clock, blanket and key are common. Large objects that are just there and not part of the child's experience, particularly where the child cannot interact with them, are less common. Various linguists have studied children, usually their own, in natural settings, and the ease with which children acquire the meanings of words. Children find the discovery of the meanings of words difficult. Do you recall the child who refers to all adult males as 'daddy' or the child who overextends a word to refer to a broader category than is appropriate in the adult language? For example, the word *ball* may be used for round stones, apples, and other round objects. From the large numbers of words available, the child focuses his or her attention on particular subsets of words. Is the selection of words acquired governed by conceptual factors broader than language or do specifically linguistic factors play a role? How do we as educators of young children attempt to understand what a child means on the basis of what he or she has said?

Around 18 months of age children begin to put words together. The amount of time a parent or carer spends talking to a child between the ages of 11 and 18 months is crucial to later language acquisition. While this finding has been reported fairly recently, the roots to this can be traced much further back. The importance of a mother or other carer talking about an object rather than the child is paramount when children are just beginning to put words together. This contributes to an increased length of sentence. Bruner (1983) was responsible for the shift in ideas about language development, taking it forward to a more functional emphasis. Inherent in his theoretical stance is that children need knowledge. Although accepting that children may have an innate knowledge of a universal grammar as Chomsky states, Bruner's stance puts language acquisition very firmly into the communicative area. In *Learning to Use Language* Bruner (1983) describes how the linguistic community arranges speech encounters so that young children can get a hold on how to make their own communicative intentions clear and how to penetrate the intentions of others. The central thread of Bruner's ideas is the important claim that the child's language acquisition device cannot function without the aid given by an adult who enters with him or her into using language communicatively. This has important implications for the ways in which educators interact with children. However much the language development of young children is studied, one important finding will always emerge: that is the role of the adult. The emerging linguistic system is an expression of the concepts that have been developed in the previous year. Hence the importance of those early months of interaction between parent and child. Included within a consideration of what the child does is the role of the parent, who talks to the child at a level simpler than normal adult-to-adult speech, but nevertheless challenges the child. As part of the monitoring of the impact of Sure Start, steps have been taken to establish a national baseline of language skills for two-year-olds (Harris 2002) The baseline seeks to quantify the typical language use, the number of words known and the age children put words together.

Transition from home to preschool

We have evidence to suggest that children's oral skills as they enter nursery school or other day care settings are not as advanced as one would expect them to be. Research by Wells (1986) carried out in Bristol to investigate language development in the years before entry to compulsory school found no clear relationship between family background and the level of language development attained. Similarly, the research by Tizard and Hughes (1984:252) found that working-class mothers were just as concerned to teach their children as the middle-class mothers were. Do early years practitioners provide the Language Acquisition Support System (LASS) described by Bruner (1983:120)? What kind of 'formats', i.e. 'standardised . . . interaction pattern between an adult and an infant that contains demarcated roles that eventually become reversible' (Bruner 1983:120), do practitioners provide? Early formats, as described by Bruner, often have a playful, game-like nature. In time these formats are assembled into higher order subroutines and in this sense can be conceived as the modules from which more complex social interactions and discourse are constructed. Tizard and Hughes describe vividly the powerful learning environment of the home as a means of providing a variety of intellectually stimulating situations within a shared context for the four-year-old girls who formed the focus of the research. Does the close mother/daughter relationship advantage girls? Are girls more linguistically mature in your setting?

Importantly, successful language acquisition depends heavily on the use of a shared and familiar context to help the partners in making their communicative intentions clear to each other. Parents are traditionally recognised as the most important players in their own child's early language acquisition. Parents speak at a level where their child can comprehend them more and move ahead with a remarkable sensitivity to the child's progress. What, then, are the implications for those of you working with very young children in an early years setting? How do you model the parent–child relationship? The research into this area is conclusive in its findings that children's home environments provide a very powerful learning environment (Tizard and Hughes 1984). Their findings on the nursery school as a learning environment are less favourable. The main reasons for this are the demands on the staff in terms of socialising the children into the routines of the nursery: by learning a new code of behaviour; needing to make themselves understood to strangers; and how to understand the intentions and communication requirements of the school staff. Does this list echo some of the statements in the chapter on personal and social development which state what Ofsted view as examples of successful social development? These findings were replicated in research by Barrett (1986) on children's introduction to reception class in schools. In the research of Tizard and Hughes (1984) the child-centred play environment was the dominant feature of the provision. This in their view led to the exclusion of children from the adult's world; consequently, opportunities to be challenged and interested by adult activities were diminished. Such adult activities in the home provided a powerful context for language development, particularly questioning by the child. Are your children, girls particularly, from socially disadvantaged backgrounds subdued, passive and lacking independence, which was a finding of Tizard and Hughes's research? In their view, staff pitched their talk to those children at a lower level, with the overall effect of lowering their expectations and standards for the working-class children. In Tizard and Hughes's view these children already appeared to be at an educational disadvantage.

Pre-school experiences

More recently, research carried out by Munn and Schaffer (1993) into the literary and numeracy events experienced by two- and three-year-old children at ten day nurseries reinforces the role of the adult in promoting what they call 'the literate culture'. Many of the findings highlight the role of one-to-one interaction between a familiar adult and the young child (Schaffer and Liddell 1984). In the research described, interest was focused around finding out whether the nurseries could provide rich opportunities for informal introductions to literacy and numeracy. How often did these opportunities occur? What were the factors associated with variations in their findings.

Data was collected via a range of quantitative measures. Munn and Schaffer suggest that the social environment of the children was a key factor. Those nurseries with a system, such as the key worker system (Marsh 1997), were more effectively placed to form close relationships with 'their' children and to get to know each child's level of competence and to provide experiences sensitively attuned to that level (Munn and Schaffer 1993:77). They further stated that the tendency to organise children into small groups and to ensure continuity of adult–child relationships was associated with enhanced numeracy and literacy experiences for children at the very earliest stages. Another finding which they suggest needs caution in interpreting was that younger members of staff more frequently provided children with numeracy and literacy experiences. They speculate that this may be a case of greater energy, enthusiasm and more recent training, but they also concede that older staff worked under less favourable conditions. These research findings have implications for what is valued in early years settings. The current dichotomy between play-based and more structured approaches may be simplifying what is a much more complicated picture. Chapter 1 has rehearsed several arguments in favour of and opposing the *status quo*. The philosophical stance taken by practitioners may have consequences for the rate of progress children make in language development during their early years sessions.

The next section examines the ways in which national initiatives have raised the status of talk in the early years and beyond. Have these moves significantly improved the quality of oral communication in our youngest children?

A small-scale research project carried out by Monaghan (1996) found that providing nursery children with plenty of first-hand experiences such as trips to a local bakery did very little to promote expressive language, and led her to suspect that in spite of good intentions many years on the findings of Tizard and Hughes's research (1984) still rang true: that one of the prime aims of nursery education to promote language development was not being fulfilled. A substantial finding from Gordon Wells's research (1986) into language at home and school was that one common factor correlating with success later in school was the child's experience of having stories read, discussing and recalling the story on a parent-to-child basis as a normal and natural part of the family experience. Donaldson (1978) also says that to achieve success in school a child's conceptual system needs to expand in the direction of increasing ability to represent him- or herself in the world at large. Stories are the means by which children are helped towards developing abstract processes and dis-embedded forms of thought. Monaghan (1996:47) claims that 'story activities should be a high priority, deserving of quality time and careful planning in the early years curriculum, with home and school working together on behalf of the child'. More recent evidence (Mills and Mills 1997) from other countries suggests that in the UK too little attention is given to helping children acquire the tools to communicate effectively. In Swiss, Hungarian and Belgian Flemish kindergartens, they claim, chil-dren become used to making extensive oral contributions and have been given all the 'necessary poise and skill' to do so. Children are taught to speak correctly and effectively to larger audiences. This, it is believed, in Switzerland is the key to the reduction of under-achievement at subsequent stages of schooling across the whole curriculum. In all three countries similar methods are used to achieve this. In almost identical ways children are taught:

- attention, listening and memory skills;

- appropriate group behaviour;

- conceptual understanding (seen as essential for subsequent mathematical suc-cess);

- phonological and motor skills (seen as essential for subsequent success in reading and writing).

(Mills and Mills 1997)

There are some indications that these practices are beginning to have an impact in the UK such as the introduction of speaking and listening as a separate strand in the early learning goals for language and literacy. Barking and Dagenham LEA have been introducing some of these ideas into their schools for some years. More and more schools in the UK are introducing 'circle time' every day to teach chil-dren to be confident in the use of precise, accurate spoken language. Research has provided some important indicators of possible ways for the early years curricu-lum to develop, particularly with regard to promoting speaking and listening. To this end I agree with Mills and Mills, but to exclude attention to reading and writing is to disregard the work of researchers such as Hall (1987) and the extent to which children engage with reading and writing from a very early age.

Planning for communication

The early learning goals for communication provide a statutory framework for considering speaking and listening. Figure 7.1 outlines the *stepping-stones* for communication skills.

Careful observation of children's level of language development on entry to preschool is central to planned activities. Figure 4.11 provides an example of a checklist used in a combined nursery centre in Stockport (Grennan 1996) to help staff identify children with particular literacy learning difficulties. The 'P' scales, introduced in 1998 to assist with target setting in special schools, are useful for those of you less familiar with the very early language utterances of very young children (Figure 7.2).

Many pre-school settings will have children for whom English is an additional language (EAL) and practices must take the needs of such children into account. In the early years it is important to recognise that sometimes children need to choose to do what they want and at other times they are supported and extended in their learning by a knowledgeable and informed adult, who may or may not be their teacher. The planning for learning will differ in some ways for these different approaches. Chapter 3 gives an outline of the differences. Planning for talking should include:

- regular story time;
- class and group discussion with effective questioning;
- adults taking time to talk to children;
- effective use of drama and role play;
- use of adult or children's spoken language as a good model.

(Ofsted 1993)

Speaking and listening for children with English as an additional language (EAL)

A key factor for children with very little command of English is that they are included in sessions with their English-speaking colleagues because they will listen and hear English modelled by peers and by adults. Role play is one of the most effective ways of encouraging first words in English, especially if the other children are articulate and confident speakers. Pairing children who speak the same mother tongue helps children to communicate with others confidently,

	Yellow	Blue	Green	Grey
1. Language for communication	Use words and/or gestures, including body language such as eye contact and facial expression to communicate.	Use simple statements and questions often linked to gestures. Use intonation, rhythm and phrasing to make their meaning clear to others.	Have emerging self-confidence to speak to others about wants and interests. Use simple grammatical structures. Talk alongside others, rather than with them. Use talk to gain attention and initiate exchanges. Use action rather than talk to demonstrate or explain to others. Initiate conversation, attend to and take account of what others say, and use talk to resolve disagreements.	Interact with others, negotiating plans and activities and taking turns in conversations.
2. Language for communication	Listen to favourite nursery rhymes, stories and songs. Join with repeated refrains anticipating key events and important phrases. Respond to simple instructions. Listen to others in one-to-one small groups when conversation interests them.	Listen to stories with increasing attention and recall. Describe main story settings, events and principal characters. Question why things happen, and give explanations.	Initiate a conversation, negotiate positions, pay attention and take account of others' views.	Enjoy listening to and using spoken and written language, and readily turn to it in their play and learning. Sustain attentive listening, responding to what they have heard by relevant comments, questions or actions. Listen with enjoyment, and respond to stories, songs and other music, rhymes and poems and make up their own stories, songs, rhymes and poems.
3. Language for communication	Use familiar words, often in isolation, to identify what they do and do not want. Use vocabulary focused on objects and people who are of particular importance to them.	Build up vocabulary that reflects the breadth of their experiences. Begin to experiment with language that describes possession.	Extend vocabulary, especially by grouping or naming. Use vocabulary and forms of speech that are increasingly influenced by experience of books.	Extend their vocabulary, exploring the meanings and sounds of new words.
4. Language for communication	Use isolated words and phrases, and/or gestures to communicate with those well known to them.	Begin to use more complex sentences. Use a widening range of words to express or elaborate ideas.	Link statements and stick to a main theme or intention. Consistently develop a simple story, explanation or line of questioning. Use language for an increasing range of purposes. Confidently talk to people other than those who are well known to them.	Speak clearly and audibly with confidence and control and show awareness of the listener, for example by their use of conventions such as greetings, 'please' and 'thank you'.

FIGURE 7.1   Early learning goals for language for communication and language for thinking.

	Yellow	Blue	Green	Grey
5. Language for thinking	Use action, sometimes with limited talk, that is largely concerned with the 'here and now'.	Talk activities through, reflecting and modifying what they are doing. Use talk to give new meanings to objects and actions, treating them as symbols for other things. Use talk to connect ideas, explain what is happening and anticipate what might happen next. Use talk, actions and objects to recall and relive past experiences.	Begin to use talk instead of action to rehearse, reorder and reflect on past experiences. Link significant events from own experience and from stories.Pay attention to sequence and how events lead into one another. Begin to make patterns in their experience through linking cause and effect, sequencing, ordering and grouping. Begin to use talk to pretend imaginary situations.	Use language to imagine and recreate roles and experiences. Use talk to organise, sequence and clarify thinking, ideas, feelings and events.

FIGURE 7.1   (continued)

P1 Children are beginning to show sensory awareness in relation to a number of people, objects and materials in everyday contexts. They show reflex response to sensory stimuli, e.g. startle response.

P2 Children perform some actions using trial and error and show reactive responses to familiar people and objects, such as reaching and holding objects, smiling and turning to familiar voices. They make sounds or gestures to express simple needs, wants or feelings in response to their immediate environment, e.g. protesting or requesting, using facial expressions to enhance meaning.

P3 Children show anticipation in response to familiar people, routines, activities and actions and respond appropriately to them. They explore or manipulate objects, toys or other equipment. They are able to communicate simple choices, likes and dislikes. They can communicate, using different tones and sounds, and use some vocalisation and/or gestures to communicate.

FIGURE 7.2   Early development 'P' scales for speaking and listening

before taking tentative steps to speak single English words. Regular small groups times or 'circle time' help to develop confidence in children. There are wider attitudinal and thinking changes related to inclusion that are explored in Chapter 2. Early Years settings are inclusive organisations that have worked well over the years to promote inclusion at all levels. There are guidelines for the inclusion of older children in school that have some pointers for appropriate practices in the early years. For example, talk in the classroom is effective for EAL children when adults interact with children in the following way:

- attend to and support the speaker only responding to what is said after carefully following and listening to the speaker's words and meaning;

- engage in dialogue;

- create meaningful social, functional and communicative situations;

- spend time with children;

- pose open questions;

- demonstrate an interest in language;

- assume that children have something important to say;

- view speaking and listening as an equal partnership and expect the child to contribute to the partnership;

- provide an atmosphere of safety in which the children feel confident and venture questions.

As well as the opportunities listed above, the following activities are designed to promote talk and can be planned into small group time or collaborative work: talk partners, snowballing, being a visiting listener, rainbowing, brainstorming, buzz groups, jigsawing, envoying, hotseating, sharing sessions, listening triads and circle time. Children are more likely to develop as confident talkers where: they feel able to make mistakes, be tentative and think aloud without being judged, their own language and way of talking are respected and where their opinions are taken seriously. Teachers listen to children and offer their own views rather than questions, and the physical environment and organisation for learning encourage collaborative talk and there is occasionally time for talk to develop beyond the task in hand. Siraj-Blatchford (1994) cites Clarke (1992) and outlines the skills required by second-language learners in order to acquire a new language:

- a new set of sounds and sound groupings, which may or may not be like those of the first language;

- new intonation patterns and their meanings and new patterns of stress and pause. These are rarely available in written form;

- a new alphabet or script;

- a new set of sound–symbol relationships and spelling;

- new vocabulary;

- new ways of putting words together (a new grammar) and organising information and communication;

- new non-verbal signals, and new meanings for old non-verbal signals;

- new social signs and new ways of getting things done through language;

- new rules about the appropriateness of language for specific situations and roles;
- new sets of culturally specific knowledge, values and behaviour.

It can be seen from the above list that the increase in phonological awareness to develop language and reading for EAL children needs to be regularly embedded in practices. Ofsted (1997c) provide an illustrative example of the way in which teachers of nursery and reception children with EAL structure their reading programme through intensive teacher–pupil interaction.

An approach which works well with young children who are reluctant communicators either to other children or to adults in the setting is that of the dialogue approach (Meadows and Cashdan 1988). The publication of *Helping Children Learn* (Meadows and Cashdan 1988:1) encapsulated many of my own beliefs about practices in nursery education at the end of the Eighties: 'we believe what is normally done in nursery schools and classes (and in playgroups and in infant school reception classes) is enjoyable and useful but not, perhaps, quite fulfilling our high hopes for its educational potential'. Indeed they observed that:

> play has been heavily idealised in much of the educational writing of the last fifty years. It has been said to be spontaneous, absorbing, refreshing, enjoyable, creative and the ideal way of learning. If children aren't enabled to play as they choose, it has been claimed their development will be impaired. Enthusiasts for play suggest that human beings have evolved so that they need to play in order to learn, to work off their surplus energy, to practice skills they will need later in life. Whilst each of these claims has some truth in it, none of them is an entirely watertight reason for elevating play into the way of learning.
>
> (Meadows and Cashdan 1988:47)

The steadfast way in which some early years educators are holding on to the belief that learning through play is *the* way of learning is one which the guidance for the Foundation Stage is helping to redress through the emphasis on providing a balance between self-directed and adult-directed learning. However, recent research (Siraj-Blatchford *et al.* 2002) provides further support for the importance of adult intervention by their formative feedback during activities and the adult–child interactions that involve 'sustained shared thinking' and open-ended questioning to extend children's thinking.

Early reading, writing and handwriting

What research tells us about early reading and writing

This is an area which is fraught with controversy. Essentially, this is because of the different beliefs which are held by educationalists and psychologists about

---

I Have a Cat

I have a cat who walks with grace
I have a cat with a blue face
I have a cat with purple eyes
I have a cat who makes sand pies

I have a cat who likes to eat snails
I have a cat with a spiky tail
I have a cat who drinks lemonade
I have a cat who plays with a spade

I have a cat who goes out to tea
I have a cat who plays in the sea
I have a cat who's name is Fred
I have a cat who sleeps on my bed.

FIGURE 7.3   Playing with language

how children learn to read and to write. An increasingly widespread view, which is beginning to influence the way in which children are introduced to the printed word, is that relating to the way in which children are taught to sound out words. The NLS advocates that children learn to identify the phonemes in their spoken language and learn how each phoneme is commonly spelt. In early speech children are concerned to understand the meanings of words and pay very little attention to the sounds that words make. But as children begin to learn to read and write words the component sounds of the words begin to take on a new meaning. Children are fascinated by rhymes and enjoy using them, in both real and invented words. Three-year-old Jake, for example, surprised his nursery teacher by describing a fly as a 'fly-osaurus' following a discussion about different names for dinosaurs in an earlier group time. Rhyme has a direct link with some aspects of learning to read. In my own teaching experience with three- and four-year-olds, poems such as the one in Figure 7.3 leave the children in paroxysms of laughter. Children's sensitivity to rhyme is directly linked to the ease with which they begin to decipher print (Bryant and Bradley 1983 and 1985). The work of Goswami and Bryant (1990) supports the research findings stated earlier that some aspects of rhyming are strong predictors of later reading ability.

To help children to understand the different sounds made by the symbols in our alphabetic system, children need to be able to distinguish separate sounds within the stream of language they hear when people talk and read aloud. This is known as 'phonological awareness'. Alphabetic letters represent sounds, and strings of letters, by representing a sequence of sounds, can signify spoken words. According to Goswami and Bryant (1990) children may recognise the word as a visual pattern without paying much attention to the individual letters or to the sounds that they represent, the assumption being therefore that children's awareness of sounds plays an important part when they learn to read and write. Children demonstrate different kinds of phonological awareness because there are different ways in which words can be divided up into smaller units of sound (Figure 7.4).

	Syllable	Onset and rime	Phoneme
'cat'	cat	c – at	c – a – t
'string'	string	str – ing	s – t – r – i – n – g

FIGURE 7.4 Three ways to divide words into component sounds (Goswami and Bryant 1990:2)

McGuinness (1997:xiii), with her cognitive and educational psychology background, states that 'children must be trained to hear the individual sounds (phonemes) of their language. They must be able to disconnect or "unglue" sounds in words in order to use an alphabetic writing system'. Her research shows that where the sequence of reading and spelling instruction is compatible with the logic of the alphabetic code *and* with the child's linguistic and logical development, learning to read and spell proceeds rapidly and smoothly *for all children*, and is equally effective for poor readers of all ages. In her recent publication *Why Children Can't Read* (1997) she provides guidance to parents. The issue, she believes, is not when children are taught to read, but that they are taught correctly. The successful conditions in which children learn to read can be summed up simply as:

- talking to your child;
- reading to your child;
- encouraging pre-writing skills.

The above are very much part of the early literacy repertoire of most early years practitioners, and generally accepted by practitioners as central to their practices. However, the area where McGuinness's views challenge some of the current practices is more interesting. For instance, teaching letter names in isolation is claimed to be harmful and should be replaced by providing the sound of the letter within a familiar word. The only function reciting the alphabet serves is to help children to find their way around a dictionary or an index where this skill is required. Are these views supported by research in the UK?

Teaching and learning early reading skills

The debate on the most effective ways of introducing the written word to children is likely to run and run. There are some references to the methods used by reception class teachers in the Ofsted (2002a) evaluation of the first four years of the NLS. Shared reading is used to teach the conventions of print. Adults repeat simple phrases to assist those who are just beginning to read. The teaching of phonics in the reception class was judged to be good. The review of practices in reception classes during the duration of the NLS states that in most classes,

- children were able to concentrate for 15 minutes for daily word and text level work, although not necessarily taught consecutively;

- most children work beyond the early learning goals;

- phonic work was limited to teaching letter–sound correspondences at a slower rate than that recommended by the Strategy.

By the fourth year of the Strategy teaching was judged to be good: skilful guided writing with good emphasis on segmenting phonemes for spelling was evident; and classroom assistants are used well to support children especially in mixed age classes. There has however been widespread criticism of some of the methods advocated by the NLS (Ofsted 2002a and Davies 2003). Essentially, Davies is promoting THRASS, which is a method of teaching all 44 sounds in the English language. He acknowledges there are gaps in the subject knowledge of many teachers as to the most effective way of teaching letter sounds to young children, primarily a misunderstanding of how to teach phonics in his view, supported to some extent by HMI's evaluation of the NLS which concludes that 'the guidance from the NLS on how to teach phonics was not helpful enough in enabling teachers to teach phonic knowledge and skills systematically and speedily from Year R onwards' (Ofsted 2002a:35). Davies claims that some of the recommended strategies to teach letter–sound correspondence will not work using some children's names for example because of the teachers' inability to identify correctly the number of phonemes in a word.

Observations of some guided reading sessions show very little difference to group reading carried out many years ago. Guidance for reception class teachers is likely to vary from that for older children. The list of teaching strategies below is a modified version of the guidance provided to Year 1 teachers for the Early Literacy Support Programme. The most effective early years practitioners do the following when working with a small guided reading group:

- strategies introduced in shared reading (whole class) are modelled in guided reading;

- introduce the book by reading through the title, talking about the type of book and looking at the pictures;

- if required locate and read new names and unknown words;

- give children time to look at the illustrations and with the guidance of an adult tell the story, encouraging children to identify words and sounds they may know;

- now give the children the opportunity to read the book independently (responses of the children to this task will inform you whether it is an appropriate strategy. The NLS advises that this should be a book unknown to the children. For children just ready to cotton on to reading a familiar text may provide more opportunities to turn on all the 'searchlights');

- always complete a reading assessment during this 10–15 minute activity.

The NLS guidance suggests that reading books that are too familiar to children will lessen their ability to decode unknown words because they will rely on other reading strategies such as contextual and grammatical knowledge. For example, children reading 'house' for 'home' are doing just that. Hence the advice to practitioners to introduce unknown texts to children in guided reading sessions. How do you view this? Part of the responsibility of the early years practitioner is to encourage children to want to read and enjoy what they are reading. Is reading enjoyable if children have to use their phonological awareness to decode unknown words too frequently? Don't we all know of children whose reading skills have developed without ever decoding a word? The searchlight model acknowledges that children learn in a variety of ways, some as a result of what they see (visual), others because of what they hear (auditory) and others by a sense of touch (kineasthetic). The introduction of *Progression in Phonics* (DfEE 1999e) to assist nursery and reception class teachers and other teachers has provided a progressive framework to teach phonological awareness. It is a useful resource as a lot of the activities are centred around playing games and are very interactive.

As part of the Family Literacy Campaign in 1995 story sacks were introduced in Swindon (Griffiths 1997). A story sack is basically a large cloth bag containing a good quality picture book and supporting materials for a young child. The project aimed to:

- promote literacy in young children and their families;

- demonstrate why story sacks offer parents rich learning materials in support of family literacy;

- show how story sacks generate confidence in parents when they help young children to learn at home from books.

(Griffiths 1997)

Time spent reading stories to pre-school children, choice of reading materials, and the degree of engagement of children in that process, are of critical importance to early literacy. The greatest progress is made when the vocabulary and the syntax of the materials are slightly above the child's own level of linguistic maturity. Whitehead (1997:48) has reviewed recent texts on early literacy development (Browne 1996, Hall and Martello 1996, Miller 1996 and Riley 1996) and concluded that current practices, according to her analysis, are likely to be underestimating young children's abilities and experiences, if not actually deskilling them. Riley, for example, suggests that the new school entrant may be very competent, but, due to insufficient awareness, reception class teachers are unable to capitalise fully on the child's prior, but highly idiosyncratic, knowledge.

An Ofsted (1997c) video showed the way in which a primary school with the majority of children from Bangladesh and Eastern European countries taught their nursery and reception aged children to read using a structured programme for the teaching of phonics. These children, who showed a remarkable ability to read fluently later in school, spent time working on:

- letter–sound correspondences, using their own names or objects;

- learning consonant and short vowel sounds in speech and in writing;

- learning the alphabetic system to aid the decoding of print;

- learning common sounds including digraphs and blends;

- phonological training where children listen for sounds and segment words into their component parts;

- learning sounds in context and at random;

- the development of a sight vocabulary of 50 to 100 core words using flash cards;

- learning simple phonetic spellings: mainly, but not exclusively, consonant–vowel–consonant words;

- early links between reading and writing.

There are overt links between the list of activities above and the list of skills required by EAL pupils listed earlier to enable them to become effective speakers of English.

Riley (1995) carried out research into the relationship between adjustment to school and success in reading at the end of reception year. She found from her 191 pupil sample that those children who entered reception class with well developed alphabetic knowledge, and the ability to write their names and to understand concepts about print, and who settled well into school, had an 80 per cent chance of reading, at least in line with their chronological age, by July. She also recognised the potential of the social and environmental impact on literacy development, as did Miller (1996:5), who claims that early reading competences in children between three and five are 'more an indicator of the sorts of informal learning which have been taking place in the pre-school years. The phonological skills are visible signs of literacy development and as such are no more than the "tip of the iceberg", whereas underneath are all the incidents and activities in daily life which will have contributed to the development showing at the "tip".'

In summing up which system is the most effective, it is worth remembering that children learn to read in a variety of ways. Thus, they need access to a variety of strategies to achieve success. The message from this chapter is to recognise the importance of the range of approaches, but to take account of the firm basis required in phonological awareness in the early stages of reading. Children's reading improves by practice and children read readily when they enjoy the activity. To ignore the attitudes needed to enjoy literacy could encourage children to turn elsewhere for the vicarious satisfaction the pleasure of reading texts such as *Where the Wild Things Are!* (Sendack 1963) provides.

The most recent survey of early years practices in the non-maintained, private and voluntary sectors (Ofsted 2001) indicates that there are still 21 per cent of settings with weaknesses in their provision for communication, language and literacy for three- and four-year olds.

Planning for early reading and writing in the nursery and reception class

The early learning goals for reading, writing and handwriting are shown below (Figure 7.5).

An important consideration is that literacy needs to be planned for every day. It is no good planning to work with a group of children each day, thereby covering all the children in the class or nursery group by the end of the week. Use the extra adults you have and provide them with focused activities so all children are introduced to key literacy experiences every day in a planned way and, in addition, have regular opportunities to sing and recite rhymes and songs, to share books with each other, alone or with other adults; and encourage children to develop independent writing, name recognition and phonic skills.

The case study below illustrates how the reception class children in a northern primary school cope with their daily literacy hour and are beginning to work towards the early learning goals identified in Figure 7.5.

During the whole class carpet session which lasts almost 40 minutes the children chant the name and sound of the letter 's' prior to answering the question, 'Where have you seen this letter?', to which the children respond with enthusiasm, 'snake', 'sandwiches', 'sunburn', 'sun' and so on. The children then go on to chant through an alphabet book, stopping at the letter 's'.

	Yellow	Blue	Green	Grey
Linking sounds and letters	Enjoy rhyming and rhythmic activities. Distinguish one sound from another.	Show awareness of rhyme and alliteration. Recognise rhythm in spoken words.	Continue a rhyming string. Hear and say initial and final sounds in words, and know which letters represent some of the sounds.	Hear and say initial and final sounds in words, and short vowel sounds within words. Link sounds to letters, naming and sounding the letters of the alphabet. Use their phonic knowledge to write simple regular words and make phonetically plausible attempts at more complex words.
Goals for reading	Listen and join in with stories and poems, one-to-one and also in small groups. Show interest in illustrations and print in books and print in the environment. Begin to be aware of the way stories are structured.	Have favourite books. Handle books carefully. Suggest how the story might end. Know that information can be relayed in the form of print. Hold books the correct way up and turn pages. Understand the concept of a word.	Enjoy an increasing range of books. Begin to recognise some familiar words. Know that information can be retrieved from books and computers.	Explore and experiment with sounds, words and texts. Retell narratives in the correct sequence, drawing on language patterns of stories. Read a range of familiar and common words and simple sentences independently. Know that print carries meaning and, in English, is read from left to right and top to bottom. Show an understanding of elements of stories, such as main character, sequence of events, and openings, and how information can be found in non-fiction texts to answer questions about where, who, why and how.
Goals for writing	Draw and paint, sometimes giving meaning to marks.	Ascribe meaning to marks.	Begin to break the flow of speech into words.	Use their phonic knowledge to write simple regular words and make phonetically plausible attempts at more complex words. Attempt writing for different purposes, using features of different forms such as lists, stories and instructions. Write their own name and other things such as labels and captions and begin to form simple sentences, sometimes using punctuation.

FIGURE 7.5   Early learning goals for reading and writing

	Yellow	Blue	Green	Grey
Goals for handwriting	Engage in activities requiring hand–eye co-ordination. Use one-handed tools and equipment.	Draw lines and circles using gross motor movement. Manipulate objects with increasing control.	Begin to use anticlockwise movement and retrace vertical lines. Begin to form recognisable letters.	Use a pencil and hold it effectively to form recognisable letters, most of which are correctly formed.

FIGURE 7.5   (continued)

> The children sing the words on the 's' page. The session moves on to other features of a big book. The children demonstrate that they know what an author and illustrator do. One child asks what the hyphen is, and is answered by another child in the group. Reading through the text together the children chorus, 'That's an exclamation mark!' when the teacher asks. I wonder if they know what function it serves? An interactive exchange with the children checks their understanding of the story. After this session the children move to group activities. They are grouped by ability, which in reality means that those who have been in school the longest demonstrate they can write two to three sentences independently with the help of a series of key word cards. The new intake, who are described as having special educational needs, are just able to make marks on paper and are expected to copy 's'. The classteacher works with another low-attaining group on their guided reading text.

The above example probably typifies the way in which literacy is taught to children under five in most reception classes of English schools, although guidance to schools says that children under five are not expected to follow the literacy hour as a blocked sequence until towards the end of their time in the reception class in preparation for the next stage (Year 1).

Figure 7.6 is an example of the weekly planning for a reception class literacy hour in a different reception class at the beginning of the spring term. There are about nine children who are in their second week of school, having just moved from the nursery class attached to the school.

Experts are very much at odds as to the most appropriate time for children to be introduced to writing. The difference in views between the UK and other European countries is widespread. Mills and Mills (1997) on the one hand are critical of the early start advocated in British nurseries compared to some other countries (Hungary, Switzerland, Flemish Belgium). British educationalists, on the other hand (Hall 1987) have shown that very young children write naturally in their play when encouraged to do so. Children begin repetitive mark making as early as 12 to 18 months when opportunities and materials are made available (Miller 1996:19). Browne (1996:67) emphasises the need for children to be given time to experiment with each stage of the writing process and to feel that their

Teachers:	Year: Reception	Term: Spring/first half
Objectives Text level work – understanding of print. • That words can be written down to be read again for a wide range of purposes • To understand and use terms correctly about books and print: book, cover, beginning, end, page, line, word, letter, title • To track the text in the right order, page by page, left to right, top to bottom, pointing while reading and telling the story, and making one-to-one correspondences between written and spoken word		
Whole class text: *Two Feet (Pascoe 1993)*		
Day 1	Spend time on title (capitals) and cover. All writing inside book obscured	
Day 2	Look at title and cover again. Concentrate on illustrations – Can the children find the hidden ducks ?	
Day 3	Read story straight through and then again. Who likes to wear wellies? Has anyone got yellow wellies?	
Day 4	Read story through. Look at descriptive words, for example, adjectives in 'Two cold, wet, muddy feet in cold, wet, muddy, blue socks' etc.	
Day 5	Read story through – show children words from p.14. Put them in the correct order.	

FIGURE 7.6 Weekly planning for shared reading (15 minutes) in the literacy hour in a reception class

written efforts are valuable if they are to continue to learn and to develop positive attitudes to writing. There is a danger that children will be expected to record before they have the necessary skills or confidence to do so. Hence the frequent over-use of work sheets. Hall and Martello (1996:15) stress that the pressure on the early years educator to produce written evidence that children are 'working', is leading to pointless work sheets and colouring in, while denying the children opportunities for talking – the most potent tool for 'learning'.

Figure 7.7 is an example of independent writing by a reception class girl towards the end of the summer term before starting in Year 1. As an observer in the classroom, I was spotted by this child and had explained to me that she was on the 'independent' table and what that meant. Hence, I was not allowed to get involved as the children had to complete their shopping lists unaided.

Practitioners working with very young three-year-olds will need to be careful not to place unduly high expectations on their children to write. There are clear developmental stages children need to go through before they are ready to over-write or copy an adult's writing. Creating opportunities for children to want to make marks is the key first step. Observe and make assessments of their attitude

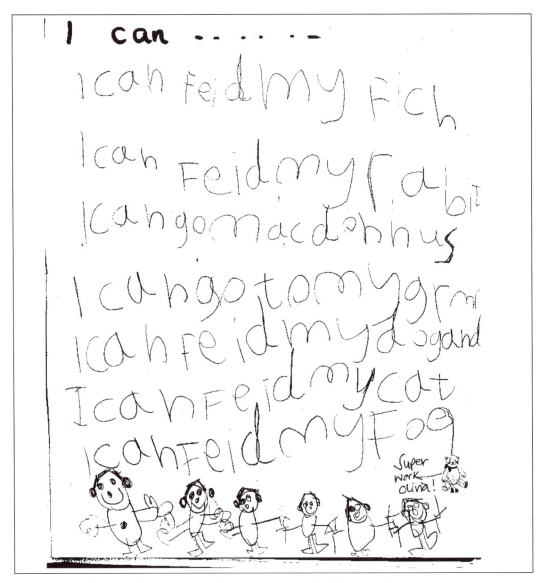

FIGURE 7.7   Example of independent writing by a five-year-old girl in a reception class

to writing. Are they interested? Do the boys show as much interest as the girls? What can you do to motivate children who do not want to paint, crayon or use a writing implement in their play? Earlier in the chapter, you may recall reading about the strategy used with an interactive whiteboard in one setting. Below (Figure 7.8) are the stages that children go through as they make marks. Use this to assess where the children in your setting are before rushing them in to some activities that will do more to demotivate them than develop writing.

THE DEVELOPMENT OF WRITING	
Stage	Indicators
1 Drawing and sign writing	• Make shapes and lines on the page • Shapes often have clear meaning to the child • Shapes do not look like letters • Understands that there is a difference between pictures and words
2 Letter-like forms	• Knows there is a difference between drawing and words • Cannot write letter shapes • Draws symbols which simulate letter shapes • Letters in own name are close approximations to letter shapes • Attempts at writing over letters shows some pencil control
3 Copied letters	• Over-writing shows good control of letter shapes • Copies letter shapes quite accurately/accurately • Copies letters from a separate piece of writing
4 Name and letter strings	• Writes letters voluntarily without copying • Writes own name • Writes lines of letters which convey meaning • Controls letter shapes quite well • May/may not group letters into a word
5 Words	• Uses strings of letters to write words • Some words can be read • Words not written as separate units in a sentence • Words written as separate units in copying sentences
6 Sentences	• Writes in sentences • Some words within sentences can be read
7 Text	• Several sentences written independently

Children in the nursery may exhibit aspects of Stages 1 and 2. The opportunities to write are likely to be met in a playful context – imaginative play in a post office for example.

FIGURE 7.8   The development of writing (Gorman 1997)

Further reading

DfEE (1999d) *Progression in Phonics*. London: DfEE.

Goswami, U. and Bryant, P. (1990) *Phonological Skills and Learning to Read*. Hove: Psychology Press.

McGuinness, D. (1997) *Why Children Can't Read*. Harmondsworth: Penguin.

Nutbrown, C. (1997) *Recognising Early Literacy Development*. London: Paul Chapman Publishing.

Riley, J. (1996) *The Teaching of Reading*. London: Paul Chapman Publishing.

Weinberger, J. (1996) *Literacy Goes to School*. London: Paul Chapman Publishing.

Developing mathematical understanding in the early years

Introduction

This chapter shares examples of good practice in early mathematical learning in nurseries and reception classes. Evidence from research citing the importance of the role of the adult as teacher, explainer and instructor is also outlined. A selection of completed examples of curriculum plans, observational checklists and ideas for schemes of work gathered from a variety of LEAs and guidance from the National Numeracy Strategy (NNS) will show how mathematical learning can be effectively promoted in a range of early years settings. The outcomes of a longtitudinal five-year research project (Siraj-Blatchford *et al.* 2002) published recently and a recent HMI evaluation (Ofsted 2002) of the first three years of the National Numeracy Strategy in reception classes are disseminated to show what is happening nationally.

Research findings

Findings from research and reports by HMI are consistent in their emphasis on the role of the adult in supporting and extending mathematical learning, including the role of parents. Research findings on the influence of children's home experiences have led to an increase in initiatives to involve parents in their children's early mathematical awareness (Basic Skills Agency 1998). Research consistently points to the need for more training for parents beyond helping in class.

The role of parents

Durkin and colleagues (1986) have documented the relatively high level of parental input around number words in informal settings, showing how children's earliest contact with number words occurs through everyday language. Munn (1994) found that some deliberate teaching of number takes place in the home setting, albeit structured around game-like and pleasurable activities. Children can learn about the importance of counting – and it is this very broad knowledge, the concept of counting, which may be the strongest predictor of school progress, 'It is not so much the component skills of counting that needs attention prior to school, but the very broadest grasp of what the activity is all about, and it is at this level that pre-school teachers usually operate' (Munn 1994). Aubrey *et al.* (1999), on the other hand, found that following a qualitative and quantitative analysis of mother–child conversations collected by Wells (1972–82) from a mathematical perspective, only 2 per cent of samples contained reference to mathematical content, mainly number, counting and comparisons of relative size.

The Basic Skills Agency (1997) piloted a series of family numeracy programmes for adults with few qualifications, and their children aged three to six. These programmes were in disadvantaged areas, and aimed to use games, role-playing, and day-to-day activities to extend understanding of numeracy. The evaluation of the 14 family numeracy pilot projects (Basic Skills Agency 1998) found that developing mathematical learning through play helps parents to improve their own numeracy skills, helps them to assist their children with numeracy activities and gives an immediate boost to children at risk of failing in numeracy. Specifically:

- the children who took part made far greater gains than their peer group not on the programme;
- 84 per cent of parents gained at least one unit of a nationally recognised qualification, which was in many cases their first ever formal qualification;
- parents increased their contact with the child's teacher and were more involved in school activities and supporting in class;
- there was a significant increase in a wide range of numeracy-related play activities at home;
- projects were successful in reaching parents who had little contact with formal agencies through the use of the community outreach workers, bilingual teachers and assistants, and by using health visitors to support self-referral.

(Basic Skills Agency 1998:4)

Current government policies further highlight the importance of the role of parents in their recommendations to schools (DfEE 1999b) to seek ways of improving the numeracy skills of parents and children together in school. This, they suggest, is likely to be more productive than adult education classes aimed specifically at parents of pre-school and primary children. Parents living in more disadvantaged areas were found to need more assistance by settings to assist their children's learning in the home. The traditional helper role in a setting was found to be insufficient in Siraj-Blatchford's research (2002:12). Research by Aubrey (1993, 1994, 1995, 1996), while not aimed at the role of parents, provides valuable insights into the mathematical knowledge children bring with them as they enter reception class. Jones (1998) has carried out an ethnographic study of the mathematical experiences of Somali pupils in a reception class which is an interesting reminder to teachers that home learning in numeracy can be very different from the school situation. Briefly, the research concludes that home numeracy learning for reception-aged Somali pupils is a much more formal affair than the usual school experience. For example, children were expected to memorise numbers after a parent had written them down. Parents were very explicit about what their expectations were of their children. This, Jones claims, was different to the school's expectations of these children, who in contrast were expected to go on to the next task without being told to by a teacher. The research reported cites an example of a Somali child sitting waiting to be told what to do next. This is a classic example of cultural differences and highlights the importance of talking to parents to find out what happens at home.

The role of the adult

Research carried out in the 1980s by Tizard *et al.* (1988) concluded that very little mathematical teaching was observed in reception classes of the sample schools in inner London. The view was widely challenged at the time by practitioners, claiming that the research underestimated the amount of mathematical learning while playing in the sand tray or with Lego, which was regarded as a necessary prerequisite to learning about numbers. More recent research would challenge the view that children playing in the sand and with Lego are laying the foundations of mathematical understanding (Munn and Schaffer 1993). A further analysis of research into the ways in which children acquire early mathematical understanding strongly supports the crucial role of the adult in introducing number concepts into children's play (Munn and Schaffer 1993, Munn 1994). By the time children are ready to leave nursery school and enter school many, according to Munn's research, are able to understand the purpose of counting if their early experiences have had some degree of adult-led interaction. Early in their time at nursery school children's responses to the question 'Why count?' ranged from comments that the children like to count or say the words when counting. From this research it would appear that children just count and perceived that they had taught themselves to count, seeing it as a linguistic rather than a functional activity. However, the overarching finding from the research is the difficulty of providing for numeracy in an unstructured environment. Generally, pre-school children, she found, had a lack of understanding of numerals, and development of quantitative understanding tends to be slow in a nursery situation. Because Munn was looking at both literacy and numeracy development her research supports the view that children have relatively little difficulty in sharing the adult's purpose of reading (i.e. to access meaning) from the earliest stages of emergent literacy. Counting, on the other hand, had no such stable framework which was shared with adults – a factor which may account for some of the difficulties which both teachers and children have with early numeracy (Munn 1994:17). Opportunities for adults and children working together playing a mathematical game in which the adult is setting the agenda has a clear purpose and provides a valuable opportunity for mathematical development. The interactive nature of such an activity with the child modelling the adult's numerical skill of counting helps the children to understand the function of counting, thus developing their numeracy understanding and helping them to count purposefully from a very early age.

An important finding from Munn and Schaffer's research (1993) were the advantages to children of an assignment system or key worker system which enabled adults to form a close relationship with their 'children' and thus put them in a better position to get to know each child's level of competence and to provide experiences appropriately attuned to that level. The case study below illustrates how an adult sensitively structures a role-play experience to include a mathematical dimension.

It is interesting to note that three- and four-year old children in the Siraj-Blatchford study were found to have mathematical experiences for the least amount of time, irrespective of the type of setting, including Early Excellence centres. Overall, children in reception classes experienced more mathematical activities than in any other setting. However, activities to promote literacy, physical and creative skills were all experienced for much more time. Could it be that the findings of Munn in the early 1990s are the same today? Is enough attention given to mathematical learning?

The Haberdashery Shop

Miss Pickles, Emma and Paul are busy counting buttons in the structured play haberdashery shop created in the Stockport nursery to help develop numeracy. Painstakingly, Miss Pickles, the headteacher, encourages Emma to count the buttons on each card and order the cards from nought to ten. Later we see Emma ordering additional button cards for the shop as she writes a list of well-formed numbers. Paul, with the help of Miss Pickles, is measuring the length of the ribbon, '54 centimetres' says Miss Pickles in a matter-of-fact tone. 'Is that long enough?'

Totally absorbed in his work Paul nods in agreement, and mutters something about 60.

Activities such as cooking and singing number rhymes help children develop a mental set towards number, but not necessarily a specific skill which can be measured. Consequently there is a danger that for assessment purposes such worthwhile mathematical activities are difficult to assess, therefore the teacher relies on his or her intuitive judgement that learning is taking place and may devalue the mathematical worth of such activities. They select instead evidence from formal recording, which is an unreliable measure of understanding in young children. A recurring theme in this review of research is the importance of mathematical games as a strategy to improve number knowledge. Recent research in New Zealand by Peters (1998) found that, once again, the children's learning was enhanced when a sensitive adult was available to support and extend the children's learning as they played games. The greatest gains were seen where the games involved enumeration, rote counting, understanding of the number sequence and recognition of number patterns. In this research the high number of parents involved released the teacher to observe what was happening in the groups. These observations formed the basis of informal discussions with parents at the end of each session. These 'debriefing' sessions were invaluable as a means of clarifying problems in the parents' style of working with the children that were then quickly overcome. Generally parents preferred not to work with their own child as they felt they had more patience with other people's children and that they tended to put more pressure on their own child. To ensure maximum involvement of parents, all sessions started at the beginning of the day. Munn (1997) outlines the implications for teaching if, as her research claims, children's counting ability is an imitative social practice with little association with quantification until there are changes in the children's social environment, such as going to school. She discusses the implications of this for teachers in the following way:

- Assess children's beliefs about counting before working on addition, subtraction or comparison of quantities.

- Take young children's counting seriously.

- Make the purpose of counting explicit for children.

- Stimulate children to develop their own numerical goals.

(Munn 1997:17)

Mathematical learning

Each sack contains 175 bulbs, the majority of which are spread out on the field near a number of holes recently dug in the ground. The Ranger gathers together a group of excitable three- and four-year-olds well wrapped up in raincoats, anoraks and boots. It is raining steadily. 'We need to put six bulbs in each hole,' instructs the Ranger. Before he can say another word, enthusiastically the children take a handful of bulbs and search out a hole in which to plant them. 'Wait a minute,' calls the Ranger, as he proceeds to explain carefully that the bulbs must be planted the correct way up. Closely examining the shapes of the bulbs the children begin to count the bulbs into each hole. 'One, two, three, four . . .' chants Luke. 'Is that enough?' questions Luke. 'No. You need two more,' replies the Ranger. Luke races off to gather two more bulbs. On return he is uncertain he has planted six bulbs altogether. He rescues the previously planted bulbs and spreads them out in front of him, counting, 1, 2, 3, 4, 5, 6 as he does so. 'I have two more,' he proudly exclaims to anyone who is listening.

A typical nursery day. What are the children learning? They purposefully explore and investigate their environment and importantly apply their knowledge of numbers and counting to the activity. Luke is just beginning to apply his understanding of numbers to a practical situation: a typical mathematical activity, where the adult structures a situation to enable the child to demonstrate his knowledge. Fundamental to Luke being able to demonstrate his previously learned ability to count and an ability to add numbers together was the role of the adult, who, in this case, presented the problem, and supported Luke in his search to find a solution. Such opportunities, as other case studies in the chapter demonstrate, are very common practices in nurseries everywhere.

Historically, it is claimed that teachers hold the view that children find arithmetic difficult because formal arithmetic has been imposed on children before they were conceptually ready for such learning. The work of Piaget is frequently cited to justify this. Particularly influential are notions associated with the idea of conservation. Piaget maintained that if children cannot conserve number, that is if they appear not to understand that the number of objects in a group remains the same however the objects are arranged, then they are not yet ready to start on school arithmetic (Piaget 1965). The practical application of this belief is manifest in mathematical schemes that start off with very concrete activities, such as matching objects on a one-to-one basis, or sorting them into sets. This is done in the belief that this is concrete rather than abstract. In reality this type of activity is abstract for most children because it had little relevance to the child's mathematical thinking, unlike an interactive session with a knowledgeable teacher whose questioning encourages children to manipulate numbers mentally. On other occasions, such as in their play, the children may have the opportunity to demonstrate their emerging competence. The case study below illustrates this beautifully.

Four children are playing skittles in one corner of the open area in the nursery hall. Alongside the skittle run is a painting easel covered with plain paper and a selection of felt pens. The three- and four-year-olds have organised themselves into two teams. One child in each team counts the skittles as the ball knocks them down and then records the number on the score sheet. The children had been introduced to formal recording of numbers in the nursery. The group confidently record their score and create a list of recognisable numbers down the paper. The activity has some purpose. This is what adults do when they play games. It has meaning for the children and it is providing an opportunity for the application of their understanding of numbers. In another part of the same nursery a small group of children are putting 'candles' on a birthday cake. They are arguing about how many are required. One child miscounts four, much to the frustration of the older child who proceeds to instruct the younger child by pointing to each candle as she counts.

Messages from research

There are clear messages from research about early mathematical development that need to be heeded by all practitioners. In summary the messages are:

- the importance of the adult in supporting, explaining and knowing children's competences in mathematics, which is most effectively achieved through a key worker system;

- the involvement of parents both with their child at home and in the setting;

- the key role of mathematical games in developing numeracy;

- understanding the range of opportunities for mathematical learning across a wide range of experiences;

- do not underestimate children's mathematical understanding on entry to reception class;

- mathematical activities must have purpose and meaning if they are to make 'human sense' to the child.

If, therefore, the creation of an environment in which children engage in computational activities is important once children enter school the results of an NFER survey (Harris and Henkhusens 1996) claiming that some infants spend only 12 minutes a day in mathematics lessons begins to explain why British schoolchildren attain less well than their international counterparts in mathematical tests. The findings are distorted by the difficulty the researchers had in quantifying mathematics lessons as many mathematical experiences are provided through thematic work. The research mentioned earlier by Munn and Schaffer (1993) raises important points in relation to how opportunities are provided for young children to acquire mathematical knowledge and understanding in a nursery setting. In their research carried out in ten day nurseries in the Glasgow area, claims are made that relative to literacy events, with which staff are more confident, numeracy events are relatively infrequent. And importantly, unless the member of staff engineers opportunities to introduce numbers through rhymes or counting in the daily activities of the day nursery, the children do not develop understanding of mathematical ideas. This was also a finding in the DfES research project (Siraj-Blatchford 2002) mentioned above.

Ofsted findings

One of the most extensive databases of information about what happens in the broad spectrum of early educational settings is that of Ofsted. A survey of mathematical development carried out by the Early Years arm of Ofsted (2001), *Nursery Education: Quality of Provision for 3 and 4 Year Olds 2000–01*, found that:

> *81 per cent of 3-year-olds* are given good opportunities to develop their mathematical abilities through games and puzzles, access to technical toys which encourage mathematical thought and everyday activities. There are too few opportunities provided for children to explore concepts of number, shape and size, or to solve problems that might involve simple adding and subtracting. However, this is not surprising given that most 3-year-olds will be at the yellow or blue *stepping-stone* level of development and are not likely to be able to solve problems involving addition and subtraction until they are in the reception class!
>
> *86 per cent of 4-year-olds* are in settings that are good at promoting mathematical development. Children are encouraged to talk about number using a variety of activities such as number rhymes, stories and games. Children use shapes in painting, cutting and drawing.

The findings do not include an evaluation of the quality of provision in the maintained sector, which includes nursery and reception classes. The longtitudinal research project completed in 2002 by Siraj-Blatchford *et al.* would suggest that the time children spend engaged in mathematical learning is significantly less than in other areas, apart from personal, social and emotional development, which is infrequently planned for as a separate activity. Evaluations of the National Numeracy Strategy (Ofsted 2000 and 2002) comment on practices in reception classes. They found that most teachers introduce elements of the daily mathematics lesson during the autumn term in short sessions through the day, usually beginning with an oral and mental starter. Further work in mathematical development is almost always done in small groups with carefully planned support from teachers and other adults. It is quoted that reception class teachers found the *Guidance on the Organisation of the Daily Mathematics Lesson in Reception Classes* (DfEE 2000) helpful because of the ways in which it emphasises how young children develop mathematical understanding and vocabulary through practical activities and play (Ofsted 2002:14). However, an inappropriate amount of time given to the area of learning was not perceived to be an issue from this evaluation. Research carried out by Rodger (1999) into the impact of inspection on the quality of provision in children's centres in Manchester found that weaknesses in the mathematical area of learning was the fourth most frequent weakness, with an equal number of children's centres being required to 'identify and implement more opportunities for children to write and to use and record numbers in their imaginative play and to provide more time for practical mathematics activities, to recognise and create patterns and to show an awareness of number operations, such as addition and subtraction'. Given the very small number of four-year-old children in the settings it was probably not surprising that these were areas of mathematics receiving less attention. The one area in which all of the centres excelled was singing number rhymes.

Early learning goals for mathematics

A major criticism of mathematics for young children, particularly in reception classes, has been the over-use of commercially produced work sheets which, while purporting to be mathematical, frequently required little more from the children than the colouring in of various objects. Such activities have been described as 'occupational' rather than educational and seriously contributed to the large amount of time children are sedentary during their school day (Ofsted 1993). Research by Aubrey (1995) indicates that practitioners follow the structure of a scheme and introduce new concepts to children as the scheme dictates, whether this is appropriate to the child or not. Practitioners are required to ensure their children meet the early learning goals through practical, first-hand experiences without resorting to the whole class teaching methodology the goals appear to endorse. Are direct whole class teaching sessions appropriate at any time for children under five? To work in an interactive way with a group of children of similar abilities, such as the four-year-olds in the term prior to starting statutory schooling, seems reasonable as long as the interest and motivation of the children can be sustained. The training materials provided for practitioners in nursery and reception classes (DfEE 1999b) has a wealth of suggested activities including whole class activities suitable for the nursery and reception years. The key principles of the mathematical curriculum in the nursery are:

- providing a wide experience of numbers, patterns, measurements and shapes in line with the Foundation Stage curriculum and early learning goals for mathematics;

- teaching mathematics and providing mathematical experiences so that children can work in small groups, as pairs or individuals and as a large group;

- enabling children to encounter mathematics in a variety of contexts, including free and structured play.

(DfEE 1999b:116)

Stepping stones	Yellow	Blue	Green	Grey
Numbers as labels for counting	Show an interest in numbers and counting. Use some number names and number language spontaneously. Enjoy joining in with number rhymes and songs. Use mathematical language in play.	Show curiosity about numbers by offering comments or asking questions. Use some number names accurately in play. Willingly attempt to count with some numbers in the correct order. Recognise groups with one, two or three objects.	Show confidence with numbers by initiating or requesting number activities. Count up to three or four objects by saying one number name for each item. Recognise some numerals of personal significance. Begin to represent numbers using fingers, marks on paper or pictures. Recognise numbers 1 to 5, then 1 to 9. Count up to six objects from a larger group. Count actions or objects that cannot be moved. Select the correct numeral to represent 1 to 5, then 1 to 9 objects. Show increased confidence in numbers by spotting errors. Count an irregular arrangement of up to 10 objects. Say the number after any number up to 9. Begin to count beyond 10.	Say and use number names in order in familiar contexts. Count reliably up to 10 everyday objects. Recognise numbers 1 to 9. Use developing mathematical ideas and methods to solve practical problems.
Calculating	Compare two groups of objects saying when they have the same number.	Show an interest in number problems. Separate a group of three or four objects in different ways, beginning to recognise that the total is still the same.	Sometimes show confidence and offer solutions to problems. Find the total number of items in two groups by counting all of them. Use own methods to solve a problem. Say with confidence the number that is one more than a given number.	In practical activities and discussion begin to use the vocabulary involved in adding and subtracting. Use language such as 'more' or 'less' to compare two numbers. Find one more or one less than a number from 1 to 10. Begin to relate addition to combining two groups of objects and subtraction to 'taking away'.
Shape, space and measures	Show an interest in shapes and space by playing with shapes or making arrangements with objects. Show an awareness of similarities in shapes in the environment.	Show interest by sustained construction activity or by talking about shapes and arrangements. Use shapes appropriately for tasks.	Sustain interest for a length of time on a pre-decided construction or arrangement. Match some shapes by recognising similarities and orientation.	Use language such as 'heavier' or 'lighter', 'greater' or 'smaller', to compare quantities. Talk about, recognise and recreate simple patterns.

FIGURE 8.1 Early learning goals for mathematical development

Stepping stones	Yellow	Blue	Green	Grey
Shape, space and measures	Observe and use positional language. Use size language such as 'big' and 'little'.	Begin to talk about the shapes of everyday objects.	Use appropriate shapes by representational models or more elaborate pictures. Show curiosity and observation by talking about shapes, how they are the same or why some are different. Find items from positional/directional clues. Describe a simple journey. Order two items by length or height. Choose suitable components to make a particular model. Adapt shapes or cut material to size. Select a particular name's shape. Begin to use mathematical names for solid 3D shapes and flat 2D shapes and mathematical terms to describe shapes. Show an awareness of symmetry. Order two or three items by length. Order two items by weight or capacity. Instruct a programmable toy.	Use language such as 'circle' or 'bigger' to describe the shape and size of solids and flat shapes. Use everyday words to describe position. Use developing mathematical ideas and method to solve problems.

FIGURE 8.1   (continued)

The materials describe three types of number work in reception:

■ using number drawn from children's own experience;

■ counting and working on the structure and properties of numbers;

■ understanding cardinal numbers – recognizing that numbers can represent groups of objects or the frequency of events.

Interestingly, they also allude to developing social skills and what children should be able to do by the end of the reception year:

■ listen and respond as part of a large group for 20 minutes or more;

■ operate effectively as part of a small group with little or no adult support;

■ engage in mathematical activity for longer than five minutes as part of a small group of children.

Assessing and planning for mathematical development

Assessment

Informal, observational assessment as outlined in Chapter 4 is an effective starting point for assessing young children's mathematical competences. However, in the new world of accountability and measuring performance many practitioners are starting to set targets for pupils in the reception class. BEAM Education has produced pamphlets to inform parents of the targets likely to be achieved by their children at the end of the reception class. An example below shows how this is phrased for parents.

About the targets

These targets show some of the things that your child should be able to do by the end of the Reception year.

Some targets are harder than they seem, e.g. a child who can count up to 20 may still have trouble saying which number comes after 15. She may have to start at 1 and count from there. Counting things you can't see can be quite difficult.

Targets – Reception

By the end of this year, most children should be able to . . .

- Say one, two, three, four . . . to twenty.
- Count up to 10 objects.
- Recognise the written numbers 1, 2, 3, 4, . . . to 9.

and so on.

A typical assessment scheme would be for observational assessments to be built into focused group activities using the *stepping-stones* charts included in Chapter 4. Evidence of achievement of the learning objective would be either ticked on a group list or individually added to a child's personal profile on a sticky label to save remembering to rewrite it. In this way, a profile of achievement for each child soon builds up. Comments such as the following may be written.

Jake 12 May 2003
Can count to 5 and point to objects
as he does this (blue achieved)

Short term planning	**Date:**
Workshop area: maths development	
Key learning outcomes:	**Adult role and planned activities:**
Resources:	
Assessment (list children assessed)	
....	
....	
....	
....	

FIGURE 8.2   Short-term planning format for a daily mathematics lesson in a reception class

Excellent practitioners are looking at ways of interpreting the *stepping-stones* to maximise children's development. In reception classes there are generally weekly numeracy plans, and in nursery classes and schools adult-focused plans for small group work. Figure 8.2 shows a typical short-term planning format and Figure 8.3 shows a completed adult-focused plan from a nursery school

Research evidence supports the view that many early years settings are lacking in opportunities for children to experience high quality mathematical learning (Munn and Schaffer 1993, Aubrey 1995). The recently introduced requirement that additional time is found for mathematical learning is an important one. NNS guidance suggests that classrooms should be organised to maximise quality teaching and learning:

- in a large group, or as a whole class, for activities where children act in unison and facilitate each other's contributions;
- in small groups, so staff can promote personal interaction to enhance learning;
- in pairs or as individuals, where the adult's role is to act as a more competent partner.

Date: **Area of learning:** Maths development

Learning objective/s:

-       To recap on previous skills to move the Pixie* forwards
-       To know how to move the Pixie backwards
-       To use a number line to predict how many presses forwards or backwards

* a programmable toy

Materials:

Pixie, 3 number lines 1–3, 1–5, 1–10.

Activity (begin, middle, end)

- Allow all children to recap moving the Pixie forward one length by pressing CM↑ GO
- Introduce the idea of Pixie moving backwards. Allow all chn to press CM↓ GO in turn. This could be in front of them or on the number line.
- Let each child choose a pair of animals and place on a number they choose. Same child counts the lengths and sends the Pixie forwards or backwards to collect.

Use knowledge of children to select which number line they use.

Evaluation

FIGURE 8.3   Adult-focused plan from a nursery school for mathematical development

     Research evidence cited earlier outlines the central importance of the role of adults in mathematical learning and the different kinds of mathematical learning children engage with: functional and computational (Munn 1994). This has implications for the most effective way in which practitioners can promote learning in the day-to-day work of the setting. Planned opportunities based on the setting's overall programme for mathematical experiences and planned and incidental opportunities for children to engage in functional mathematics appear to be important. An important element of assessment will therefore be judging whether the child is operating at a functional level of mathematical understanding and whether or not the child is ready to consider computation. Whatever the focus, evidence suggests that planning needs to contain particular elements if the children are to progress most in their learning. As indicated in Chapter 3 the stages of planning are consistent across all areas of learning. Although the guidance produced by QCA (2000) states explicitly that all areas of learning should have equal priority, it is generally understood by practitioners that there should be a higher priority given to communication, language and literacy and mathematical development.

Planning for mathematical learning

Following the Foundation Stage planning structure recommended by QCA (2001) in which settings are advised to have long-, medium- and short-term plans, this section provides examples of medium- and short-term plans. The aspect of the area of learning planned for is number (Figure 8.4), based on the Tower Hamlets curriculum framework (Field and Lally 1996).

The planning examples provided in this chapter are typical of settings and highlight the mathematical ideas to be introduced to children during adult-

NUMBER (1)			
Learning intention/ knowledge/skills/attitude	Areas and resources inside and out for spontaneous learning	Planned activities and experiences	Adult input and specific language input
To understand the purpose of numbers – that you count to find out how many there are	• Role play involving counting e.g. – post play – delivering letters to numbered destinations – train and bus play with tickets – delivery person delivering correct number of articles to different points – parking numbered bikes in their allocated space	• Cooking – counting the ingredients, explain why precision is necessary • Consistently use repertoire of number rhymes – 5 Little Ducks; 10 Green Bottles; 5 Little Speckled Frogs. 10 in the Bed etc. • Make a big book of rhymes used so that children see number rhymes written whilst saying the rhyme.	• Model counting in a wide range of contexts, especially activities children are involved in – the number of jumps, steps, bangs on the drum, shapes cut from play-dough, number playing, prints made on papers, buttons to do up etc. • Use stories with numbers e.g. *The Shopping Basket* by John Burningham (1993)
To be able to repeat numbers in correct order			
To be able to count a collection of objects accurately, matching one number to one object	• Construction equipment • Displays of numbers– numerals and objects, preferably interactive where children can sort and count		• Encourage children to move object to show they have counted it
To know that the last number said is the number that are in the set	• Number jigsaws and other number matching activities where children can practice what they know	• Build with the children and encourage them to talk about their constructions *'How many bricks have you used for this part? Can you make this match it? How long is this wall? Can you make another wall 6 bricks long?*	• Ask children to count various things where there is a need to know e. g. *'How many pieces of paper do we need so that each child in the group has a piece?'*
To be able to count a collection of objects and check the total	• Interesting collections of objects with sorting trays which will encourage discussion, classification and may be counted, e.g. small metal objects, shells, fridge magnets	• Introduce numeral cards to use with rhymes – e.g. 10 Green Bottles, each with a numeral for children to hold	• Encourage children to make sensible estimates before counting
To know what number comes before/after another number		• Make number lines, using chalk outside or large tiles inside with children's footprints etc. *'What number comes next?'*	• Have a number line for children to put their label on each day to record how many children are present

FIGURE 8.4   Number planning for younger/less able children (Field and Lally 1996)

Group: **Week beginning:**
Focus activity:
Learning objective(s) including National Curriculum if appropriate:

Activity:

Key vocabulary:

Assessment notes:

Next steps/comments:

FIGURE 8.5   Format for small group time plans

directed activities. It is common for nursery staff to identify adult-focused or small group time plans such as Figure 8.2 earlier or Figure 8.5 above.

The National Numeracy Strategy

Many children under five are in reception classes and will be included in the National Numeracy Strategy recently implemented in all primary schools. Central to the strategy is direct teaching, whereby an adult instructs, explains and demonstrates mathematical ideas to a class of children and to small groups of children. Because this is a requirement for older pupils in school, young four-year-olds in mixed age classes will be involved from the beginning of the year in which they start in the reception class. Evidence from the National Numeracy Project suggests that frequently the youngest four-year-olds are excluded from the first part of the hour and work with another adult or the teacher on more appropriate activities. A disturbing finding in some schools is that the school puts pressure on the reception class staff to implement the hour in the same way as the rest of the school as soon as possible. There is no such requirement in literacy, and the *National Numeracy Strategy: Framework for Teaching Mathematics* (DfEE 1999b) states quite categorically that:

> your aim should be to prepare children, by the end of reception, for the dedicated mathematics lesson of about 45 minutes that will be part of each day in **Year 1**. For example, you will need to help them learn how to listen, how to show and talk about what they

have been doing in front of other children, how to find and use the equipment that they need, how to take turns and so on.

(DfEE 1999b:27)

The guidance provided for schools required to implement the numeracy strategy is a useful document for those working in the non-statutory sector. A particularly pertinent statement is: 'in the early years children will use oral methods, in general moving from counting objects or fingers one by one to more sophisticated mental counting strategies' (DfEE 1999b:6) (See Figure 8.7). Examples of activities to promote mathematical learning are provided to fit in with the wide range of practical activities traditionally associated with nursery education. Figure 8.6 gives a list of activities suitable for different types of groupings of children.

A useful strategy will be to use these activities as a basis for your curriculum planning to ensure that your children are getting the rich, practical opportunities necessary to develop mathematical understanding. Some activities, such as singing and counting rhymes, lend themselves to whole-class work. You may need too to demonstrate how to play skittles outside. It will be most economical of your time to do this for the whole group, but be aware that this will be too much for

	Large group work	Small group work	Individual or paired work
Adult-directed activity	• Number songs and rhymes • Chanting the numbers • Counting claps, jumps • Identifying what is in a cloth bag	• Comparing sets • Recognising coins • Dice activities • Preparing food – weighing and measuring	• Making number tiles • Playing track games • Dominoes • Making shape patterns • Using bricks
Adult-supported structured activity	• Sharing news • Feedback on work done in small group • Passing-the-teddy type games	• Building brick towers and structures • Creative art • Threading beads • Sand and water play	• Number jigsaws and puzzles • Drawing or 'writing' • Structured equipment
Child-led activity	• Some outdoor games (informal racing, climbing, etc.)	• Playing shops • Some use of manipulative materials (dough, clay . . .) • Some sand and water play	• Role play • Small world play • Some outdoor play with large toys and apparatus

FIGURE 8.6   Mathematical activities for the nursery (DfEE 1999b)

Children's own experience of numbers
- **Numbers as labels:** *house numbers, bus numbers, telephone numbers, car numbers, price labels . . .*
- **Numbers associated with collections:** *101 dalmations, three bears . . .*
- **Counting small collections or events:** *counting strawberries into bowls, steps going upstairs.*
- **Numbers implying an order or position:** *ages (my sister is three, my mum is twenty-four . . .) positions in a race or in a football league.*

Counting numbers and the structures of the number system
- *Chanting the numbers to 10, to 20, then to 100*
- *Realising that in each decade the units digits repeat (71, 72, 73 have the same units as 1, 2, 3)*
- *Counting in multiples of 10, 20, 30, 40 . . .)*

Numbers of sets as objects
- *Matching the number 4 to four objects*
- *Recognising that a tower of 4 bricks is taller than a tower of 3 and shorter than a tower of 5*
- *Realising that 4 things can be split into 3 and 1 or 2 and 2*

FIGURE 8.7   Contexts for number work in the reception class (DfEE 1999b)

some children, who will need reinforcement and support as they try to do this. The key objectives for the reception year are the same as the early learning goals for mathematical development (see Figure 8.1 earlier in the chapter).

I hope there will be a top-down effect on nursery education as a consequence of the introduction of the National Numeracy Strategy, but it will be a welcome one which acknowledges the importance of practical, first-hand mathematical experiences and the role of the knowledgeable adult in supporting and extending mathematical learning in the early years. There may too be a reduction in reception classes of the worksheet-based activities that are mistakenly described as mathematical. An understanding of the mathematical potential across the curriculum will be necessary to ensure that children's interests and developing understanding are successfully scaffolded by an adult, whether the mathematical experience is planned or incidental.

Further reading

Aplin, R. (1998) *Assisting Numeracy. A Handbook for Classroom Assistants.* London: BEAM Education.

DfEE (1999) *The National Numeracy Strategy.* Sudbury: Cambridge University Press.

DfEE (1999) *Guide for your Professional Development: Book 4 Raising Standards in the Early Years, in Key Stage 1 and in Special Schools.* London: DfEE.

Montague-Smith, A. (1997) *Mathematics in Nursery Education.* London: David Fulton Publishers.

Thompson, I. (ed.) (1997) *Teaching and Learning Early Number.* Buckingham: Open University Press.

Knowledge and under-standing of the world

Introduction

This chapter shows how knowledge and understanding of the world provides the basis for relevant first-hand experiences. The opportunity to apply communication, numeracy, literacy, observational and investigative skills to practical situations is at the heart of knowledge and understanding of the world. One can see the close links between this area and aspects of personal, social and emotional development with regard to the community, family and other cultures and beliefs. Consequently, the area of learning which forms the focus for this chapter is fundamental to young children's learning. The activities and experiences in which children take part allow them to deepen their understanding about themselves, their friends and families. For example, watching the traffic passing and counting the lorries rumbling past provides a context for the application of basic skills in a meaningful way. The activity is about recording how many vehicles they see. It is also about observing similarities and differences between different types of vehicles. That such activities, like counting the bulbs mentioned in Chapter 8, are described as geography or mathematics, or personal and social development, is largely irrelevant. The subject or area of learning label is for the adults to know about for their record keeping and to inform their planning. The child benefits from the richness and first-hand nature of the experiences. He or she uses all their senses to hear the traffic, to see the different vehicles, to record the number seen or simply to tell someone about it. The experience is everyday, within the child's understanding and importantly will have some meaning for that child, who will begin to identify with the world around him or her.

I am reminded as I begin to write this chapter of Ben (six years old) at the end of his nursery experience. Fortunately for him his parents want him to go to school in the area. There is no suitable school catering for his special needs and so he stays in the nursery full-time until a suitable school can be found. He has his own teacher for two hours every day. His parents want him to go to the school his brothers attend, across the road from the nursery. The head of the school is not so sure. Ben remains in the nursery. Ben is a paraplegic. He has profound hearing loss and is partially sighted. His communication skills are minimal. He communicates via signing (a little) and expresses delight by hugging anyone around. He has just spent half an hour of his daily two hours allocation of a special educational needs support teacher in the quiet room, where they work through a programme of literacy and numeracy activities recommended by the support service. He can count to five now. The support teacher is a very experienced former nursery teacher. She is making little headway with Ben as she struggles to sustain his attention on the picture book they are sharing.

Ben and she go outside and head for the climbing platform in the middle of the field near the railings which separate the nursery field from the main road. She cajoles him to climb to the centre where they can easily see both main roads coming to a junction. Once again she gets out the picture book and encourages Ben to point to the lorry and say 'l-o-r-r-y'. Squirming and wriggling Ben's attention wanders. Suddenly, rumbling round the corner comes a builder's lorry. Pointing excitedly Ben cries out, 'LORRY!' and hugs his teacher, who smiles and glows at this tremendous achievement.

By providing a context to enable children to find out about themselves, where they live, what people around them do and how they make sense of the environment you are helping children to make sense of the world. You are recognising that 'children learn most effectively when they are actively involved and interested' (Ball 1994). In this chapter I will be looking at learning in this area in an holistic manner. I realise that by doing this I may be perpetuating the difficulties practitioners find in providing appropriate activities. However, I believe it is essential to do this for the following reasons:

- the nature of the experience, whether it is adult-led or child-initiated is paramount;
- learning about the world around them will always require children to use many skills and to develop many ideas.

There are broadly five strands which can be applied to knowledge and understanding of the world: science; geography; history; design technology; and information and communication technology. For those of you working with children of five in reception classes you may wish to take these into account when you are planning learning to promote these early learning goals and to take into account continuity and progression with the next stage of learning. Figure 9.1 shows the early learning goals.

Although each goal has its own set of skills and concepts which require particular kinds of activity to develop children's understanding in that aspect of the area of learning it is unlikely that these will be provided for in an isolated way. Many of

	Yellow	Blue	Green	Grey
Exploration and investigation	Show curiosity and interest by facial expressions, movement or sound. Explore objects.	Show curiosity, observe and manipulate objects. Describe simple features of objects and events. Sort objects by one function. Talk about what is seen and what is happening.	Examine objects and living things to find out more about them. Notice and comment on patterns. Show an awareness of change.	Investigate objects and materials by using all of the senses as appropriate. Find out about, and identify, some features of living things, objects and events they observe. Look closely at similarities and differences, patterns and change. Ask questions about why things happen and how things work.
Designing and making skills	Investigate construction materials. Realise that tools can be used for a purpose.	Join construction pieces together to build and balance. Begin to try out a range of tools and techniques safely.	Construct with a purpose in mind, using a variety of resources. Use simple tools and techniques competently and appropriately.	Build and construct with a wide range of objects, selecting appropriate resources, and adapting their work where necessary. Select tools and techniques they need to shape, assemble and join materials they are using.
Information and communication technology (ICT)	Show an interest in ICT	Know how to operate simple equipment.	Complete a simple program on the computer and/or perform simple functions on ICT apparatus.	Find out about and identify the uses of everyday technology and use ICT and programmable toys to support their learning.
A sense of time	Remember and talk about significant things that have happened to them.	Show interest in the lives of people familiar to them. Begin to differentiate between past and present.		Find out about the past and present events in their own lives, and in those of their families and other people they know.
A sense of place	Show interest in the world.	Comment about where they live and the natural world.		Observe, and find out about and identify, features in the place they live and the natural world. Find out about their environment and talk about those features they like and dislike.
Cultures and beliefs	Express feelings about a significant personal event.	Describe significant events for family or friends.	Gain an awareness of the cultures and beliefs of others.	Begin to know about their own cultures and beliefs and those of other people.

FIGURE 9.1   Early learning goals for knowledge and understanding of the world (QCA 1999b)

the skills are process skills which are common to several areas of learning. For example:

- collaborating;
- exploring;
- making choices;
- organising;
- explaining;
- talking and communicating;
- sharing;
- observing;
- taking responsibility;
- asking and answering;
- recording;
- interpreting;
- predicting;
- recalling and reflecting.

Learning in this area should be first-hand and practical. You may need to be outside with your children to be sure that they develop a firm understanding of the idea, or develop the skill. You will need to visit shops and parks, travel on a bus and observe the sky, the trees and the litter scattering along the footpaths. You will need to provide opportunities for children to observe closely, to touch, to feel, to smell and to listen. Alongside the learning goals for physical development many of the goals in this area of learning will be most successfully achieved in the outdoor environment. While many young children will talk about where they live and the route they take between home and the nursery or how they travel to their nursery, it is necessary to relive the experience with your children in the nursery to observe their reactions, to provide the name for the landmarks they pass by every day. Involve the children's parents if you really have problems getting out and about.

Research findings

The quality of provision is improving. Five years ago, Ofsted (1997b:13) found that learning in this area was the weakest in the inspection of nursery settings, with 40 per cent of settings having some weaknesses. The nature of those weaknesses are not defined in the report. A survey (Rodger 1999) of the impact of inspection on provision in 30 children's centres in the north-west of England also found this area of learning problematic. It was found that the settings provided too few opportunities for children to play with programmable toys, to question children as to why things happen and how things work or to provide opportunities for children to talk about their past. In the scientific area there were too few opportunities to look at changes and differences and to record observations in pictorial form and too few opportunities for the children to explore and observe. The results of a more recent survey (Ofsted 2001:13) are more encouraging. The survey found that 90 per cent of settings were effective in encouraging four-year-olds to talk about their own lives and their environment. Children were encouraged to record their observations and learned to use a variety of materials in learning about technology, such as cutting and folding paper, building with blocks and construction toys and learning about nature through exploring the life cycles of tadpoles and caterpillars.

One of the most important findings from research carried out in the field of environmental cognition and the development of spatial awareness is that young children are good at learning (Palmer 1994). They are ready to use geographical concepts as early as four to five years of age. An important finding by Blades and Spencer (1987) of children's ability to cope with recognising syllables on a map was that almost half of four-year-olds were able to do this. A frequent criticism of introducing children under five too soon to such activities is that they cannot understand the abstract concept of a map. Research carried out by Rodger (1995) with children under five in a reception class showed how competent the children were in constructing their own abstract symbols of features in the school environment.

There is some evidence that the process skills of science are being subsumed within the ever familiar work sheet. What needs to be guaranteed for the under fives is the opportunity to engage in enquiry (Ellis and Kleinberg 1997). An essential of enquiry, whether it be scientific, technological or historical, is that children are encouraged to talk. Ellis and Kleinberg describe the 'get this done and move on to the next stage' syndrome in early years classes. The most recent Ofsted survey of standards and quality for reception class pupils (Ofsted 1993) claimed that speaking and listening was not emphasised enough in about half of the classes in their survey. They also found at this time that there was an under-emphasis on science and technology. Certainly, about one-fifth of settings inspected were found to have weaknesses in the opportunities they provided for children to question or to talk about their experiences and their work (Ofsted 1997b).

The Reggio Emilia approach

To those of you who are unfamiliar with the Reggio system (Edwards *et al.* 1998), I am including a very short review of the basic tenets of the approach to early childhood education implemented in a unique collection of schools for young children in northern Italy. It is appropriate to include it in this chapter because of the importance attached to the outdoor environment. Essentially, the Reggio Emilia approach's principal educational aim involves children in long-term projects to develop their intellect through a systematic focus on symbolic representation.

> Young children are encouraged to explore their environment and express themselves through all of their available 'expressive, communicative, and cognitive languages', whether they be words, movement, drawing, painting, building, sculpture, shadow play, collage, dramatic play, or music, to name a few.
>
> (Edwards *et al.* 1998:7)

Several examples of such projects are included in the book and are relevant to this chapter in that they take the topic-based approach to early learning to be the centre of all learning. For instance, one example cited by Katz (1998) describes four- and five-year-old children carrying out a study of a neighbourhood super-market. The core of the programme, unlike the pre-planned experiences we offer in the UK, was one of problem-solving and problem-setting. Rules and routines were less important than the creation of the effective adult–child relationship. Recording of the activities and representations created by the children formed the basis of the documentation, unlike our curriculum planning which generally includes information about the way in which we intend children to reach particular goals. I have some reservations about the fervour with which the Reggio Emilia approach is capturing the hearts of early years educators the world over. Haven't we in the UK been tinkering with such an approach to the early years curriculum since Plowden (CACE 1967)? Has it been tried and found less than perfect? I leave that for you to debate as you study the early learning goals for knowledge and understanding of the world in the next section.

Unlike other areas of learning described so far in this book, in this chapter I have identified a range of common experiences for under fives and outlined through the accompanying planning what learning opportunities are provided. My underlying philosophy throughout the book is very much one of the vital importance of the role of the adult. Without their presence in some of the activities cited below there would be missed opportunities for learning. The case studies are of investigating the school building, water play, mini-beast hunt, making orange juice and the use of the outdoor environment.

Planning for knowledge and understanding of the world

The learning goals require children to interact with their environment. They could not be more quintessentially child-friendly. Why then, one is tempted to ask, do practitioners find this a difficult area of learning to provide for? General planning principles are outlined in Chapter 3 along with examples of different formats for short- and medium-term planning. It is for you to decide which planning format you wish to use. Indeed it may be that you have no time to complete detailed written plans as I am outlining throughout this book (Ofsted 1999b). It is important that you know what the purpose of the activity is that you are providing. Knowing what you are doing and anticipating what the children will learn and may need to extend their learning ensures that you have all the resources necessary gathered together. To have intentions for the children's learning will also make you think about the questions you are asking and the encouragement you are providing for the children to carry on. The planning is only a scaffold for the interaction you have with your children, whose interest may go beyond your planned learning intentions. This is an important consideration when working with children under five. A strong finding from the research carried out by Siraj-Blatchford *et al.* (2002) was that adults have a powerful role to play in encouraging shared thinking. Good outcomes for children are also linked to practitioners having good curriculum knowledge (Siraj-Blatchford *et al.* 2002).

Investigating the school building

This activity required the children to investigate the immediate environment around the school building (Figure 9.2). The children in this class benefited from the outdoor dimension to the drawing task. The main reason for this was the freedom it gave to the children. Plenty of space and a challenge were provided in the task. Unusually, in this particular group of children they all made a reasonable attempt at the task. The class teacher was amazed to see some of the attempts by children who had not put marks of any kind on a piece of paper before this opportunity. Much of the learning in this sequence of activities was oral as well as recorded in pictorial or written form.

Water Play

'We're making lemonade and fizzy drinks' says Alex.

Alex and his three friends are playing in the water tray on the verandah of a Stockport nursery school one summer afternoon. They are engrossed in their investigation. Why is this? The water is blue, the various contraptions in the water are yellow and red. Alex holds his hand under the water and over and over again he keeps putting a yellow beaker under the water.

'Look' he says to no one in particular.

'It is another colour, it is another colour. My hand is another colour.'

Cautiously, and only after watching Alex for a few seconds Jane the nursery nurse intervenes and allows Alex to pursue this line of investigation, while the others produce jugfuls of lemonade. With support Alex puts various other objects under

Context

Twenty-four reception-aged children in their first term in school complete their first activity of a half-termly investigation of the immediate environment around the school. They are all sitting outside on the playground drawing the external view of the school building with a pencil on a piece of A4 paper attached to a clipboard.

In the classroom these children are very noisy and at times quite disruptive as they flit from one activity to another. Only half of the classroom is available to the children in their working time. The carpeted area, which takes up almost half of the classroom, is unused except for the short times in the day when children gather together in the whole class.

1. Learning objectives
- to observe, talk about and to draw the outside of the school building;
- to find out about the school environment;
- to observe features in the environment;
- to look closely at similarities and differences;
- to know that buildings are made from different materials, and to know what these materials are called.

2. Activity/organisation
The children have examined photographs of buildings and have talked about their features. The children have walked around school and used photographs of features to help to develop their observational skills.

The children sit on the ground with clipboards on their knees or they kneel and place the clipboard and the paper on the ground.

The children draw their representation of the school building.

3. Resources
Clipboard
A4 white cartridge paper
A pencil with a sharp point

4. Assessment/differentiation
Jake, Oscar and Eva only started school this week – targeted for personal and social development (cooperation, self-esteem and concentration).

Assessment by outcome. All the children concentrate and spend 12 minutes on the drawing activity, before engaging in discussion with the classteacher and classroom assistant about the various shapes of the windows, the different colours of the bricks, the array of pipes and gutterings, the door and the footsteps on the playground.

Only a few children identified that the walls were built from different bricks.

5. Evaluation
High level of interest and concentration shown by the children.

No one was tempted to run around the playground (although all children did this before returning to their classsroom). The skill with which the children were able to represent the building was a surprise to the classteacher. Many children were able to do this.

FIGURE 9.2   Lesson planning for observational drawing of a school building

the water and begins to deduce that they are a different colour when he does this. Using observational skills he is beginning to enquire, to ask questions, to investigate and to want to find a solution to this phenomenon.

Countless such opportunities arise in children's self-initiated learning, particularly when they play. Do you value these opportunities as well as the planned tasks you provide? At times such as this one you need to take a different approach to your teaching. You must value these free choice moments of learning alongside the planned adult-directed experiences. Curiosity is an important prerequisite to scientific thinking.

The mini-beast hunt

The children have been finding out about mini-beasts (see Figure 9.3 for the medium-term planning). They have read stories, such as *The Very Hungry Caterpillar* (Carle 1995) and *The Bad Tempered Ladybird* (Carle 1985). They know that insects are found outside and they sometimes fly. A small group of children armed with information books, pooter and magnifying lens set off to gather ladybirds.

Topic: mini-beasts	Area of learning: KUW	Term: summer 2/2
Learning intentions	Areas/resources, inside/out. Spontaneous learning	Planned activities/ experiences
Knowledge and understanding of the world To find out and identify things: wings, legs, body, head, colour, size. To look closely at similarities and differences, pattern and change, different mini-beasts. To find out where mini-beasts live. *Language and literacy* To talk about mini-beasts. To listen to stories about mini-beasts. To learn new words to describe mini-beasts. To use information books. To label their drawings. To write their name on drawings. *Mathematics* To count spots on ladybird. To count wings, legs on other insects. To compare size (ant and ladybird).	Collection of mini-beasts indoors. Designated area outside with insect-attracting plants. Displays of magnifers, pooters, Petri dishes and containers. Displays of models made by the children. Displays of pictures of mini-beasts, stories and information books.	1. Read *The Bad Tempered Ladybird Carle (1985)*. 2. Observe mini-beasts in natural setting. 3. Identifying mini-beasts in information books. 4. Develop observational skills through drawing from direct observation. 5. Make a ladybird with coloured playdough.

FIGURE 9.3   Medium-term planning for the mini-beast hunt

Very carefully they are collected in transparent containers and taken back to the classroom for further observation. Great care and concern are shown by the teacher and the children as they allow the ladybirds to rest on their hands while they count their spots and legs, talk about the colour of their bodies and their relative size compared to a butterfly which was found outside earlier in the day. The children are engrossed. They are using and acquiring a range of scientific and language skills initially. The teacher does not want to lose the momentum of their interest and enthusiasm, so she quickly provides each child with a selection of coloured play-dough to make their version of the ladybird.

Making orange juice

The planned activity in a nursery class for knowledge and understanding of the world focused on the goal asking questions 'to find out why things happen and how things work'. This nursery frequently planned a teacher-focused activity with the purpose of helping the children investigate how various toys, machines and pieces of equipment worked. Individual members of staff would work with a small group of children throughout the week until all children had had a go. The focus for the week was making orange juice which was part of a wider topic on fruits.

In preparation for the activity the nursery nurse had gathered together an electric juice extractor, a simple plastic cover to fit over a jug to collect juice, several oranges and a selection of mugs and bowls. The children gathered round as she demonstrated what the electric juice extractor could do. She then involved the children in squeezing juice from half an orange into a bowl. A discussion followed to establish what the children did compared to what was happening with the electric juice extractor. Some children made good attempts to use the word 'extractor' and several said 'squeeze' as they squeezed their oranges to make a drink.

The children's conversations generated by this activity were a good indication of the value of a practical experience as well as providing the opportunity to raise questions about how the juice came out of the orange. These children did not individually record what they did, but jointly with their teacher composed the sequence of steps necessary to get the juice from the orange to the mug. The teacher described pictorially and added some simple sentences, which she read back to the children later as they reviewed their morning's activities on the carpet.

The fact this was a planned activity introduced by the nursery nurse, rather than arising from the interests of the children at that time, made it no less relevant or interesting to the children. The activity itself provided excellent motivation to find out something new and encourage the children to talk. A view not commonly shared in the early years is that some children do not have many worthwhile preschool experiences to build experiences upon. Take, for example, the oldest child in a family of four siblings living with a lone parent and a dying grandmother. How much attention is given to this child's early experiences? Another child I recall had been fostered by several families, with his reception classroom and teacher being the only security and stability in his life at that point in time. Proudly, he showed me all the special places for him in this room as if this was his home. As early years educators we do have to compensate for the impoverished home experiences of some children by intuitively knowing what interests and motivates such children. Knowledge and understanding of the world provides a practical, relevant and first-hand context in which children learn and can apply a range of basic skills.

Further reading

De Boo, M. (1999) *Enquiring Children, Challenging Teaching*. Buckingham: Open University Press.

Johnston, J. (1996) *Early Explorations in Science*. Buckingham: Open University Press.

Palmer, J. (1994) *Geography in the Early Years*, Chapter 1: 'The Young Child in the Geographical World'. London: Routledge.

Physical development

planned and purposeful activity that provides opportunities for teaching and learning, both indoors and outdoors

(QCA 2000:11)

Introduction

Although not solely the domain of physical development, this chapter has a focus on the importance of the outdoor environment in planning an appropriate curriculum for the Foundation Stage. Examples of the ways in which settings are addressing this recommendation are included from nursery, reception and pre-school settings. In my experience, it is an aspect of early years practice which has improved considerably in the past few years. Partly as a result of the expectations of the inspection system for schools, which requires inspectors to judge the impact of the outdoor environment on children's learning. Schools with weaknesses in this aspect of the Foundation Stage curriculum are very likely to have making improvements as a key area for development in their post-Ofsted action plan. Another factor is the dissemination via LEAs and universities of the practices of other countries. There will be few early years practitioners who have not heard of *The Reggio Emilia Approach* (Edwards, Gandini and Forman 1998). The physical development area of learning has also 50 *stepping-stones*, which is significantly more than some other areas of learning.

In her book about outdoor play Bilton (1998) identifies a set of key principles which need to underpin outdoor play. These are:

- indoors and outdoors need to be viewed as one combined and integrated environment;
- indoors and outdoors need to be available to the children simultaneously;
- outdoors is an equal player to indoors and should receive *planning, management, evaluation, resourcing, staffing and adult interaction on a par with indoors;*

- outdoors is both a teaching and learning environment;
- outdoor design and layout need careful consideration;
- outdoor play is central to children's learning, possibly more to some children than others;
- the outdoor classroom enables children the opportunity to utilise effective modes of learning – play, movement and sensory experience;
- children need versatile equipment and environments;
- children need to be able to control, change and modify their environment;
- staff have to be supportive towards outdoor play.

(Bilton 1998:viii)

All children need regular opportunities to be physically active and this is recognised in the statutory Framework for the early years curriculum (QCA 2000). This view is endorsed by Manners and Carroll (1995:21) who preface their chapter on a framework for physical education in the nursery with the following quotation by Tanner (1978):

> . . . since the large movements of the body ripen first, the gross-motor activity precedes competency in respect of fine-motor and language development. It may, therefore, be suggested that physical play is not only a prerequisite for physical and emotional development, but it is also the most accessible and natural vehicle to use in the promotion of the development of the children's intellect.

(Tanner 1978)

Since the previous edition of this book was published there has been the introduction of a 'new wave' of learning styles into the primary curriculum and into the Foundation Stage curriculum. (Call 2003). Brain-based learning or accelerated learning is an educational fashion item at the present time. Am I alone in being astonished at how this repackaging and renaming of what early years practitioners have always known, although not always practised if they were reception class teachers, to be effective learning? That is that 'the brain thrives on variety and stimulation. Monotony of surroundings, toys that do only one thing, a classroom display kept up for too long, are soon disregarded by the brain' (Brierley 1987:110). The place of physical development in the curriculum for three- to five-year-olds is securely assured now that there is a statutory requirement for settings to implement it.

To judge the appropriateness of the curriculum for three-year-olds to whom the early learning goals apply, one must observe and take account of the learning characteristics of those children. Indeed, all children under five have boundless energy and a need to move. In fact, they will seldom be still. Physical development should be considered in all areas of learning. As children explore, they make use of growing physical competence. Discovering, problem-solving, investigating, exploring and observing are fundamental characteristics of the young learner. Exploration is essential if children are to build up in the brain a representation or 'model', sensed by sight, touch and movement. 'A child does not learn from a passive kaleidoscope of experiences but from the outcomes of actions that he or she has initiated' (Brierley 1987:75). A cautious interpretation of the early learning goals is required to achieve appropriate experiences for children in early years settings.

Planning for physical development

A focus on physical development requires children to have the opportunity to move freely, develop a sense of space, to become aware of the effect of exercise on their bodies and to use equipment, tools and materials. A twice-weekly PE lesson in the hall for reception class children is not enough to develop these all-round physical skills. Many practitioners know this and have taken steps to give their children daily outdoor time as part of the planned curriculum. The guidance for the Foundation Stage (QCA 2000) also acknowledges this and has 'planned and purposeful activity outdoors' as one of the strands of an effectively structured curriculum. Guidance to registered inspectors states that they must 'evaluate how schools include the outdoor environment in their planning' (Ofsted 2001c). Settings plan for the use of the outdoor environment in several ways, as shown in the examples in Figure 10.1.

The focused planning sheet is used with each group of children throughout the week, and assessment of the children's physical, and personal, social and emotional, development is made and transferred to each child's record of achievement. In this particular setting, the staff record achievement on a sticky label and transfer this to the physical development sheet in each child's record of achievement. Another way of recording the assessment information is to highlight and date the achievement using the list of *stepping-stones* for physical development and for personal, social and emotional development referred to in Chapter 4. All the area and small group planning sheets in this setting are used in this way. Alongside the adult-directed activity, the children are developing their movement skills by climbing, sliding and running around the outdoor area. Each week the setting has two focused outdoor activities which require direct teaching and assessment of achievement as part of the ongoing assessment scheme.

In other settings planning for outdoor learning may be an additional column on a weekly plan and show how the outdoor environment is contributing to learning. Where the quality of outdoor learning is very high, there is a separate plan for the week, and the activities listed on the weekly plan as outdoor activities are extended on the weekly outdoor plan to show learning intentions linked to the

Week beginning: *7 May 2002*   Area of learning: *Physical/PSE*

Learning objective/s
- *To improve hand/eye co-ordination (yellow SS) 340s*
- *Persevere in repeating some actions when developing a new skill (blue SS) 440s*
- *Show increasing control when using equipment (blue SS) 440s*
- *Have a positive approach to new experiences (yellow SS) 340s*
- *Persist for extended periods of time at an activity of their choosing (green SS)*

Materials:
Selection of balls
Bucket and hoop
Cordoned off outside area

Activity:
1. to throw a ball with control to a friend using an underarm throw;
2. to catch a ball;
3. to throw a ball at a given target.

The children are encouraged to stand in a hoop and try to get the ball into the bucket (move the bucket further away to provide challenge for the more confident children).
Children encouraged to work in pairs to throw and catch balls.

Evaluation:
Miss Smith's Group
Alex, David and Simon achieved green PSE SS for this. They showed good skills in throwing, but were less confident in catching: they need to do this again. (PD blue SS)

Trevor, Peter, Neil and Stephen had to be persuaded to join in as they found the activity too difficult (WT yellow SS in PSE and PD)

FIGURE 10.1   Outdoor planning examples: Area Planning sheet – Outdoors, Boston Nursery School

stepping stones and the adult-focused activities. Figure 10.2 shows this method of planning for one day.

There are 50 *stepping-stones* for physical development. This is the highest number of all the areas of learning apart from the three priority areas: communication, language and literacy; mathematical development; and personal, social and emotional development. This poses quite a challenge for those practitioners who are restricted in their outdoor provision.

The early learning goals focus on children's developing physical control, mobility, awareness of space and manipulative skills in indoor and outdoor environments. They include establishing positive attitudes to a healthy and active way of life.

Spring term Week 3 and 4	Personal, social and emotional development	Communication, language and literacy	Mathematical development	Knowledge and understanding of the world	Physical development	Creative development
Monday	*Learning intention* Seek out others to share experiences. (Y SS) Display a high level of involvement in activities. (G SS) *Activity* Ring games Wooden house role play	*Learning intention* Listen to instructions (Y SS) Explain what is happening and what might happen next (B SS) Question why things happen (B SS) *Activity* Take part in ring games.	*Learning intention* Observe similarities in shapes in the environment (Y SS) Use shapes appropriately for tasks (B SS) *Activity* Sorting wooden blocks by shape/or size and shape. Look for square, round and rectangular shapes outside.	*Learning intention* Show an interest in the world in which they live (Y SS) Notice differences between features of the local environment (B SS) *Activity* Each group to visit the local parade of shops	*Learning intention* Observe the effect of activity on their bodies (B SS) 4 YOs Negotiate an appropriate pathway when walking, running or using wheeled toys. *Activity* Use a stethoscope to compare the heart rate of adult before and after they have run around the nursery. Ride the wheeled toys around the roadway.	*Learning intention* Join in favourite songs (Y SS) Show an interest in the way musical instruments sound (Y SS) Explore and learn how sounds can change (B SS) Play alongside other children who are engaged in the same theme (G SS) *Activity* Making music using a line of bells strung between two trees Ring games. Role play in wooden house

key: Y SS=Yellow *stepping stones*, B SS=Blue *stepping stones*, G SS=green *stepping stones*,

FIGURE 10.2 Planning for outdoor learning in all areas of learning

	Yellow	Blue	Green	Grey
Movement	Respond to rhythm, music and story by means of gesture and movement. Manage body to create intended movements. Combine and repeat a range of movements. Can stop.	Move freely with pleasure and confidence. Move in range of ways, such as slithering, shuffling, rolling, crawling, walking, running, jumping, skipping, sliding and hopping. Use movement to express feelings. Adjust speed or change direction to avoid obstacles. Sit up, stand up and balance on various parts of the body.	Go backwards, sideways as well as forwards. Experiment with different ways of moving. Initiate new combinations of movement and gesture in order to express and respond to feelings, ideas and experiences. Jump off an object and land appropriately.	Move with confidence, imagination and in safety. Move with control and co-ordination. Travel around, over, under and through balancing and climbing equipment.
A sense of space	Move spontaneously within available space. Negotiate an appropriate pathway when walking, running or using a wheelchair or other mobility aids. Judge body space in relation to spaces available when fitting into confined spaces or negotiating holes and boundaries.	Negotiate space successfully when playing racing and chasing games with other children. Demonstrate control where necessary to hold a shape or fixed position. Mount stairs, steps or climbing equipment using alternate feet. Show respect for other children's personal space when playing among them. Collaborate in devising and sharing tasks, including those which involve accepting rules.		Show awareness of space, of themselves and of others.
Health and bodily awareness	Show awareness of own needs with regard to eating, sleeping and hygiene. Often need adult support to meet those needs.	Persevere in repeating some actions/ attempts when developing a new skill. Show an awareness of healthy practices with regard to eating, sleeping and hygiene. Observe the effects of activity on their bodies.	Show increasing control over clothing and fastenings. Show a clear and increasing preference for the left or the right hand. Show some understanding that good practices with regard to exercise, eating, sleeping and hygiene can contribute to good health.	
Using equipment	Operate equipment by means of pushing and pulling movements.	Construct with large materials such as cartons, long lengths of fabric and planks. Show increasing control in using equipment for climbing, scrambling, sliding and swinging.	Manipulate materials and objects by picking them up, releasing, arranging, threading and posting them. Show understanding of how to transport and store equipment safely.	

FIGURE 10.3   Early learning goals for physical development

	Yellow	Blue	Green	Grey
Using tools and materials	Engage in activities requiring hand–eye co-ordination. Use one-handed tools and equipment.	Demonstrate increasing control and skill in the use of mark-making implements, blocks, construction sets and 'small world' activities. Understand that equipment and tools have to be used safely.	Practise some appropriate safety measures without direction supervision. Explore malleable materials by patting, stroking, poking, squeezing, pinching and twisting them. Manipulate materials to achieve a planned effect. Use simple tools to effect changes to materials. Show understanding of how to transport.	

FIGURE 10.3   (continued)

The goals are broadly similar to the desirable learning outcomes (SCAA 1996) with the addition of two goals focusing on the importance of keeping healthy and recognising that changes happen to their body when they are active. How then are practitioners to provide continuity and progression through the goals for physical development? Do you decide to have a progressively more advanced sequence of learning outcomes for each child to follow, or do you decide with your team to identify learning outcomes for three-, four- and then five-year-olds? One way is to have a curriculum plan which identifies a sequence of learning objectives, appropriate activities, resources and how the adult will support learning. *Planning for Progress: An Early Years Curriculum Framework* (Field and Lally 1996) takes this approach. Figure 10.4 gives an example from their framework of the way in which children might develop jumping skills.

An alternative approach is to refer to the developmental scales for children and compare what they suggest children should be able to do at certain stages and match these to the appropriate learning goal. Wetton (1997) has used this approach when identifying what children should be able to do on entry to pre-school at three years of age. She suggests that the majority of children should be able to perform the following.

Gross motor and locomotor skills
- walk forwards, backwards and sideways;
- walk on tiptoes;
- show a basic running style;
- climb up steps or a ladder with one foot leading, maximum step depth 21 cms;
- climb down a ladder, one foot leading, with hand support;

Learning intention/ knowledge/skills/attitude	Areas and resources inside and out for spontaneous learning	Planned activities and experiences	Adult input and specific language input
• To observe others jumping and imitate. • To explore different ways of jumping. • To know how to land safely. • To be aware of others when jumping. • To develop control and coordination. • To know about distance, direction and height. • To evaluate and refine movements. • To plan and carry out a sequence. • To respond to instructions. • To work with confidence.	• A variety of surfaces for jumping – grass, safety surface, soft play equipment, tarmac. • Hoops on the ground to jump into. • Hopscotch. • Obstacle courses that involve jumping into, onto and around objects. • Stepping stones (marked in chalk etc.) to jump along.	• 'Who can jump the furthest?' Mark lengths of jumps and compare. • 'Which parts of your body can you use to help you jump?' Help the children to identify which they are and teach them to thrust from hips, knees and ankles, to use upward swing of arm and to keep head up. • Jumping along a wavy line. Turning jumps to face a different direction. • Jumping using hands and feet (bunny hops) along the ground and on benches. • Encourage the children to jump in different ways. • Make obstacle courses with the children which involve a variety of jumping actions. • Make jump sequences with children. Start with joining two jumps together, then two that are different, then three or more in the same direction.	• Introduce a vocabulary to help children to describe and compare their jumps: higher, longer, further, star, twisted, leap, hop, tuck, etc. • Safety – ensure children never jump onto an unstable surface; that areas which encourage children to jump are not main thoroughfares; that children develop an awareness of others when jumping. • Teach children to land with slightly bent knees and ankles and head up. • Evaluate with the children. Encourage them to make suggestions about how they could improve their jumps.

FIGURE 10.4 Developing jumping skills (Field and Lally 1996:5)

■ pivot round and round on feet;

■ walk up and down mounds;

■ jump up and down on the spot on two feet;

■ jump a distance of 36 cms;

■ jump down from one foot to two feet from a height of 45 cms;

■ balance walk along a plank at a height of 18 cms from the ground;

■ balance on one leg for 4 seconds;

■ crawl through a barrel or drain-pipe;

■ climb through the lowest rungs of a climbing frame.

Children will vary in their ability to complete the above movements. In terms of their fine motor skills the following are suggested as achievable by three-year-olds on entry to the preschool.

Fine motor skills
- place three blocks on top of each other;
- make a straight road with ten building blocks, having been shown an exact replica;
- affix a piece of construction apparatus to a hole in another;
- assemble a six-piece jigsaw;
- paint a person with a head and two other body parts identifiable;
- grip and make marks on a paper with a thick soft pencil;
- hammer shapes into a pegboard;
- make a ball with clay or playdough;
- pour water from a jug with a spout into a large container;
- thread beads onto a lace.

Children should also be given opportunities to perform the following.

Eye–hand and eye–foot co-ordination skills
- catch a large ball thrown by an adult between their extended arms;
- catch a small ball thrown by an adult between extended arms;
- kick a standing ball with force;
- pedal a tricycle along a wide chalked or painted line;
- push a ball away from self across the floor surface;
- pull an empty truck around obstacles.

(Wetton 1997:10)

Wetton (1997) makes two important points about the ways in which early years practitioners need to ensure that children are provided with the opportunity to develop their gross and fine motor skills. Where children demonstrate a lack of physical competence in any of the skills listed above they 'should be targeted for special attention if they cannot accomplish them' (Wetton 1997:11). In addition to 'targeting' the provision of a 'rich environment where they [the children] can choose to play is necessary. Such an environment would be carefully structured both indoors and outdoors with varied forms of play activities, so providing the children with an opportunity to practice their emerging motor patterns at their own rate of learning when they are biologically capable of achieving them'. (Wetton 1997:13)

What inspectors look for in physical development planning and provision

There are two specific features which a registered nursery inspector or a primary registered inspector will look for in planning. These are a clear indication of what the children should learn from the activities and detail to show how the children will be grouped and how the staff will be deployed. An understanding of the early learning goals and how progression is achieved will also be required. Observation of teaching should show that it is meeting young children's needs to be able to move around easily. So there should be a carefully planned outdoor area and sufficient space indoors for such a purpose. The arrangements made to compensate for lack of an outdoor play space are important. For example, how do the children use large apparatus? Are they provided with regular opportunities for visits to local parks, sharing play space with another nursery or making use of indoor space for gross motor activity? To provide some indicators of minimal resources Wetton (1997:17) suggests the following minimum indoor equipment for gross motor and locomotor play:

- the provision of a multi-purpose climbing frame (with a slide and a balance bar attachment);
- the provision of toys with wheels;
- the provision of large building blocks;
- the freedom to walk about the establishment without restriction;
- a space and a suitable surface for rough and tumble play;
- a space for adult-directed activities.

While this chapter is about planning for physical development it is vital, for those with children under five in a school setting, that negotiation with colleagues and headteachers, relating to the time allocated to physical development is undertaken to ensure that children have regular access to the outdoor environment.

The outdoor environment

The outdoor environment has a vital role to play in the all-round development of the child and not just in their physical development. Case studies included in Chapters 6 and 8 and above demonstrate the fundamental role of the outdoors in early learning. Because provision for outdoor learning is of paramount importance I want to begin this section of the chapter with an overview of basic provision for high quality learning outside, and to continue with examples of the creative ways in which one LEA ensures that planning for outdoor learning enables children to develop their physical skills. Literacy and numeracy activities taking place outside will be included to show how important the outdoor environment is for the development of basic skills.

Resourcing the outdoor environment

An ideal outdoor environment according to Fisher (1996:64) contains: a garden area, trees, bushes and seats, large apparatus, an area for small apparatus, an area for tricycles and trucks, a large sand pit, an area for water play, an area for construction, an area for imaginative play and an area, in the shade, for mark-making, reading and talking. Brown *et al.* (1997) in his guidance to early years practitioners in Manchester identifies five key experiences for the delivery of the physical education curriculum, four of which mainly happen in the outdoors, the fifth being dance, which normally takes place indoors. The four separate environments are indicated in Figure 10.5 and the following extract.

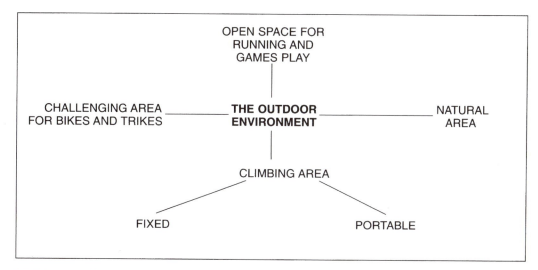

FIGURE 10.5   Key environments for the outdoor area (Brown *et al.* 1997)

The open space

This should be the largest area, made up of an open flat space which will be either grass, tarmac or a combination of both and sited to make use of existing walls and fences which help to keep balls and other small equipment in the area. As well as developing a range of skills, this area should offer opportunities for children to feel the joy of unimpeded running.

The challenge area for bikes and trikes

This should be a complex system with humps, roundabouts, junctions, corners and bridges allowing the children the opportunities to push, pull, peddle, ride, overtake and make decisions. It could be designed to include different textures of road surface. The road system could include road markings and signs. In addition to the use of traditional wheeled toys this area could provide stimulating experiences for children in wheelchairs.

The natural area

This should be an area containing a range of natural features such as trees, shrubs, hills, mounds, grass and earth. It gives children opportunities to investigate, explore, design, construct and experiment. Brantfield nursery in Kendal is a good example of the creative way in which the outdoor environment has been developed. It is provided with a playground containing a covered sand pit to cope with a variety of weather conditions, water facilities for play and a separate covered play area adjoining a play house fitted with kitchen and dining furniture and fittings. On the top of the mound a treehouse is linked into the trees and to a platform/lookout area. Elsewhere there are timber climbing frames, swings and tableaux depicting Robin Hood and Treasure Island. The outdoor area has been developed over a period of time and reflects the school's commitment to environmental education. Readily available large tractor tyres are a good, vandal proof resource for water play.

The climbing area

Fixed equipment on a safer surface would provide height and particularly opportunities to climb, swing and circle the apparatus. Portable apparatus gives opportunities for a range of low level movements such as crawling, balancing, pushing, pulling and sliding through a range of tunnels.

A dilemma faced by many early years practitioners is timetabling the use of the outdoor environment. The following choices are suggested as possible. Perhaps you can accommodate all four, but more likely you may only be able to manage one choice. Nonetheless, it should be possible to provide outdoor activity very regularly in your setting. The choices are:

- children choosing to work outside or to work indoors;
- an adult may select a group to work outside while the majority of children work indoors;
- the adult may select a group to work indoors while the majority of children work outside;
- all the children work outside.

Wherever possible it is desirable to have a minimum of two adults outside, one managing the area whilst the other focuses on the targets. With very small groups one adult may be sufficient.

Literacy and numeracy in the outdoor environment

Many years ago I attended a lecture about ways of promoting early reading and writing skills through the environment. This was innovative at the time but now is more commonplace in most early years settings, or is it? Prior to the implementation of the National Literacy Strategy I may have said this, but increased emphasis on phonological awareness may be reducing the time available to explore the environmental print around school. The curriculum for the early years requires that settings give an increased emphasis to literacy and numeracy. How then can this be achieved within the local environment? The case studies in Chapter 8 provide exemplars of the ways in which this can be achieved. I have also observed children hunting for the words of the week outside as part of a treasure hunt game.

Case Study

The case study below tracks the actions taken by a nursery headteacher following a full inspection which identified as a key issue improvement of the out environment – by implementing the plans that are already in place to provide a small adventure playground.

> The main objective in the action plan was to purchase and plan for the use of a small adventure playground. Estimates were received from a commercial company to provide the nursery with playground equipment. Guidelines were drawn up to assist the staff in their planning for regular use of the outdoor area by all children. Health and safety guidelines were also drawn up. The outdoor environment was planned into all activities using the format in Figure 10.6.

A survey carried out by Ofsted (1997b) into the quality of education in institutions inspected under the nursery education funding arrangements found that promotion of the physical area of learning was secure in 77 per cent of settings with little difference in the provision across all types of setting. The provision for physical development had improved by 2001 (Ofsted 2001b) with about 90 per cent of providers in the private and voluntary sectors encouraging the full range of learning to promote physical development. It indicated that about 10 per cent of providers had limited space with a lack of large-scale equipment. Nine per cent of settings provided poorly for outdoor play in 1997; it is a pity the follow-up survey did not comment on the rate of improvement or otherwise. The comment on the lack of space suggests that there had been limited improvement over the past five years. Given the statistics which highlight the lack of physical activity taken by many young children in their everyday lives, the number of children living in homes without gardens, the increased use of the car for transport and the limited opportunities for children to play outdoors for very valid safety reasons, it is vital that children under five have access to provision which allows them to run, jump, climb and walk around freely on a regular basis. There are variations in the extent to which children from particular socio-economic groups respond to outdoor play. Dramatic play for boys increases with regular access to the outdoor environment.

TOPIC: GROWING				
Intended learning based on *stepping-stones*	Activity (* adult focus)	Language and communication skills	Resources	Outdoor
PSED To show a willingness to tackle problems and enjoy self-chosen challenges (Y) To be curious and explore (Y) Talk freely about their home and community (B)	Exploring objects in the sand and finding seeds and bulbs Looking at photos of themselves as babies*	Naming unfamiliar objects – seed, bulb Then and now. Small and little, big and tall	Change sand tray each day – compost, soil, sand and gravel. Seeds and bulbs and a plant with roots Collection of photographs to include some of the staff as adults and children	One sand tray outside
CLL Use words and gestures (Y) Use action, sometimes with limited talk, that is concerned with the here and now Show interest in books, handle books carefully and hold correct way and understand the concept of a word (Y & B) Ascribe meanings to marks (B)	Talking about the seeds as they are planted*. 4YOs record in diary. Listen and hold book during small group story time* (*Titch*)	Diary, book, pages, pictures	Compost, plant pots, seeds and labels	Repeat seed planting activity outside*
MD Use maths language in play (Y) Use some number names accurately in play (B) Count up to six objects (G)	Collection of large seeds or other natural objects for children to sort and count* Counting game using dice (4YOs)	Numbers to six Positional vocabulary More than, less than when planting and as appropriate	Counting game – Spiders Seeds and other natural objects	Counting outside – steps across the tarmac Counting seeds one by one as planted
KUW Show curiosity, observe and manipulate objects (B) Show interest in the lives of people familiar to them (B) Investigate objects and materials by using all of their senses (G)	Use tools as they plant seeds Talk about their homes and families as they sort photos* Describe the seeds*	Trowel, fork, plant pot, compost Names of their family Hard, soft, rough, smooth	As above, all equipment for planting seeds	
PD Operate equipment by means of pushing and pulling movements Use movement to express feeling (B) Persevere in repeating some actions (B)				Free play on the climbing equipment*
CD Begin to differentiate colours (Y) Show an interest in what they see, hear, smell, touch and feel (Y) Choose particular colours for a purpose (G)				

FIGURE 10.6 Example of a weekly planning framework including the outdoor environment

Boys spent their time outdoors engaged in physical play, whereas girls engaged in material play (Bilton 1998).

Ofsted (1999c) have recently reported on the improvements there have been in provision for physical development and note that, although there have been some improvements and increased opportunities to use climbing apparatus and to practise balancing, improvements overall have been disappointing, especially in independent schools, private day nurseries and private nursery schools. The solution to this in their view is one of giving this aspect greater priority when purchasing resources and planning activities. Too many institutions still have poor facilities for physical development.

Further reading

Bilton, H. (1998) *Outdoor Play in the Early Years*. London: David Fulton Publishers.

Brown, M. *et al.* (1997) *Education and Physical Education in the Early Years*. Manchester: Manchester City Council Education Department.

Wetton, P. (1997) *Physical Education in the Early Years*. London: Routledge.

Creative development

Introduction

Creative development has been given a variety of definitions. The widely acknowledged definition of HMI (DES 1985:17) stated that this area of learning was concerned with 'the capacity to respond emotionally and intellectually to sensory experience; the awareness of degrees of quality; and the appreciation of beauty and fitness for purpose'. An important strand of HMI's definition was the way in which the knowledge and skills acquired could make a valuable contribution to other areas of learning and experience. In the High/Scope curriculum (Hohmann, Banet and Weikart 1979:172) the key experience of getting to know and representing emphasises the importance of the sensory experience. It is vital for all nursery-aged children, but particularly three-year-olds to have sensory experiences as this is how children begin to construct their mental representation of an object intellectually. The imitation of actions and sounds and role-playing are other key experiences linked to this area of learning. An awareness of the processes by which children become creatively and aesthetically aware is just as important as the products of creativity. The early learning goals appear to recognise this in their description of the goals as 'relating to the stimulation of curiosity and engagement with a wide range of sensory experiences. They focus on the development of children's imagination and creativity and their ability to explore, express and share ideas and feelings through different forms of communication' (QCA 1999:12). The way in which practitioners achieve this through the experiences they provide for children is crucial. For very young nursery children the provision of a wide range of sensory experiences to allow them to choose what is interesting to them is necessary. Knowledge and understanding of the schema which such young children exhibit provides a sound basis on which to justify the apparent randomness of early learning.

The early learning goals

The early learning goals for creative development are listed in Figure 11.1. Guidance provided by QCA (2001:20) identifies the four different aspects of creative development. This is how the *stepping-stones* are reflected in Figure 11.1. This is a slight variation on the components of creative development identified by Duffy (1998) listed in a previous edition.

Research into the contribution of creative development to the all-round development of young children is outlined and followed by case studies demonstrating good practice along with some examples of planning.

Research findings

The recent emphasis on learning goals and learning outcomes is very much at odds with the views of earlier research in the area of creativity (Lowenfield 1957, Kellogg 1969). Teachers were warned not to 'accelerate children out of their biological art stage'. This was a view which dominated the practices of early years educators until very recently and was very much current within the early years orthodoxy of ten to fifteen years ago. The work of Mann and Taylor (1973), Vygotsky (1978) and Athey (1990) all support the views taken in this chapter that children who function well creatively are those who are talked to about what they are doing. 'Young children enjoy discussing their art work as they are in the process of creation, and cognitive growth is assisted by the integration of language and motor processes (Mann and Taylor 1973:36). Brierley (1987:76) said that 'building up knowledge of the world through our senses by trial and error is the basis of all later intellectual activity'. Joicey (1986) claimed that 'we are all guilty of looking without seeing'. How do we develop young children's observational skills? Gentle (1985:63) argues that 'the main purpose of the teacher's work with young children is to extend and enrich their sensory experience'. Thus it is imperative that development of all the senses are given high priority in the early stages of education and that educators understand that the range of sensory experiences which children bring to the nursery setting will be diverse.

Children are continually learning to represent. Bruner (1990) suggests that the process of representation can be thought of in three ways:

- through the enactive mode;
- through the iconic mode;
- through the symbolic mode.

	Yellow	Blue	Green	Grey
Exploring media and materials	Begin to differentiate colours. Use their bodies to explore texture and space. Make three-dimensional structures.	Differentiate marks and movements on paper. Begin to describe the textures of things. Use lines to enclose a space, and then begin to use these shapes to represent objects. Begin to construct, stacking blocks vertically and horizontally and making enclosures and creating spaces.	Explore what happens when they mix colours. Understand that different media can be combined. Make constructions, collages, paintings, drawings and dances. Use ideas involving fitting, overlapping, in, out, enclosures grids and sun-like shapes.	Explore colour, texture, shape, form and space in two or three dimensions.
Music	Join in favourite songs. Show an interest in the way musical instruments sound. Respond to sound with body movement.	Sing a few simple, familiar songs. Sing to themselves and make up simple songs. Tap out single repeated rhythms and make some up. Explore and learn how sounds can be changed. Imitate and create movement in response to music.	Begin to build a repertoire of songs. Explore the different sounds of instruments. Begin to move rhythmically.	Recognise and explore how sounds can be changed. Sing simple songs from memory. Recognise repeated sound patterns to match movements to music.
Imagination	Pretend that one object represents another, especially when objects have characteristics in common. Notice what adults do, imitating what is observed and then doing it spontaneously when the adult is not there.	Use one object to represent another, even when the objects have few characteristics in common. Use available resources to create props to support role-play. Develop a repertoire of actions by putting a sequence of movements together. Enjoy stories based on themselves and people and places they know well. Engage in imaginative and role play based on their own first hand experiences.	Introduce a story line or narrative into their play. Play alongside other children who are engaged in the same theme. Play co-operatively as part of a group to act out a narrative.	Use their imagination in art and design, music, dance, imaginative and role-play and stories.
Responding to experiences and expressing and communicating ideas	Show an interest in what they see, hear, smell, touch and feel. Use body language, gestures, facial expression or words to indicate personal satisfaction or frustration.	Further explore an experience using a range of senses. Begin to use representation as a means of communication. Describe experiences and past actions, using a widening range of materials.	Try to capture experiences and responses with music, dance, paint and other materials, or words. Develop preferences for forms of expression. Talk about personal intentions, describing what they were trying to do. Respond to comments and questions, entering into dialogue about their creations. Make comparisons.	Respond in a variety of ways to what they see, hear, small, touch and feel. Express and communicate their ideas, thoughts and feelings by using a widening range of materials, suitable tools, imaginative and role play, movement, designing and making, and a variety of songs and musical instruments.

FIGURE 11.1   Early learning goals for creative development

Representations within the creative area of learning are represented through the symbolic mode. Children, for example, are encouraged to develop symbolic codes through drawing and painting, dancing and imaginative play. It is important that what is described as creativity is truly creative. Duffy (1998) reminds us that much of what happens in the early years in the name of creativity is little more than 'time filling . . . or decoration rather than being truly creative, intellectual activities'. How often have you seen the identical row of Father Christmases where the children have, if lucky, been allowed to stick the pre-cut features on the face and added their allocation of white whiskers?

Two-dimensional and three-dimensional representations

Three-dimensional experiences

Three-dimensional experiences are provided for children who are allowed to feel through direct bodily contact with a range of surfaces, and through manipulating a range of substances such as playdough, clay and sand. Prentice (1994:132) states that children should have opportunities to:

- look at, collect, handle, talk about a wide range of objects which have different functions, which come from diverse cultures and which were made at different times in different ways;

- gain an understanding of similar and contrasting shapes and structures, rough and smooth textures, angular and curved forms, drawn, painted and printed surface decoration, through their own making and through an introduction to the work of adult artists and designers;

- make things on both large and small scales;

- work individually and collaboratively;

- become familiar with plastic and resistant materials, a range of sharpening and cutting tools and processes, including new technologies;

- participate in experimental ways of working, e.g. group constructions of an ephemeral nature, perhaps out of doors, on an environmental scale, through which ecological issues could be raised together with an involvement of the performing arts.

Two-dimensional experiences

Liam has just started nursery and is investigating the painting easel and a variety of painting tools. Quizzically he gazes at Jack, who is four, painting a self-portrait. Jack selects a long-handled brush from a selection in a pot in the tray along the bottom of the easel. He wets the brush in a pot of water next to the pot, makes sure there isn't too much paint on it by brushing it into a sponge for that purpose, also on the tray. He then reflects on the colour of his skin before mixing two powder paints together from a selection of options contained in small quantities in plastic lids, also along the bottom of the painting easel. He washes and cleans his brush and repeats the process to get his paint the correct colour for his eyes. To no-one in particular he says, 'My face is not white.' Mixing the powders together with the water on his brush a pale pink mixture emerges on his palette. Confidently, Jack makes a circular shape on his paper. He then turns to Liam and tells him that he must clean his brush and wipe his palette to make an eye colour. By the time the children in this school are seven the quality of their painting is outstanding. The techniques for painting from observation are applied consistently throughout the school. The skills are gradually taught and children expect to be able to make a representation which has some meaning to them.

A typical event! Jack was applying previously learned skills of mixing paints, selecting the appropriate brush and managing his palette with a lot of skill. To some extent he was scaffolding Liam's learning by enabling Liam to imitate what he was doing. The point of this case study is that the skills are taught to the children by imitation and demonstration and the child then has the confidence to try for himself. The resources allowed Liam to select the appropriate brush, choose his own colours and to make his own unique representation of himself. This led to a high level of motivation. Other ways of mark-making were available to the children. Sponge painting, finger painting and various pencils, crayons and pens all ensured that the children could experiment with the effects of different media. Matthews (1994) identified a sequence of stages which children go through in their development of drawing (Figure 11.2).

Planning for two- and three-dimensional art work

In the following example I have gone through the curriculum planning process from the scheme of work to long-term planning and then to medium-term planning for a range of art and design activities based on the theme of toys carried out in a nursery school shortly before the end of the autumn term. Figure 11.3 is an extract from the creative arts scheme of work relating to art.

Five areas were provided for the week covering:

- painting
- malleable
- collage
- design/3D
- fine motor

Children	
Birth -1 year	• imitate actions and movement using their whole body • are aware of patterns which have strong contrasts and resemble the human face • make intentional marks, for example, with food using finger and hand • are aware that movements result in a mark
1-2 years	• make a variety of marks, sometimes described as scribbling • are aware that different movements make different marks • grip pen or crayon using palm of hand • make marks which record and represent the movement of their bodies and other objects • draw overlapping and layered marks
2-3 years	• use pincer grip to hold graphic materials • produce continuous line and closed shape to represent inside and outside • combine lines and shapes • produce separate but linked shapes
3-4 years	• name marks, and symbolic representation is emerging • experiment with the variety of marks that can be made by different graphic materials, tools and surfaces • unaided, use a circle plus lines to represent a person, often referred to as a 'tadpole person' • start to produce visual narratives
4-5 years	• are able to produce a range of shapes and sometimes combine them, for example, to produce a sun • draw shapes and figures that appear to float in space on the page • draw figures which include more details, such as arms, legs, hands, fingers, eyebrows • subdivide space on page to show higher and lower
At 6 years	• draw figures that are grounded and use lines for ground and the sky • display depth by making figures in the distance smaller to indicate further away • include more detail in their drawings, for example, windows, doors and chimneys on buildings • drawings have more narrative features, for example, may feature a number of episodes of the same story

FIGURE 11.2   The development of drawing (J. Matthews, *Helping Children to Draw and Paint in Early Years.* London: Hodder and Stoughton, 1994)

Each area in the creative room in the nursery provided a different activity each day. The weekly planning identified the activity, resources, purpose of the activity, adult role and comment/evaluation of learning and was completed in advance by the member of staff responsible for the creative room as indicated in Figure 11.4, which shows the planning for one day only.

Area of learning – Art	Learning outcomes
Exploring and experimenting	1. To explore and experiment with a variety of media. 2. To talk about colour, texture, shape, form and space in 2D and 3D. 3. To be able to mix colours to achieve a new colour or shade. 4. To explore and experiment with a variety of tools, materials and techniques.
Technique	5. To be able to select the appropriate tool, material, technique for the activity.
Comparison	6. To be able to talk about the work of others and be aware of similarities and differences.
Expression	7. To be able to talk about and describe their responses to what they can see/hear/touch/feel. 8. To be able to express ideas in a visual form. 9. To be able to talk about their work. 10. To show confidence and enjoyment in the creation of models and pictures. 11. To have experience of the work of famous artists.

FIGURE 11.3   Creative arts scheme of work

AREA: Green		FOCUS: Toys	SKILL: Painting	
ACTIVITIES	RESOURCES	PURPOSE	ADULT ROLE	COMMENT
Painting Can you do a marble painting?	Marbles, paints, tray, paper.	Encourage children to explore and develop the technique of rolling to make a design.	Discuss the activity with the child.	
Malleable Come and roll the dough and make pretend mince pies.	Playdough, cutters, book, boards, trays, microwave.	To develop social skills and language.	Talk about the activity on offer and ask questions.	
Collage We are weaving using Christmas colours.	Trellis, various materials, paper.	To describe their responses to the colours and different materials and to explore and experiment with different techniques.	To support and interact where needed and to name colours and textures of materials.	
Design/3D Come and help to design a train.	Big boxes, tubes, card, Sellotape.	To become familiar with different shapes and to use tools to make the train.	To provide correct language and to talk about the sequence.	
Fine motor Observe and draw old bear.	Charcoal, paper, old teddy, book.	To observe and draw in detail.	Discuss what they are doing and to look at the book.	

FIGURE 11.4   Daily plan for creative activities

Imaginative play

Imaginative play provides children with the opportunity to represent the world away from the reality of it. Children act out scenes from home in their role-play. They acquire understanding of other cultural traditions and roles. Communication is creative and achieved in many ways through language and action. It is exploratory and enjoyable. How much importance do you attach to imaginative play in your setting? Does it have a high status and how do you communicate this? As well as providing an opportunity to develop a range of social, emotional and language skills it provides children with the opportunity to rehearse their own developing understanding of the world. It provides a context for learning many basic skills both with and without adult intervention. For example, in Chapter 8 we see the nursery teacher extending mathematical learning in the haberdashery shop. Should imaginative play opportunities be planned or part of children's spontaneous activity? In a book on curriculum planning it might appear illogical to support the latter viewpoint. However to some extent I do. Within all the planned activity available to the children there must be time for children to be children and to consolidate and practise skills acquired through interaction with another child or adult. Imaginative play can do this up to a point. The problem has arisen over the years where educators have only taken that standpoint and not included opportunity for planned play in their planning. A consequence of this is a devaluing of play as a means of learning. Too little attention is given to the purposes of play, with the result that inexperienced and ill-informed colleagues may be dismissive of play as a means of learning.

Raising the role and status of imaginative play

A survey of reception and nursery teachers attending an in-service course (Rodger 1996) came up with the following list of necessary conditions for improving the role and status of play:

- write a policy for play indicating its contribution to learning. This needs to go beyond the creative area of learning;
- give someone responsibility for promoting play in your setting;
- always include imaginative play in your long-, medium- and short-term planning;
- identify outcomes from play experiences which contribute to all areas of learning;
- create time to review and reflect upon the value of play in your setting;

- keep parents informed of the important role of play in early learning;

- learning in the early years setting needs to be organised to ensure that children have a broad and balanced curriculum which allows them to have access to adult-directed and *self-initiated* activities. Play is the most worthwhile self-initiated activity.

Planning for imaginative play

The medium-term plan outlined in Figure 11.5 is adapted from *Planning for Progress* (Field and Lally 1996), the Tower Hamlets early years curriculum planning guidance. I include this example because it is possible to see how progression in children's learning can be taken account of in planning.

Role play/imaginative play (1)			
Learning intention/ knowledge/skills/attitude	Areas and resources inside and out for spontaneous learning	Planned activities and experiences	Adult input and specific language input
• To be able to observe people in different roles. • To be able to choose/make appropriate props for role play. • To be able to act in role and know how to behave e.g. mothers/babies; doctors/patients; shopkeeper/ customer. • To know and be able to use language appropriate to specific roles. • To be able to take on a role with rules that govern it e.g. as a customer needing to use a basket and pay for goods.	• Role play areas set up to reflect different social situations – shop/clinic/office. • A flexible routine to give children time to observe and be able to participate regularly in role play. • Good quality resources for role play with real things as often as possible.	• Visits to local environment – school secretary, cafe, shops, Post Office, Police Station, Fire Station, baby clinic etc. • Visits from local people to the class – mother and baby, police officer, nurse etc. • Activities based in home corner where appropriate vocabulary and behaviour can be developed e.g. in cooking, washing dolls and clothes, feeding babies etc. • Take children out to shop at the local supermarket/ market. Make shopping lists before leaving.	• Adults model different roles and introduce the language of roles *'How much is...?'* *'I would like...'* *'Please may I have...?'* • Provide possibilities to extend role play e.g. with blocks, using outside area, making props. • Talk about range of jobs adults do and how they are done e.g. looking after a baby, being a post person. Help children understand people's role in society, challenge stereotypes. • Model interactions with different people in the context of role play. • Talk about what happens at home, babies routine. • Measure and weigh food.

FIGURE 11.5   Planning for progression in imaginative play (Field and Lally 1996)

Music

Children are expected to be able to listen attentively to, and explore how sounds can be made louder/quieter, faster/slower, longer/shorter, higher/lower and to recognise patterns in music, movement and dance. The example in the case study below is from a lesson taught by a teacher to reception and Year 1 children. While it is inappropriate for very young three-year-olds to be expected to sit and participate in a 45-minute lesson as this was, there are elements of this experience that are relevant when presented to a very small group of children or when an adult joins a group of children choosing to explore sound in the music area.

> The children in this large group were very familiar with the story of the farm cat who liked to try to climb the trees and catch the birds. The problem was that the cat was too old and kept falling down the tree. The teacher used this story as a stimulus to teach the children about ascending and descending rhythms. Using a xylophone she played four ascending notes and then four descending notes and encouraged the children to listen at first and then to identify whether the rhythm she played was ascending or descending. This activity maintained the children's attention for 10 minutes.

Figure 11.6 illustrates part of a creativity scheme of work in a nursery school, with a list of progressive learning outcomes used by practitioners as a basis for planning and monitoring coverage of the scheme.

Creative development is vital for young children to provide them with the opportunity to express themselves. Nursery settings were reported to be good at providing for high quality art work and sensory experiences by Ofsted (1999c), although too few opportunities are still provided for children to engage in drama, dance and role play. In a more recent survey (Ofsted 2001:**10**), children were found to be given opportunities to 'use their imagination and respond in several ways to what they see, hear, feel and touch'.

Further reading

Duffy, B. (1998) *Supporting Creativity and Imagination in the Early Years*. Buckingham: Open University Press.

Area of learning – music	Learning outcomes
Sound	1. To experiment with sounds. 2. To experiment with body sounds. 3. To experiment with mouth sounds. 4. To experiment with environmental sounds. 5. To experiment with instrumental sounds.
Music and sounds	1. To listen/respond and identify a variety of music, e.g. taped music sounds, voice, body sounds, instruments.
Rhythm	1. To develop concepts of rhythm. 2. To develop concepts of long/short in contrast. 3. To develop concepts of long/short in sequence. 4. To develop concepts of long/short together. 5. To develop concepts of rhythmic patterns.
Pitch	1. To develop concepts of pitch. 2. To develop concepts of quiet sounds. 3. To develop concepts of loud sounds. 4. To develop concepts of getting louder/quieter. 5. To develop concepts of loud and quiet together. 6. To develop concepts of high/low in contrast. 7. To develop concepts of getting higher, getting lower.
Tempo	1. To develop concepts of tempo. 2. To develop concepts of slow/fast in contrast. 3. To develop concepts of maintaining a heavy pulse. 4. To develop concepts of getting faster/getting slower.
Knowledge of musical language and instruments	1. To use appropriate language to describe sounds/music. 2. To be familiar with a variety of musical instruments. 3. To be able to use a selection of instruments appropriately. 4. To be able to express their ideas and feeling through music.

FIGURE 11.6   Creativity scheme of work – music

References

Abbott, L. and Rodger, R. (eds) (1994) *Quality Education in the Early Years*. Buckingham: Open University Press.

Abbott, L. and Gillen, J. (1997) *Educare for the Under Threes – Identifying Need and Opportunity*. Report of the research study by the Manchester Metropolitan University jointly funded with the Esmee Fairbairn Charitable Trust. Manchester: Manchester Metropolitan University.

Ackers, J. (1994) '"Why involve me?" Encouraging children and their parents to participate in the assessment process', in Abbott, L. and Rodger, R. (eds) *Quality Education in the Early Years*. Buckingham: Open University Press.

Adams, J. (1994) 'She'll have a go at anything: towards an equal opportunities policy', in Abbott, L. and Rodger, R. (eds) *Quality Education in the Early Years*. Buckingham: Open University Press.

Adams, M. J. (1990) *Beginning to Read*. London: MIT Press.

Adelman, C. (1981) (ed.) *Uttering, Muttering*. London: Grant McIntyre.

Anderson, B. F. (1975) *Cognitive Pyschology*. New York: Academic Press.

Anning, A. (1995) *A National Curriculum for the Early Years*. Buckingham: Open University Press.

Anning, A. (1997) 'Developing the school curriculum', School Curriculum and Assessment Authority Conference, *The Primary Curriculum: The Next Steps*. London: SCAA.

Anning, A. (1998) 'Appropriateness or effectiveness in the early childhood curriculum in the UK: some research evidence', *International Journal of Early Years Education* 6(3), 299–314.

Athey, C. (1990) *Extending Thought in Young Children*. London: Paul Chapman Publishing.

Athey, C. (1997) 'Graphic representation: innate or acquired?' *British Association for Early Childhood*. Text of a lecture given at the Museum of Childhood, Bethnal Green, 16 July 1997.

Atkinson, S. (1992) *Mathematics With Reason*. London: Hodder and Stoughton.

Atkinson, S. (1995) *Behind the Scenes at the Museum*. London: Black Swan.

Aubrey, C. (1993) 'An investigation of the mathematical knowledge and competencies which young children bring to school', *British Educational Research Journal* 19(1), 27–41.

Aubrey, C. (1994) 'An investigation of children's knowledge of mathematics at school entry and the knowledge their teachers hold about teaching and learning mathematics, about young learners and mathematics subject knowledge', *British Educational Research Journal* 20(1), 105–120.

Aubrey, C. (1995) 'Teacher and pupil interactions and the process of mathematical instruction in four reception classrooms over children's first year in school', *British Educational Research Journal* 21(1), 31–48.

Aubrey, C. (1996) 'The nature of teaching mathmetics subject matter in reception classrooms' in Broadhead, P. (ed.) *Researching the Early Years Continuum*. BERA Dialogues 12. Avon: Multilingual Matters.

Aubrey, C. (1997) 'Children's early learning of number in school and out', in Thompson, I. (ed.) *Teaching and Learning Early Number*. Buckingham: Open University Press.

Aubrey, C., Alfrey, M., Godfrey, R., Godfrey, J. (1999) 'Children's early numeracy experiences in the home'. Paper presented at *Third Warwick International Early Years Conference*.

Baddeley, G. (ed.) (1992) *Learning Together Through Talk: Key Stages 1 and 2*. London: Hodder and Stoughton.

Ball, C. (1994) *Start Right: The Importance of Early Learning*. London: RSA.

Barrett, G. (1986) *Starting School: An Evaluation of the Experience*. London: AMMA.

Bartholomew, L. (1997) 'Transition from nursery to primary school: conducive to learning? The story of O', *International Journal of Early Childhood* **29**(2), 1–7.

Basic Skills Agency (1997) *Update. New Initiative: Family Numeracy*. London: Basic Skills Agency.

Basic Skills Agency (1998) *Family Numeracy Adds Up*. Slough: National Foundation for Educational Research.

Bennett, N., Desforges, C., Cockburn, A., Wilkinson, B. (1984) *The Quality of Pupils' Learning Experiences*. London: Laurence Erlbaum Associates.

Bennett, N. and Kell, J. (1989) *A Good Start? Four-year-olds in Infant Schools*. London: Blackwell.

Bennett, N., Wood, L., Rogers, S. (1997) *Teaching Through Play. Teachers' Thinking and Classroom Practice*. Buckingham: Open University Press.

Bilton, H. (1998) *Outdoor Play in the Early Years*. London: David Fulton Publishers.

Birmingham City Council Education Department (1997) *Baseline Assessment for the Primary Phase*. Birmingham: BCCED.

Blades, M. and Spencer, C. (1987) 'The use of maps by 4- to 6-year-old children on a large scale maze', *British Journal of Developmental Psychology* **5**, 19–24.

Blatchford, P. and Plewis, I (1990) 'Pre-school reading-related skills and later reading achievement: further evidence', *British Educational Research Journal* **16**(4), 425–428.

Blenkin, G.M. and Kelly, A.V. (eds) (1992) *Assessment in Early Childhood Education*. London: Paul Chapman Publishing.

Blenkin, G. M. and Kelly, A. V. (1997) *Principles into Practice in Early Childhood Education*. London: Paul Chapman Publishing.

Bogue, E. G. (1985) *The Enemies of Leadership: Lessons for Leaders in Education*. Bloomington: Phi Delta Kappa Educational Foundation.

Bredecamp, S. (ed.) (1987) *Developmentally Appropriate Practice in Early Childhood Programs Serving Children from Birth Through Age 8*. Washington DC: National Association for the Education of Young Children.

Brierley, J. (1987) *Give Me a Child until He Is Seven. Brain Studies and Early Childhood Education*. London: The Falmer Press.

Broadhead, P. (1997) 'Promoting sociability and cooperation in nursery settings', *British Educational Research Journal* **23**(4), 513–531.

Brown, M. *et al.* (1997) *Education and Physical Education in the Early Years*. Manchester: Manchester City Council Education Service.

Brown, R. (1973) *A First Language: The Early Stages*. Cambridge, Mass: Harvard University Press.

Browne, A. (1996) *Developing Language and Literacy 3–8*. London: Paul Chapman Publishers.

Bruce, T. (1987) *Early Childhood Education*. London: Hodder and Stoughton.

Bruner, J. (1983) *Child's Talk. Learning to Use Language*. London: W. W. Norton.

Bruner, J. (1990) *Acts of Meaning*. Cambridge, MA: Harvard University Press.

Bryant, P. E. and Bradley, L. (1983) 'Psychological strategies and the development of reading and writing' in Martlew, M. (ed.) *The Psychology of Written Language*. Chichester: Wiley.

Bryant, P. E. and Bradley, L. (1985) *Children's Reading Problems*. Oxford: Basil Blackwell.

Burningham, J. (1993) *The Shopping Basket*. London: Red Fox.

Call, N. (2003) the official Braingym website. www.braingym.com.

Carle, E. (1985) *The Bad Tempered Ladybird*. London: Putnam.

Carle, E. (1995) *The Very Hungry Caterpillar*. Leamington: Scholastic.

Central Advisory Council for Education (CACE England) (1967) *Children and their Primary Schools* (The Plowden Report). London: HMSO.

Chomsky, N. (1972) (2nd edn) *Language and Mind*. New York: Harcourt.

Clarke, P. (1992) *English as a Second Language in Early Childhood*. Australia: Multicultural Resource Centre.

Cleave, S. and Brown, S. (1991) *Early to School. Four Year Olds in Infant Classes*. Windsor: NFER-Nelson.

Clough, P. and Nutbrown, C. (2002) *The Index for Inclusion: Personal Perspectives from Early Years Educators*. Research paper, *Early Education* **36** (Spring).

Curtis, A. M. (1986) *A Curriculum for the Pre-school Child*. London: NFER/Nelson.

Dale, P. S. (1976) (2nd edn) *Language Development*. London: Holt, Rinehart and Winston.

David, T. (1996) 'Curriculum in the early years', in Pugh, G. (ed.) *Contemporary Issues in the Early Years*, 85–101. London: Paul Chapman Publishing.

David, T. (ed.) (1999) *Young Children Learning*. London: Paul Chapman Publishing.

David, T., Curtis, A., Siraj-Blatchford, I. (1993) *Effective Teaching in the Early Years: Fostering Children's Learning in Nursery and Infant Classes*. London: OMEP.

David, T. and Nurse, A. (1999) 'Inspections of under fives' education and constructions of early childhood', in David, T. (ed.) *Teaching Young Children*. London: Paul Chapman Publishing.

Davies, A. (2003) *Why all Teachers of English Should be Trained to Use the THRASS 'Periodic Table of Phonics'*. Paper presented at a Standards and Effectiveness Unit seminar, DfES, 17 March 2003.

De Boo, M. (1999) *Enquiring Children, Challenging Teaching*. Buckingham: Open University Press.

Department for Education and Science (1985) *Curriculum 5–16*. London: HMSO.

DES (1989) *A Survey of Education for Four-year-olds in Primary Classes*. Ref. 339/89/NS. London: Department for Education and Science.

Department for Education (1990) Starting with Quality: The Report of the Committee of Enquiry into the Quality of the Educational Experience offered to 3- and 4-year-olds. London. HMSO.

DfE and Ofsted (1995) *Governing Bodies and Effective Schools*. London: DfE.

Department for Education and Employment (DfEE) (1997) *Early Years Development Partnership and Plans*. London: DfEE.

DfEE (1998a) *Numeracy Matters*. London: DfEE.

DfEE (1998b) *Early Years Development and Childcare Partnership*. Planning Guidance. Sudbury: DfEE.

DfEE (1998c) *Self-appraisal Schedule*. London: DfEE.

DfEE (1998d) *Guide for Providers Claiming Nursery Education Grant*. Sudbury: DfEE.

DfEE (1998e) *The National Literacy Strategy*. London: DfEE.

DfEE (1998f) *Supporting the Target Setting Process*. Nottingham: DfEE.

DfEE (1999a) *Requirements of Nursery Education Grant 1999–2000*. Nottingham: DfEE.

DfEE (1999b) *The National Numeracy Strategy*. Sudbury: Cambridge University Press.

DfEE (1999c) *The National Curriculum. Handbook for Primary Teachers*. London: DfEE.

DfEE (1999d) *The National Literacy Strategy. Supporting Pupils Learning English as an Additional Language*.

DfEE (1999e) *The National Literacy Strategy Phonics. Progression in Phonics*. London: DfES.

DfEE (1999f) *Tomorrow's Children. The review of pre-schools and playgroups*. Nottingham: DfEE Publications.

DfEE (2000) *Guidance on the Organisation of the Daily Mathematics Lesson in Reception Classes*. London: DfEE.

DfEE (2001a) *Schools: Building on Success*. London: The Stationery Office.

Department for Education and Skills (DfES) (2001b) *Special Educational Needs Code of Practice*. Nottingham: DfES.

DfES (2001c) *Guidance on the Threshold Process in 2001 (round 2) in England*. London: DfES.

Desforge, M. and Lindsay, G. (1995) *Infant Index Teacher's Handbook*. www.shef.ac.uk/education/publications/journalarticles.shtml.

Dodwell, E. (1997) 'Building on emergent bilingualism', *Education* 3–13, 27–31.

Donaldson, M. (1978) *Children's Minds*. Glasgow: Fontana/Collins.

Donnelly, J. (2003) *Schoool Improvement Plan*. Sunderland: Pennywell Early Excellence Centre.

Downes, G. (1978) *Language Development and the Disadvantaged Child*. Edinburgh: Holmes McDougall.

Drifte, C. (2001) *Special Needs in Early Years Settings*. London: David Fulton Publishers.

Drummond, M. J. (1993a) *Assessing Children's Learning*. London: David Fulton Publishers.

Drummond, M. J. (1993b) 'Scales of injustice. Assessment in the early years', *Times Educational Supplement* 19 March 1993.

Drummond, M. J., Lally, M., Pugh, G. (1989) *Working with Children. Developing a Curriculum for the Early Years*. London: NES/NCB.

Duffy, B. (1998) *Supporting Creativity and Imagination in the Early Years*. Buckingham: Open University Press.

Durham County Council (1999) *Flying Start – Baseline Assessment for the Primary Phase*. Durham County Council: Durham.

Durkin, K., Shire, B., Reim, R., Crowther, R., Rutter, D. (1986) 'The social and linguistic context of early number word use', *British Journal of Developmental Psychology* **4**, 269–288.

Early Childhood Education Forum (1998) *Quality in Diversity in the Early Years*. London: National Children's Bureau.

Early Childhood Mathematics Group (1998) *Learning Mathematics in the Nursery: Desirable Approaches*. London: BEAM/Early Childhood Mathematics Group.

Early Years Curriculum Group (1989) *The Early Years Curriculum and the National Curriculum*. Stoke on Trent: Trentham Books.

Early Years Curriculum Group (1995) *Four-Year-Olds in School: Myths and Realities*. Oldham: Madeleine Lindley.

Edgington, M. (1998) 'Baseline assessment: avoiding the pitfalls', *Early Years* **24**, 3–5.

Edwards, A. and Knight, P. (1994) *Effective Early Years Education*. Buckingham: Open University Press.

Edwards, A. D. and Westgate, D. P. G. (1994) *Investigating Classroom Talk*. London: The Falmer Press.

Edwards, C., Gandini, L., Forman, G., (eds) (1998) *The Hundred Languages of Children. The Reggio Emilia Approach – Advanced Reflections*. London: JAI Press.

Eisner, E. W. (1985) *The Educational Imagination: On the Design and Evaluation of Educational Programmes* (2nd edn). New York: Macmillan.

Eisner, E. W. (1996) *Cognition and Curriculum Reconsidered*. London: Paul Chapman Publishing.

Ellis, S. and Kleinberg, S. (1997) 'Helping teachers support young children in science enquiries', *Education* **3–13**, 59–64.

Ensing, J. (2000) 'The Foundation Stage', *Early Education* **32** (Autumn).

Field, C. and Lally, M. (1996) *Planning for Progress. An Early Years Curriculum Framework*. London: Tower Hamlets Inspection and Advisory Service.

Fisher, R. (1996) 'Building bridges in early literacy', *International Journal of Early Years Education* **5**(3), 189–197.

French, L. and Song, M. J. (1998) 'Developmentally appropriate teacher-directed approaches: images from Korean kindergartens', *Journal of Curriculum Studies* **30**(4), 409–430.

Galton, M. and Williamson, J. (1992) *Group Work in the Primary Classroom*. London: Routledge.

Garton, A. F. and Pratt, C. (1989) *Learning to be Literate. The Development of Spoken and Written Language*. Oxford: Basil Blackwell.

Gelman, R. and Gallistel, C. R. (1978) *The Child's Understanding of Number*. Cambridge, Mass: Harvard University Press.

Gentle, K. (1985) *Children and Art Teaching*. Beckenham: Croom Helm.

Ghouri, N. (1998a) 'Formality "damages" under fives'. *Times Educational Supplement*. 6 November 1998.

Ghouri, N. (1998b) 'Key stage zero for early years'. *Times Educational Supplement*. 9 December 1998.

Ghouri, N. (1999a) 'Key Stage zero for nurseries'. *Times Educational Supplement*. 26 February 1999.

Ghouri, N. (1999b) 'Pay threat of baseline tests'. *Times Educational Supplement*. 26 February 1999.

Ghouri, N. (1999c) 'Playgroup closures'. *Times Educational Supplement*. 19 March 1999.

Gifford, S. (1997) ' "When should they start doing sums?" A critical consideration of the "emergent mathematics" approach' in Thompson, I. (ed.) *Teaching and Learning Early Number*. Buckingham: Open University Press.

Gorman, T. (1997) 'Assessing young children's writing', *Basic Skills*, September/October, 1997, 17–19.

Goswami, U. (1998) *Cognition in Children*. Hove: Psychology Press.

Goswami, U. and Bryant, P. (1990) *Phonological Skills and Learning to Read*. Hove: Psychology Press.

Grennan, T. (1996) *Check List for the Identification of Children with Special Educational Needs*. Stockport: Hollywood Park Combined Nursery Centre.

Griffin, B. (1997) 'The contribution made by educarers to the social, construction of identity' in Abbott, L. and Gillen, J. (eds) *Educare for the Under Threes – Identifying Need and Opportunity*. Manchester: Manchester Metropolitan University.

Griffiths, N. (1997) 'Story sacks', *Basic Skills*, September/October, 1997, **10**.

Hackett, G. (1998) 'Ministers undecided on nursery syllabus'. *Times Educational Supplement*. 4 December 1998.

Hall, N. (1987) *The Emergence of Literacy*. Kent: Hodder and Stoughton.

Hall, N. and Martello, J. (1996) *Listening to Children Think: Exploring Talk in the Early Years*. London: Hodder and Stoughton.

Halsall, R. (1998) *Teacher Research and School Improvement*. Buckingham: Open University Press.

Hannon, P. and James, S. (1990) 'Parents' and teachers' perspectives on pre-school literacy development', *British Educational Research Journal* **16**(3), 259–270.

Harris, F., (2002) *Sure Start Language Measure*. Department of Langauge and Communication, Science, City University. London: City University.

Harris, A., Jamieson, I., Russ, J. (1996) *School Effectiveness and School Improvement*. London: Pitman.

Harris, S. and Henkhusens, Z. (1996) *Mathematics in Primary Schools*. Slough: National Foundation for Educational Research.

Hirst, K. (1998) 'Pre-school literacy experiences of children in Punjabi, Urdu and Gujerati speaking families in England', *British Educational Research Journal* **24**(4), 415–429.

Hodge, M. (1998) Letter to Wendy Scott, Chief Executive, The British Association for Early Childhood Education, 6 November 1998.

Hofkins, D. (1998) 'Fragile consensus on early learning', *Times Educational Supplement*. 22 May 1998.

Hohmann, M., Banet, B., Weikart, D. P. (1979) *Young Children in Action*. Ypsilanti, Michigan: The High/Scope Press.

Hook, S. (1999) 'Quango stands by early years formality'. *Times Educational Supplement*. 22 June 1999.

Hopkins, D. (ed.) (1994) *Schools Make a Difference: Practical Strategies for School Improvement*. London: Resources Base/LWT.

Horbury, A. and Cottrel, K. (1997) 'Cultural factors affecting the acquisition of reading strategies in bilingual children', *Education 3 to 13*, 24–26.

Houston, M., Pepper, D., Watson, L. (1995) *That's My Letter. The Foundations of Emergent Literacy Pre-school. A project in a Leith Primary Nursery Class*. Lothian: Lothian Regional Council.

Hurst, V. and Lally, M. (1992) 'Assessment in nursery education: a review of approaches' in Blenkin, G. M. and Kelly, A. V. (eds) *Assessment in Early Childhood Education*. London: Paul Chapman Publishing.

Johnston, J. (1996) *Early Explorations in Science*. Buckingham: Open University Press.

Joicey, H. B. (1986) *An Eye on the Environment: An Art Education Project*. London: Bell and Hyman with WWF.

Jones, L. (1998) 'Home and school numeracy experiences for young Somali pupils in Britain', *European Early Childhood Research Journal* **6**(1), 63–71.

Jordan, J. (1998) 'Family literacy for linguistic minorities', *Basic Skills* January, 1998, 9–11.

Jorde-Bloom, P., Sheerer, M., Britz, J. (1991) 'Leadership style assessment tool', *Child Care Information Exchange* **87**, 2–15.

Katz, L. (1998) 'What can we learn from Reggio Emilia?' in Edwards, C., Gandini, L. and Forman, G. (eds) *The Hundred Languages of Children*. London: JAI Press.

Kellogg, R. (1969) *Analyzing Children's Art*. Palo Alto, California: National Books.

Leeds City Council Education Department (1997) *Baseline Assessment Scheme*. Leeds: Leeds City Council.

Lindon, J. (1993) *Child Development from Birth to Eight*. London: National Children's Bureau.

Lindsay, G. and Desforges, M. (1998) *Baseline Assessment: Practice, Problems and Possibilities*. London: David Fulton Publishers.

Lowenfield, V. (1957) *Creative and Mental Growth*. New York: Macmillan.

MacGilchrist, B. and Mortimore, P. (1997) 'The impact of school development plans in primary schools', *School Effectiveness and School Improvement* 8(2) 198–218.

McGuinness, D. (1997) *Why Children Can't Read*. Harmondsworth: Penguin.

McNeil, D. (1970) *The Acquisition of Language*. New York: Harper and Row.

Macpherson Sir William, of Clunie (1999) *The Stephen Lawrence Inquiry: Report of an Inquiry*, London: The Stationery Office.

Manchester City Council Education Department (1997) *Assessment in the Early Years. Trialling Materials*. Manchester: MCCED.

Mann, M. and Taylor, A. (1973) 'The effects of multisensory learning systems on the concept formation of young children', *Journal of Research and Development in Education* 6(3), 1–39.

Manners, H. K. and Carroll, M. E. (1995) *A Framework for Physical Education in the Early Years*. London: Falmer Press.

Marsh, C. (1997) 'Adult roles and interactions' in Abott, L. and Gillen, J. (eds) *Educare for the Under Threes – Identifying Need and Opportunity*. Manchester: Manchester Metropolitan University.

Matthews, J. (1994) *Helping Children to Draw and Paint in Early Years*. London: Hodder and Stoughton.

Matthews, P. and Smith, G. (1995) 'OFTSED: Inspecting schools and improvement through inspectors', *Cambridge Journal of Education'*, **25**, 23–44.

May, H. and Carr, M. (1997) 'Making a difference for the under fives? The early implementation of Te Whaariki, the New Zealand National Early Childhood Curriculum', *International Journal of Early Years Education* 5(3), 225–235.

Meadows, S. and Cashdan, A. (1988) *Helping Children Learn*. London: David Fulton Publishers.

Mearing, A. (ed.) (1998) 'Learning together' in *Basic Skills* 14–15. London: The Basic Skills Agency.

Merttens, R. (1998) *Britain's Early Years Disaster – A Response to the Report by Clare and David Mills*. Oxford: The Gatsby Charitable Foundation.

Miller, L. (1996) *Towards Reading*. Buckingham: Open University Press.

Mills, C. and Mills, D. (1997) *Britain's Early Years Disaster*. Oxford: The Gatsby Charitable Foundation.

Misrahi, B. (1997) 'The inspection of day-care: locking cupboards or opening ideas?', *Early Childhood Development and Care* 131, 77–92.

Monaghan, V. (1996) 'The development of language in story', in Broadhead, P. (ed.) *Researching the Early Years Continuum*. Clevedon: Multilingual Matters.

Montague-Smith, A. (1997) *Mathematics in Nursery Education*. London: David Fulton Publishers.

Morris, E. (1997) 'Developing the primary school curriculum: the next steps', Conference address Com/97/894. London: SCAA.

Morris, E. (1998) 'Excellence in the early years', Conference address. Penn Green Centre, Corby.

Munn, P. (1994) 'The early development of literacy and numeracy skills', *European Early Childhood Research Journal* **2**(1), 5–18.

Munn, P. (1997) 'Children's beliefs about counting' in Thompson, I. (ed.) *Teaching and Learning Early Number*, 9–19. Buckingham: Open University Press.

Munn, P. (1998) 'Baseline testing cost for mental arithmetic. Report on British Psychological Conference'. *Times Educational Supplement*. 18 September 1998.

Munn, P. and Schaffer, H. R. (1993) 'Literacy and numeracy events in socially interactive contexts', *International Journal of Early Years Education* **1**(3), 61–80.

Nabuco, E. and Sylva, K. (1996) *The Effects of Three Early Childhood Curricula on Children's Progress at Primary School in Portugal*. Paper presented at ISSBD, Quebec.

National Association for the Education of Young Children (1989) *Anti-Bias Curriculum: Tools for Empowering Young Children*. USA: NAEYC.

National Primary Centre and Oxfordshire Education Department (1995) *Nursery Education Curriculum for the Early Years*. Westminster College, Oxford.

Nelson, K. (1973) 'Structure and strategy in learning to talk'. *Monograph of the Society for Research in Child Development*. **38**(149).

Neugebauer, R. (1985) 'Are you an effective leader?' *Child Care Information Exchange* **46**, 18–26.

New Zealand Ministry of Education (1993) *Te Whāariki: Draft Guidelines for Developmentally Appropriate Programmes in Early Childhood Services*. Wellington: Learning Media.

Nicholson, R. (2001) *Planning for Foundation Stage Learning*. Wandsworth Council.

Nutbrown, C. (1994) *Threads of Thinking*. London: Paul Chapman Publishing.

Nutbrown, C. (ed.) (1996) *Respectful Educators: Capable Learners: Children's Rights and Early Education*. London: Paul Chapman Publishers/Sage.

Nutbrown, C. (1998) Discussion Paper. *Baseline Assessment in the Early Years*. London: British Association for Early Childhood Education.

Office for Standards in Education (1993) *First Class: The Standards and Quality of Education in Reception Classes*. London: HMSO.

Office for Standards in Education (1995) *The Ofsted Handbook. Guidance on the Inspection of Nursery and Primary Schools*. London: HMSO.

Office for Standards in Education (1996a) *Raising Achievement of Bilingual Pupils 1995–96*. London: Ofsted.

Office for Standards in Education (1996b) *Primary Subject Guidance*. London: Ofsted.

Office for Standards in Education (1997a) *The Quality of Education in Nursery Voucher Settings*. London: DfEE.

Office for Standards in Education (1997b) *The Quality of Education in Institutions Inspected Under the Nursery Education Funding Arrangements*. London: Ofsted.

Office for Standards in Education (1997c) *Literacy Matters. Commentary to accompany the Ofsted Video*. London: Ofsted.

Office for Standards in Education (1998a) *Guidance on the Inspection of Nursery Education Provision in the Private, Voluntary and Independent Sectors*. London: The Stationery Office.

Office for Standards in Education (1998b) *Inspecting Subjects 3–11. Guidance for Inspectors*. London: Ofsted.

Office for Standards in Education (1998c) *Are You Ready for Your Inspection? A Guide for Nursery Education Providers in the Private, Voluntary and Independent Sectors.* London: Ofsted.

Office for Standards in Education (1998d) *The Annual Report of Her Majesty's Chief Inspector of Schools. Standards and Quality in Education 1996/97.* London: The Stationery Office.

Office for Standards in Education (1999) *Raising the Attainment of Minority Ethnic Pupils.* London: Ofsted.

Office for Standards in Education (1999a) *The Annual Report of Her Majesty's Chief Inspector of Schools 1997/98.* London: The Stationery Office.

Office for Standards in Education (1999b) *Update April Nursery Inspection Guidance.* London: Ofsted.

Office for Standards in Education (1999c) *The Quality of Nursery Education. Developments since 1997–98 in the Private, Voluntary and Independent Sector.* London: Ofsted.

Office for Standards in Education (2000) *School Evaluation Matters.* London: Ofsted.

Office for Standards in Education (2001a) *Evaluating Educational Inclusion*: Ref No: HMI 235. http://www.ofsted.gov.uk

Office for Standards in Education (2001b) *Nursery Education: Quality of Provision for 3- and 4-year-olds 2000–01.* London: Ofsted.

Office for Standards in Education (2002) *Early Years Early Days.* London: Ofsted.

Office for Standards in Education (2002a) *The National Literacy Strategy: The First Four Years 1998–2002.* HMI 555. London: Ofsted.

Office for Standards in Education (2002b) *The National Numeracy Strategy: The First Three Years.* London: Ofsted.

Office for Standards in Education (2003) *Inspecting Schools: Framework for inspecting schools.* HMI 1526: London: Ofsted.

Office for Standards in Education (2003a) *Standards and Quality in Education. The Annual Report of Her Majesty's Chief Inspector of Schools 2001/02.* London: The Stationery Office.

Office for Standards in Education (2003b) *The Education of Six-year-olds in England, Denmark and Finland.* HMI 1660. London: Ofsted.

Office for Standards in Education and Coopers and Lybrand (1994) *A Focus on Quality.* London: Ofsted.

Osborn, A. F. and Millbank, J. E. (1987) *The Effects of Early Education.* Oxford: Clarendon Press.

Ouston, J., Earley, P., Fidler, B. (1996) *OFSTED Inspections. The Early Experiences.* London: David Fulton Publishers.

Ouston, J., Fidler, B., Earley, P. (1997) 'What do schools do after Ofsted inspections – or before?' *School Leadership and Management* **17**(1), 95–104.

Palmer, J. (1994) *Geography in the Early Years.* London: Routledge.

Panorama (5 October 1998) *Failing at Four.* BBC.

Parsons, S. and Parsons, B. (1998) *Influences on Adult Basic Skills.* London: Basic Skills Agency.

Pascal, C. and Bertram, T. (1997) 'A curriculum for lifelong learning' School Curriculum and Assessment Authority Conference *The Primary Curriculum: The Next Steps.*

Pascoe, G. (1993) *Two Feet.* London: Heinemann.

Perkins, M. (1995) 'Early experiences of classroom literacy', *European Early Childhood Education Research Journal* **3**(2), 79–90.

Peters, S. (1998) 'Playing games and learning mathematics', *International Journal of Early Years Education* 6(1), 49–58.

Piaget, J. (1959) *The Construction of Reality in the Child*. New York: Basic Books.

Piaget, J. (1965) *The Child's Conception of Number*. London: Routledge and Kegan Paul.

Pollard, A. (1997) *Reflective Teaching in the Primary School*. London: Cassell.

Pound, L. (1999) *Supporting Mathematical Development in the Early Years*. Buckingham: Open University Press.

Prentice, R. (1994) 'Experiental learning in play and art', in Moyles, J. (ed.) *The Excellence of Play*. Buckingham: Open University Press.

Pugh, G. (1996) *Evaluations of Nursery Vouchers: Lessons from Phase One*. London: National Children's Bureau.

Pugh, G. (1997) 'A curriculum fit for young children' School Curriculum and Assessment Authority Conference. *The Primary Curriculum: The Next Steps*.

Qualifications and Curriculum Authority (1997) *Looking at Children's Learning*. Ref: COM/97/805. Sudbury: QCA.

Qualifications and Curriculum Authority (1998a) *An Introduction to Curriculum Planning for Under Fives*. London: QCA.

Qualifications and Curriculum Authority (1998b) Conference to discuss review of early learning. Various venues. QCA.

Qualifications and Curriculum Authority (1998c) *Baseline Assessment Scales for Children with Special Educational Needs, Teacher's Guide*. Middlesex: QCA.

Qualifications and Curriculum Authority (1999a) *The Review of the Desirable Outcomes for Children's Learning on Entering Compulsory Education*. London: QCA.

Qualifications and Curriculum Authority (1999b) *Early Learning Goals*. QCA/991436. London: QCA.

Qualifications and Curriculum Authority (2000) *Curriculum Guidance for the Foundation Stage*. London: QCA/DfES.

Qualifications and Curriculum Authority (2001) *Planning for Learning in the Foundation Stage*. London: QCA.

Qualifications and Curriculum Authority (2002) The Foundation Stage Profile. London: QCA.

Reynolds, D., Creemens, B. P. M., Peters, T. (eds) (1990) *School Effectiveness and Improvement: Proceedings of First International Congress*, London 1988. Cardiff: University of Wales College.

Richards, C. (ed.) (1982) *New Directions in Primary Education*. Basingstoke: The Falmer Press.

Riley, J. (1995) 'The relationship between adjustment to school and success in reading by the end of the reception year', *Child Development and Care* 114, 25–38.

Riley, J. (1996) *The Teaching of Reading*. London: Paul Chapman Publishing.

Rodd, G. (1997) *Leadership in Early Childhood*, 2nd edn. Buckingham: Open University Press.

Rodger, R. (1994) 'A quality curriculum for the early years: raising some questions', in Abbott, L. and Rodger, R.(eds) *Quality Education in the Early Years*, 14–36. Buckingham: Open University Press.

Rodger, R. (1995) 'Subjects in the early years curriculum?' in *European Early Childhood Education Research Journal* 3(1), 35–45.

Rodger, R. (1996) *The Role and Status of Play*. Unpublished results of a survey into nursery and reception class teachers' priorities regarding the role and status of play in their settings. Bolton: Bolton Local Education Authority.

Rodger, R. (1999) Improvement through inspection: the impact of nursery education inspections on the quality of provision in thirty children's centres in the North West of England. Presentation *Third Warwick International Early Years Conference*. April 1999.

Rodger, R. and Barnes, S. (1997) 'Our very best show' in Moylett, H. *Working with the Under Threes: Training and Professional Development*. Buckingham: Open University Press.

Rodger, R., Abbott, L., De Jonckeere, S., Griffin, B., Marsh, C., Ackers, J. (1995) *An Identification of Factors Contributing to Quality Educare for Children under Five*. Manchester: Didsbury School of Education, The Manchester Metropolitan University.

Roffey, S. (2001) *Special Educational Needs – the Early Years*. London: David Fulton Publishers.

Roffey, S. and O'Reirdan, T. (1997) *Infant Classroom Behaviour*. London: David Fulton Publishing.

Royal Society of Arts (1994) *Start Right. The Importance of Early Learning*. London: RSA.

Russell, S. (1996) *Schools' Experience of Inspection in Ofsted Inspections. The Early Experience*. London: David Fulton Publishers.

Sainsbury, M. (1998) *National Foundation for Educational Research Evaluation of the National Literacy Project*. Summary Report. Sudbury: DfEE.

Sammons, P., Hillman, J., Mortimore P. (1995) *Key Characteristics of Effective Schools: A Review of School Effectiveness Research*. London: Institute of Education/Ofsted.

Santen, L. V. and Auty, M. (1997) *Nursery Planning for Learning Outcomes. A Detailed Examination of the Planning Process Undertaken by One Nursery*. Oxford: National Primary Centre and Oxfordshire LEA.

Schaffer, H. R. (1990) *Making Decisions about Children*. Oxford: Blackwell.

Schaffer, H. R. (1992) 'Joint involvement episodes as a context for development' in McGurk, H. (ed.) *Childhood Social Development*. Hove: West Sussex LEA.

Schaffer, H. R. and Liddell, C. (1984) 'Adult–child interaction under dyadic and polyadic conditions.' *British Journal of Developmental Psychology* **2**, 33–42.

Scheerens, J. (1992) *Effective Schooling: Research, Theory and Practice*. London: Cassell.

Schneider, B. H. (1993) *Children's Social Competence in Context*. Oxford: Pergamon.

School Curriculum and Assessment Authority (SCAA) (1996) *Nursery Education: Desirable Outcomes for Children's Learning on Entering Compulsory Education*. DFEE: London.

School Curriculum and Assessment Authority (SCAA) (1997a) *The National Framework for Baseline Assessment*, Ref: COM/97/807, London: SCAA.

School Curriculum and Assessment Authority (SCAA) (1997b) *Developing the Primary Curriculum: the Next Steps*. London: SCAA.

School Curriculum and Assessment Authority (SCAA) (1997c) *Supporting Bilingual Pupils in the Primary School*. London: SCAA.

Schweinhart, L. and Weikart, D. (1997) *Lasting Differences: The High/Scope Pre-school Curriculum Comparison Study Through Age 23*. Ypsilanti. Michegan: The High/Scope Press.

Scott, Wendy. (1998) A message from the new Chief Executive. *Early Education News*. London: The British Association for Early Childhood Education.

Scott, W. (1999) 'Key Stage zero for nurseries'. *Times Educational Supplement* 26 February 1999.

Sefton LEA (1996) *Baseline Assessment for the Early Years*. Sefton: Sefton Council.

Sendack, M. (1963) *Where the Wild Things Are!* Glasgow: Harper Collins.

Sharp, C. (1988) 'Voluntary Organisations Liaison Council for under fives', *Co-ordinate*, **11**.

Sharp, C. (1998) *Age of Starting School and the Early Years Curriculum*. Paper prepared for the National Foundation for Educational Research's Annual Conference. October 1998.

Siraj-Blatchford, I. (1994) *The Early Years: Laying the Foundations for Racial Equality*. Stoke: Trentham Books.

Siraj-Blatchford, *et al.* (2002) *Researching Effective Pedagogy in the Early Years*. London: DfES.

Slavin, R. E. (1991) *Student Team Learning: A Practical Guide to Cooperative Learning* (3rd edn). Washington WA: National Education Association.

Stevenson, C. (1987) *Four Year Olds in School. Policy and Practice*. DES Statistics Bulletin. London: NFER/SCDC.

Stockport Metropolitan Borough Council Education Department (1996) *Baseline Assessment Guidance*. Stockport: Stockport MBCED.

Suggate, J., Aubrey, C., Pettitt, D. (1997) 'The number knowledge of four and five year olds at school entry and at the end of their first year', *European Early Childhood Education Research Journal* **5**(2), 85–101.

Sylva, K. (1994) 'A curriculum for early learning' in *Start Right: The Importance of Early Learning*. London: RSA.

Sylva, K. (1997) 'The early years curriculum: some evidence-based proposals' School Curriculum and Assessment Authority conference. *The Primary Curriculum: The Next Steps*. London: SCAA.

Sylva, K., Melhuish, E., Sammons, P., Siraj-Blatchford, I. (1999) *The Effective Provision of Pre-school Education (EPPE) Project*. Unpublished report, Institute of Education, London.

Tamburrini, J. (1982) 'New directions in nursery education', in Richards, C. *New Directions in Primary Education*. Basingstoke: The Falmer Press.

Tanner, R. (1978) *Education and Physical Growth*. London: Hodder and Stoughton.

Taylor, G. (1999) 'Emotional factors affecting learning' in *British Association for Early Childhood Education*. **11** (Summer).

Teacher Training Agency (2000) *Raising the Attainment of Minority Ethnic Pupils*. Guidance resource materials for providers of initial teacher education. London: Teacher Training Agency.

Thomas, W. and Collier, J. (1997) *School Effectiveness for Language Minority Students*. Washington, DC: National Clearing House for Bilingual Education.

Thompson, I. (ed.) (1997) *Teaching and Learning Early Number*, 20–29. Buckingham: Open University Press.

Times Educational Supplement (1998) 'Quality fears on assessment at five.' April.

Tizard, B. and Hughes, M (1984) *Young Children Learning*. London: Fontana.

Tizard, B., Blatchford, P., Burke, J, Farquhar, C., Plewis, I. (1988) *Young Children at School in the Inner City*. Hove: Hove Local Education Authority.

Tooley, J. and Darby, D. (1998) *Educational Research. A Critique*. London: Ofsted.

Tymms, P. (1997) 'Monitoring the progress of children during their first years in school', *OMEP Current Research in Early Childhood*, Update **90**, 1–2.

Tymms, P. (1999) *Baseline Assessment and Monitoring in Primary Schools: Achievements, attitudes and value-added indicators*. London: David Fulton Publishers.

Tymms, P. and Merrel, C. (1996) *Baseline Assessment and Value Added: A Report to the School Curriculum and Assessment Authority* (with D. Williams). Durham: University of Durham.

Venning, A. (1999) 'First steps in reading at three', *Times Educational Supplement*. 25 June 1999.

Vygotsky, L. V. (1978) *Mind in Society: The Development of Higher Psychological Processes*. Cambridge, MA: MIT Press.

Vygotsky, L. V. (1986) *Thought and Language*. Revised and edited by Alex Kozulin. Cambridge, Mass: MIT Press.

Ward, D. (2003) *Foundation Stage Profile*, in *Times Educational Supplement*, January.

Wells, G. (1972–82) 'Language at home and school', *Newsletter of the Child Development Society* **30**.

Wells, G. (1986) *The Meaning Makers. Children Learning Language and Using Language to Learn*. London: Hodder and Stoughton.

Wetton, P. (1997) *Physical Education in the Early Years*. London: Routledge.

Whitehead, M. (1997) 'Early literacy: taking stock', *OMEP Current Research in Early Childhood*. Update **88**, 1–3.

Wilkinson, J. E. *et al.* (1998) *Assessment of Children on Entry to School: A Review of Baseline Assessment in Scotland*. www.scre.ac.uk/forum/forum1998/wilkinson.htm/

Wirral Metropolitan Borough Council (1996) *Starting Points: Teacher's Guide*. Wirral: WMBC.

Wolfendale, S. (1993) *Baseline Assessment: A Review of Current Practice, Issues and Strategies for Effective Implementation*. Stoke on Trent: Trentham Books.

Wood, L. and Attfield, J. (1996) *Play, Learning and the Early Childhood Curriculum*. London: Paul Chapman Publishing.

Index